DON'T BE ON THE WRONG SIDE OF THE SPLIT IN THE EXECUTIVE SUITE

Today American management is becoming increasingly divided. There are those who are sticking with and are stuck with the ways that used to assure top performance and profits. And there are those who have learned to employ personal styles and professional strategies that satisfy the demands of a maturing corporate world and the technology, economy and society of today.

The difference between these two executive camps is the difference between failure and success now and in the future. That is why *The Managerial Challenge* was written—to help make you aware of the choices and moves that can make all the difference to your company and to you.

ABOUT THE AUTHORS: THE MANAGERIAL CHALLENGE: A PSYCHOLOGICAL APPROACH TO THE CHANGING WORLD OF MANAGEMENT is the joint work of ROHRER, HIBLER & REPLOGLE, INC., an organization of 100 corporate psychologists who have served as consultants to over 1,000 companies. Their previous work, the bestselling MANAGERS FOR TOMORROW, with over 200,000 copies in print, is also available in a Mentor edition.

Books from the MENTOR Executive Library

☐ **THE ART OF BEING A BOSS by Robert J. Shoenberg.** A uniquely valuable guide to the executive ladder, from first step to top rung. Explains everything you need to know to get ahead in the corporation—and be as effective a leader as possible once you get there. (#ME1990—$3.50)

☐ **TRADEOFFS: Executive, Family, and Organizational Life by Barrie S. Greiff, MD and Preston K. Munter, MD.** An authoritative guide to achieving a harmonious balance between career, family, and personal priorities. An essential tool in the survival kit of any modern executive. (#ME1960—$3.50)

☐ **WORKAHOLICS by Marilyn Machlowitz.** This in-depth survey will provide you with such essential information as: the characteristics of workaholics, how a person becomes one; the four types of work addicts; how productive they really are; how to work or live with one. (#ME1979—$2.95)

☐ **HOW TO GET A BETTER JOB QUICKER by Richard Payne.** Follow this employment expert's remarkable step-by-step plan that has helped thousands move up the ladder of success. (#ME1988—$2.50)

☐ **HOW TO KEEP SCORE IN BUSINESS by Robert Follett.** Accounting illiteracy has been the stumbling block of many promising managers, but with this comprehensive guide, you'll be able to avoid disastrous pitfalls as you learn everything you need to know to survive and prosper in the world of finance. (#ME1860—$2.50)

THE MANAGERIAL CHALLENGE

A Psychological Approach to the Changing World of Management

By The Staff of
Rohrer, Hibler & Replogle, Inc.

FOREWORD BY DANIEL T. CARROLL

A MENTOR BOOK
NEW AMERICAN LIBRARY
TIMES MIRROR
NEW YORK AND SCARBOROUGH, ONTARIO

Copyright © 1981 by Rohrer, Hibler & Replogle, Inc.

Library of Congress Catalog Card Number: 81-85137

MENTOR TRADEMARK REG. U.S. PAT. OFF. AND FOREIGN COUNTRIES
REGISTERED TRADEMARK—MARCA REGISTRADA
HECHO EN CHICAGO, U.S.A.

SIGNET, SIGNET CLASSICS, MENTOR, PLUME, MERIDIAN AND NAL
BOOKS are published *in the United States* by
The New American Library, Inc.,
1633 Broadway, New York, New York 10019,
in Canada by The New American Library of Canada Limited,
81 Mack Avenue, Scarborough, Ontario M1L 1M8

First Printing, December, 1981

1   2   3   4   5   6   7   8   9

PRINTED IN THE UNITED STATES OF AMERICA

TABLE OF CONTENTS

NOTE

To avoid the awkward "he or she"
and to avoid the banal word "person,"
we will use "he" in this text to refer
to a human being, whether male or
female.

PREFACE

As corporate psychologists, we at Rohrer, Hibler & Replogle, Inc. have learned a great deal from our clients and with them about the task of managing an enterprise. Since our founding in 1945, our work has brought us face-to-face with every conceivable problem and opportunity in the world of business and management.

It is a given that the world of management changes and that the survivors are those who have most successfully anticipated and adapted to change. In this book, we describe the practical experiences that have led us to what we consider to be the best of both the old and new ways of organizing and managing. It would be presumptuous to say that we have learned all there is to know about managing an organization; but we can say that the lessons we have learned, the operating principles we have seen used, and the reasons for the mistakes that we and our clients have made add up to the fund of information that we want to share with those interested in good management. We believe it is particularly important to share these insights now because of the accelerating curve of management change. Management effectiveness in meeting that change is going to be increasingly important for survival, let alone growth.

As with our first book, *Managers for Tomorrow,* published

in 1963, the development of *The Managerial Challenge* involved many of our staff. We designed a procedure that tapped the experience and knowledge of all the staff so that when a stand was taken on some principle, the book would truly represent RHR's stance.

This book is neither an exhaustive exposition of one subject nor a scholarly examination of all the factors and conditions that management must cope with in the immediate future. Instead, it is a book that is intended to stimulate readers to think more clearly and deeply about their management actions and practices. We hope that it will encourage them to reexamine even some of the most successful practices of the past in order to determine their effectiveness in the future. To those who expect a "how to" exposition of pat formulas, only disappointment is in store; but to the successful manager or executive who wants additional questions raised so that they may be examined, this volume may be a challenging resource.

We especially appreciate Mr. Daniel Carroll's foreword for its reflection of his studied approach to the art and science of creating effective organizations. He is presently president and chief executive officer of Hoover Universal, Inc. and was formerly president of the managing consulting division of Booz, Allen, & Hamilton. Appreciated too are the contributions of the RHR writers and their colleagues who together have gleaned the best experiences and most insightful knowledge of our staff of corporate psychologists. Finally, there are those dedicated and often-unsung heroes, the secretaries and typists in our many offices, whose skills and conscientiousness, sometimes even embarrassing in their perfectionism, are not forgotten.

Allen S. Penman, Chairman
Rohrer, Hibler & Replogle, Inc.

FOREWORD

In a welcome addition to the literature on change in the world of management, the staff of Rohrer, Hibler & Replogle, Inc. has perceptively and responsibly linked the individual to the job, to the organization, and indeed to the business world at large. The result is a book for the curious, the secure, and the ambitious among practitioners of management, and for anyone interested in how managers function. Even though the subject legitimately embraces several social science and even technological fields, it is clearly within the grasp of this talented group of psychologists.

First they provide a reasonable and challenging assessment of the contemporary scene and the way individuals are reacting to it. The authors have done a particularly fine job of identifying changing life-styles, and provide sound counsel on how to deal with what amounts to a radically different value system. As a sometimes student of management and a full-time practitioner I am impressed with RHR's emphasis on encouraging employee involvement in the design of the organization culture and pleased that they do not fall into the trap of assuming that the prevailing value system will persist indefinitely.

A valuable discussion of the growing preoccupation with the fit between individual and job follows. Fortunately for us, the authors go beyond the usual exhortation for care and sensitivity and bring up the importance of defining more realistically both sides of the fit: namely, the actual expectations for the job and the prospective capabilities of the individual rather than simply his or her work history. This segment also deals with performance appraisals, and traces accurately the four-stage evolution through which this frequently erratic process has gone.

The segment on managers is probably the one to which many readers will devote particular attention. After all, it talks directly and intimately about the roles to which likely readers will have aspired, and I think there will be more than an historical interest in the evolution of managers from experts to motivators and then to professionals. Readers will find a useful catalog of training flaws, training options and, significantly, the likely yields from those options—especially the contrast between the real yields and the perceived ones. Certainly RHR's high regard for the "behavior analysis" procedure should be provocative to anyone concerned with performance correction or performance improvement.

The "Organization" segment integrates three subjects of great consequence: the information or decision-making fabric of organizations, the evolutionary nature of the organization style and practice, and the usually ignored matter of organization effectiveness. Taken together, they raise questions about the productivity of one's organization and its readiness for a future that the authors make surprisingly predictable. Anticipating the organizational consequences of the radical change from limited data automation to the era of widespread modeling, for instance, should stimulate the development of an organization plan that accommodates a business universe of better data, more time for managerial reflection, and a sharp rise in the anxiety levels in both "data-centered" professionals and their decision-maker counterparts. Likewise, considering the "crisis" of organizational change should elicit reflection on one's own position within the organization and on the evolutionary course the organization itself is taking.

Particularly vital to organization practitioners, RHR's thoughtful description of the "biological model" reminds one of the unending complexity of organization design and the importance of accepting that complexity instead of rejecting it by reverting to the "structural model." And the authors correctly stress the inescapable and essential nature of organization purpose, without which there is slim chance of lasting succeses.

The "leadership" segment incorporates an RHR survey of the concerns of top managers, offering not merely a catalog of current issues but insight into fundamental management styles and methods. Moreover, in an exceedingly fine summary of a subject of great currency, this segment deals with directors and their changing role in organization theory and practice.

In my view, *The Managerial Challenge,* while incisive and compelling for us all, will be especially encouraging and inciting to the venturesome—who, after all, are our hope and our future.

Daniel T. Carroll
Ann Arbor, Michigan
June 1981

PART ONE
The Individual

CHAPTER I.
The Individual in the Organization

1. INTRODUCTION

Changes in the world of management begin with changes in the world of the individual in the organization, whether executive, manager, or blue-collar worker. These are not changes in human nature itself, of course; for it, as the old adage maintains, never changes. But these are essentially changes in the values by which more and more Americans live, the values that, held to be inviolable by the individual, are determinants of so much of human behavior.

The overall reason for so much change is that we are in the midst of a cultural revolution. Massive and fundamental changes affect every aspect of organizational life. Interpersonal relations are different. The traditional American work ethic that puts a value on work itself is often questioned. The national commitment to free enterprise has been eroded by government itself. What many individuals expect from the workplace is dramatically altered from the expectations of a decade ago. Changes such as these, taken together, amount to a groundswell, if not an earthquake, and cause grave concern in the world of management.

This chapter, therefore, will examine these changing values

and how they affect organizational life; to do so is to examine some of the basic causes of change in the world of management.

2. AREAS OF CHANGE

The Need to Influence Conditions

Many individuals today want to have some say in what personally affects them. At its worst, this is a demand; at its best, it is a responsible desire to influence events, situations, laws, selection of officials, or any of the host of factors that impinge on one's life by injunction, control, or pressure.

Of course, the desire, if not necessarily the need, to be a responsible citizen who contributes to the quality of society in America is ideologically nothing new. It is as old as the democratic processes which legally guarantee and consistently support freedom of speech and the secret ballot. What is fairly new, however, and bids fair to become more and more entrenched in our value system in the next decade, is the emphasis on the rights of the individual. Even though these have always been guaranteed by the Constitution and the Bill of Rights, it took the decisions of the Warren and Burger courts to create Title VII, the ERA, and other translations of old ideas into the language of today.

There now is a burgeoning of movements that express the urgent desires of many individuals to create equal employment opportunities, to desegregate schools, and to establish equality of the races and sexes. We are at the apex, for the moment at least, in the history of efforts to resist oppression, destroy dictatorships, and free the individual from dominance. In the broad perspective of history, the struggle of the individual to control his own destiny is continuous.

In any such struggle there is bound to be a spectrum of individuals ranging from the noble to the selfish, from those to whom involvement means the responsible exercise of their rights to those for whom involvement means attaining their goals by any means at any cost. For the latter, the individual's right to freedom provides a hunting license for obtaining indulgences and prerogatives at the expense of others. And so the nobler aspects of involvement—self-fulfillment, self-realization, and doing one's thing as one's right—are, of course, vitiated.

Why this shift in attitude, this need to influence the conditions of one's life? The cause may well come from the powerful confluence of the psychological and sociological forces that characterize our present cultural revolution.

Psychological Forces

The desire to have one's say is enhanced by a trend in psychological theory and practice. This trend probably began with Sigmund Freud's attack on the Victorian autocratic family structure and its concept of family power, discipline, and absolute parental authority. The exposure of resulting repressed fears, inhibitions, and anxieties, pulled into the daylight of consciousness by the therapy of the psychoanalytic couch, may have contributed mightily to the mental health of many; but an unexpected concomitant attitude has also developed—namely, the feeling that what I am, who I am, what I feel, and what I think, supersedes all else. The individual's personal satisfactions and his right to have personal control over what he does are now regarded as the basis for a well-adjusted life.

There are undoubtedly still other contributory causes, but the psychology of fulfillment or self-realization seems a natural outgrowth of Freud's theories. What's important, says this psychological trend, is how you feel—about yourself, others, your experiences, the world of events. One's personal reactions are somehow thus deified.

This psychology of self-determination may be perverted from a wholesome desire to be responsible for one's behavior to an unwholesome egocentricity that demands to be indulged. Thus psychological theory, inherently not at fault, can be twisted into a justification for troublesome behavior.

The point here is not to decry the tendency to be self-centered. The point is rather to describe the individual in the organization who is influenced by the kind of thinking that urges him to want to influence whatever affects him. Examples are numerous: personnel directors are finding more and more job seekers who are more concerned with who their colleagues will be than with what they will be doing. Other job seekers care more about whether the job duties are fulfilling than about the amount of the compensation. Students are often represented at college trustee meetings, and employees are increasingly selected to sit on company advisory boards.

Sociological Forces

The demand to influence conditions is intensified by the feeling that the members of any group must hang together to avoid hanging separately. At least this defensive attitude is partly why so many people today want to be in on what affects them. Society must always, of course, have leaders who in effect determine what its members do. If the leaders harbor nefarious motives or practice repressive procedures, the only protection, short of revolt and rebellion, is for the members to unite. So on the unwarranted assumption that somehow or other the bosses, the leaders, the heads of any organization, are probably up to no good and need to be watched very carefully, even monitored, many individuals today seek involvement in a great number of "protest" groups as a self-protective measure.

Another factor in the cultural revolution is the shift in attitude toward the sources of authority. The authority of those who used to be obeyed without much questioning—the father in the family or the father figures in the church, in the school, or on the job in the person of the boss—is replaced by the authority of peer groups whose standards and expectations now so often both prescribe and proscribe behavior. The individual today will probably move from one influence or consensus group to another throughout his life. He will be influenced primarily by his personal relations within the groups on the job, in his neighborhood, and in other associations.

The Demand for Quality of Life

Another major change is in how work itself is valued. Traditionally, work of any kind, so long as it provided a livelihood, was considered a good thing. Stemming from the background of our Pilgrim and Puritan founders, the idea of work as a noble activity has been an accepted concept. Thus to say "He's a hard-working person" is to commend him; but to say "He's out of work" or, worse yet, "He doesn't want to work" is either to pity him or reject him. Whether the work is interesting or intrinsically valuable is not a significant consideration.

Now, for many Americans quality of life is an important

value, both on and off the job. They want a life that allows opportunity for leisure, whether that means community work or the pursuit of hobbies, a life that fosters close family relations, and a life that provides fulfilling employment, work that is inherently interesting, allows for personal growth and challenge, and realizes one's potential. In other words, "What I do on the job is what's right for who I am."

This more recent attitude toward work rearranges priorities. Now many individuals demand that their participation in the organization contribute to their "quality of life," a euphemism that means, in effect, "I enjoy what I am doing; I find my colleagues stimulating; I'm learning; I'm fulfilling my ambitions; and I'm realizing my potential." In Chapter X, a number of chief executive officers (CEO's) who were interviewed by RHR consultants about what they considered would be major influences in the 80s that would affect their jobs, cite this very expectation for quality of life by an increasing number of employees at all levels, nonmanagers as well as managers. It seems highly probable that the work ethic for many is becoming old-fashioned. The hairshirt philosophy of yesteryear—"If it's fun, it must be evil; if it's rough on you, it's good for you"—is becoming passé.

To be sure, there is a segment of the workforce who are workaholics, those hard-driving, intense individuals to whom little matters except work. Yet, interestingly enough, the pattern of the workaholic is becoming a matter of increasing concern. The workaholic is more and more frequently written about, studied by physicians, psychologists, and psychiatrists, provided with in-house exercise facilities, and adjured to take vacation time more often—actions that imply that working hard is an increasingly questionable activity. Studies of the psycho-physical effects of stress are proliferating; biofeedback (a system for learning to control the involuntary reactions of the autonomic nervous system such as vasoconstriction, "fast heart," and adrenaline secretion) is becoming popular. The implicit assumption is that the human organism can only withstand the rigors of stressful work with difficulty. Thus stress, which was once considered necessary for developing strength and character, is now often seen as a potential threat.

The demand for quality of life in the job scares some managements, upsets some, and is scorned by some; in general, it raises questions about why an organization must please its members. In fact, this new value is one that enlightened managements can turn into an asset, a positive force for building morale. Of course, management first needs to accept certain realities: many people don't want to move, even for a promotion or for training as part of a career-development plan. Many are concerned, and properly, about doing work that has some intrinsic value, about feeling a sense of purpose, about being wholly committed to what they're doing. Certainly such desires are good, but they do mean that managements must make an effort to help employees have a meaningful part in what the company is doing rather than just having a job. It is also probable that those who are looking for a quality-of-life dimension to work are more fast-tracked, begin with a better educational background; in short, it's a reasonable assumption that such employees are even desirable if management can be flexible enough to pay the price of adapting to their reasonable demands.

Participative Management

Closely allied to the demand for quality of life on the job is a high valuation on participation in the managing process. The individual of the future may want to be involved in the policy and procedural decisions that affect him. He may want the opportunity of having some say in whatever controls him, perhaps his job assignment or even his formal appraisal.

Managements may react to these developments with fear, scorn, passivity, or puzzlement. But again, there are several positive steps that can be taken: first, selection must be improved so that only those capable of participating in the process of managing will do so; second, the training and educational programs of the organization must be modified so that, instead of concentrating as usual on skills training and management practices, they will emphasize philosophy and principles, thus concentrating more on the reasons *why* than on merely *how*; third, the criteria for promotion must more explicitly define the qualities of performance inherent in being an effective participant in managing; fourth, management must be flexible, for adjusting to the need or demand of employees to influence policies, procedures, and plans requires the kind of flexibility that expresses a stronger value system and a deeper commitment than does a more narrow-minded and absolutist position.

Changes in Status Symbols

To many individuals, success is not so much symbolized anymore by title, salary, house size, number of cars, or clothes as it is by one's amount of leisure time, by the freedom to pursue one's private interests. Personnel managers report that more frequently job seekers are not motivated to move to another location because, for personal reasons, "Here is where I want to be." More and more candidates seem unimpressed in their application interviews, certainly unpersuaded, by an organization's locations, the size of a position's salary, or opportunities for advancement.

Changes in Ideology

A basic shift in ideology may underlie these changes. William F. Martin and George Cabot Lodge[1] call it a shift from the American "individualistic ideology" to "communitarianism." In their report on their 1975 survey, they define the two ideologies as follows:

Ideology I—Individualism
   "The community is no more than the sum of the individuals in it. Self-respect and fulfillment result from an essentially lonely struggle in which initiative and hard work pay off. The fit survive and if you don't survive, you are probably unfit. Property rights are a sacred guarantor of individual rights, and the uses of property are best controlled by competition to satisfy consumer desires in an open market. The least government is the best. Reality is perceived and understood through the specialized activities of experts who dissect and analyze in objective study.

Ideology II—Communitarianism
   Individual fulfillment and self-respect are the result of one's place in an organic social process; we "get our kicks" from being part of a group. A well-designed group makes full use of our individual capacities. Property rights are less important than the rights derived from membership in the community or a group—for example, rights to income,

[1]William F. Martin and George Cabot Lodge, "Our Society in 1985— Business May Not Like It," *Harvard Business Review*, November–December, 1975.

health, and education. The uses of property are best regulated according to the community's need, which often differs from individual consumer desires. Government must set the community's goals and coordinate their implementation. The perception of reality requires an awareness of whole systems and of the interrelations between and among the wholes. The holistic process is the primary task of science.

Martin and Lodge found that although 62 percent of the 1,-800 respondents (top to middle management and professionals) felt that Ideology I dominated Americans today, that "many sense its replacement by a new set of value definitions based on the communitarian principles of Ideology II," and that "73 percent anticipate that Ideology II will dominate in 1985."

The significance of such a possible shift in ideology is that the trend toward communitarianism is no mere transient deviation from normal behavior or a fad that will disappear like fog in the heat of reality. Instead this is probably a deeply felt, well-rationalized philosophy of life, an ideology that cannot be restrained or exorcised by laws and regulations. And the behavior that it stimulates or condones is not easily melded into harmony with contrary behavior. Perhaps this burgeoning ideology is even the underlying cause of some labor strife, although wages or fringe benefits often seem to be the surface subjects of conflict.

A New "Ruling Class"?

Another socio-psychological phenomenon of American society that management will have to live with in the 80s is the emergence of a so-called ruling class. These are the trained and educated professionals "whose power comes from the manipulation of words, symbols, and ideas."[2] Such household names as Andrew Young, Gary Trudeau, Governor Jerry Brown, Milton Friedman, and Henry Kissinger, as well as many others, unheralded and unknown, make up a "huge community of America's educated that is now influencing opinions, policies, pleasures, and the way of life for an entire

[2]"Our New Elite, For Better or Worse," *U.S. News & World Report*, Feb. 25, 1980, p. 65 ff.

society."[3] Also to be included in this elite are many members of top management whose breadth of interest and concern gives them an impact on legislation, city development, or social issues.

The emergence of what *U.S. News & World Report* calls "our new elite" is not necessarily a threat to organizational development. Societies have always been ruled—the Greeks by statesmen, medieval England by priests, America of the late 1800s by industrialists. What is significant, however, is that ideologies affecting the work ethic, values, and demands for involvement may be promulgated, perhaps inadvertently, by the new elite and thus may create another factor in American society that management must face.

3. IMPLICATIONS FOR MANAGEMENT

Fad, Fancy, or Fact?

The changing values are unlikely to be a fad. The chief reason for such a judgment is in the very nature of values, which by definition are what people believe in, even hold sacred, and will certainly fight for. Values are not changed like clothes to suit the season or one's friends.

Nor are the changing values a fancy, a miragelike phenomenon. It could be an American fancy stirred up by crepe-hanging conservatives—Americans generally panic easily —were it not also for value changes in other parts of the world. Bertrand LeGendre says,[4] "A gulf separates the professional aspirations of French youth from the realities of the workaday world." And he concludes, "Their [the youth's] desacralization of work and the priority they accord to family and leisure are opening the way to behavior changes which politicians and economists might be wise to take into account. The 35-hour week probably isn't the only demand along such lines which will be made in the years to come." Another bit of evidence: One chairman in the RHR survey whose company has gone international since the late 20s says, "The issue of individual independence will not go away very soon. We

[3]Op. cit., p. 65.
[4]"Vanishing Work Ethic," English edition of *Le Monde*, August 12, 1979.

see it in Europe, where the average workweek is 36 hours. Already in England there is a movement to no weekend work and no shift work. This will come more and more in the United States. There is a strong trend toward less and less sacrifice." In the December 18, 1978, issue of the *Wall Street Journal*, a study released by the Labor Department and done by the University of Michigan Institute of Social Research reports that, "American workers are less satisfied with their jobs than they were five years ago." Dissatisfaction was greatest among college graduates and centered for all workers on the need for more money and for improvements in medical insurance, retirement programs, and paid vacations. In short, the changing values in a growing segment of the American workforce appear to be a worldwide ground swell, not a fancy.

There is therefore little doubt that changing values are a fact. Rather dramatically, Patricia Skalka[5] states a not-so-mythical case of a modern family's expectations:

Place: An American home   Date: Something in the future

It's 6:00 A.M. on a Wednesday, and husband and father, Harry H. is out the door, on his way to work. What he does is unimportant to the scenario, what is important is that Harry is largely able to set his own hours on the job. Because of this flexibility, Harry will be home in midafternoon, just about the time his two children come home from school. Weather permitting, they're planning a bike ride together, then, while they talk about school and friends, they'll all help start dinner, maybe hamburgers on the grill.

Meanwhile, wife and mother, Margaret, will have left for her permanent part-time job, 9:00 to 4:30, five days a week, an arrangement that keeps both adults and children happy and allows for needed extra income. In four months, when Margaret has their third child, she'll be eligible for an extended pregnancy leave, which, though largely unpaid, will not alter her job status when she decides to return to work—something she'll be able to do because of the on-the-premises day care facilities provided by her employer. Furthermore, Harry, too, will be eligible for pater-

---

[5]Patricia Skalka, a free-lance writer and instructor at Columbia College, writes in *Passages* for August, 1979, a publication of Northwest Orient Airlines.

nity leave of up to six months, should any problems develop and he is needed at home. Of course, all expenses for the delivery will be covered by one or the other's employee insurance, as will the cost of the counseling Harry and Margaret will seek in a few years when their eldest child develops a drug habit, and the family, torn by guilt and uncertainty, can no longer cope with their routine lives. When the crisis occurs, the parents again will be able to utilize emergency leave plans instituted by their employers, to spend needed time with their children.

Harry and Margaret are not real people, but the family benefits they enjoy in the above scenario are very real. Probably no worker in this country has all these benefits right now, but more and more people are sharing in at least some of these or similar programs. Policies advocating autonomy, flexibility, more employee control and more concern for quality of life, both on and off the job—policies that would have raised eyebrows in personnel departments and caused ulcers in some managers 20 or even 10 years ago—are now becoming, if not commonplace, at least respectable and approachable.

The Need for Perspective

Certainly a major concern of management is to maintain perspective in the face of the changes brought by the cultural revolution. Overreaction against changing values is futile. One extremist, the sole owner of a foundry, simply surrendered to excessive union demands, closed his shop doors, sold his machinery, and retreated to a farm where he now breeds horses and raises apples. A similarly futile overreaction is a supine acceptance of different values such as a management might make by psychologically abdicating responsibility or by managing by consensus. Obviously, overreaction rather than sensible perspective willl mean ruination for any organization.

Since any revolution, almost by definition, involves exaggerations, extremes, and presumed ultimates, keeping a levelheaded perspective is an appropriate response. After all, the superiority of American achievements speaks loudly for the value of the work ethic, for our democratic system, and for consistent and strenuous efforts to protect the constitutionally guaranteed rights of the individual. Just because flaws are found in some concepts and laws as they are implemented and just because inevitable changes occur with experience and circumstance, there is no reason to presume that the value changes sought by the cultural revolution or by the new "ruling class" are automatically either good or bad. A sensible perspective rejects overreaction, respects our American heritage, recognizes the validity of some needed changes, and stimulates participation in the evolution, not the revolution, of our society.

For example, it is an overreaction to see Ideologies I and II, cited above, as a conflict between free enterprise and socialism, between democracy and communism. This is not at all an inevitable choice. Perspective requires a recognition that the points of view in Ideologies I and II are stated in overly simplified and extreme terms. Of course, all individuals in our society are dependent on others (Ideology II), but all Americans also have equal opportunity (Ideology I) to make their own independent way (at least we work constantly to realize this ideal). In short, a sane perspective is to be careful that in changing the bath water (and it may need changing), the baby is not also thrown out.

Interestingly, the CEO's interviewed by RHR (see Chapter X) are strongly committed to defining the good in the American way of life. They recognize the validity of some needed changes—for example, including more employees in the decision-making process and in the responsibility for implementing decisions. Any student of management knows of the proliferation of accommodations to value changes such as "flex time," dental care for the family, beefed-up medical services, job-sharing, employee assistance programs (alcoholism, family budgeting, family planning, marriage counseling, etc.), career planning, rehabilitation programs for the unskilled, and so on. The list of specific adjustments is long. But the CEO's reject outright the extremist position that all society's problems can be solved by an omniscient, all-powerful government. They consider such a solution an abdication of personal responsibility.

Perspective also requires a realization that such adjustments and adaptations as these cannot detract from the basic job of management to preserve and develop the organization. Without such a perspective, management is no longer managing by controlling progress toward selected goals.

What to do—General Considerations

In addition to developing a sensible and knowledgeable perspective on the changing individual, which is a necessary but still an armchair solution, management must act in positive ways. An excellent starting point for action and for planning is to review the organization's present philosophy, policies, and procedures. This is not as obvious and banal a proposal as it sounds. Such a review is meant to be a thorough reexamination, a testing, a real wrestling with conflicts or ambiguities. Even though the review may seem to be forced by a possibly unwelcome circumstance, it can have only beneficial results. It is interesting that the RHR interviewers of top men were repeatedly told, "These questions you're asking me about what the 80s will hold for our organization are provocative. All of our top people should discuss them." In other words, to question the status quo (once described as Latin for the "mess we're in") may be painful, awkward, time consuming, and/or dismaying, but hardly ever futile.

1. *Review the Philosophy.* A review of the philosophy of the organization may uncover the assumption that the workforce today is identical in drive, interest, and expectation with the workforce of the 30s when the work ethic was still rarely questioned. Or it may highlight any restrictive resentments of management for today's fringe benefits package that one perhaps always wished for but could never get. Also it may usefully explore the question of the organization's philosophy. Is it negativistic, a rationale for a consistent reluctance to make any change or adaptation to today's world; or is it positive, viewing change as a possible challenge?

Furthermore, the organization's philosophy about people may have been softened by frequent thoughtless concessions to the workforce's demands so that an expectation of a day's pay for a day's work has become almost willy-nilly a day's pay for some work. For it is one's philosophy that justifies actions and makes them purposive and controlled. When matters such as societal changes are disturbing or are creating organizational problems, the starting gate on the road to solution is one's philosophy.

A critical point to be made here is that adapting successfully to individuals' value changes requires an understanding first of all of one's own values. For there is little use in devising superficial adjustments to a conflict in values without any understanding. Unfortunately there is no practical way to avoid the difficult task of self-examination. "Why do I believe as I do?" is a question harder to answer than "What do I believe?"; but unless the management of an organization, faced with value conflicts among themselves as well as between themselves and those they manage, understands the "why" of their own values, there is little likelihood of successful adjustment.

2. *Review the Policies.* A review of policies, the rules by which the organization lives, may produce a revitalization of an organization's behavior. Are affirmative action plans effective? How well are we involving minorities? Are we reluctantly law-abiding or vigorously pro-American and pro-free-enterprise? What about our good citizen posture? How many management people are involved in civic and social betterment programs? In our performance appraisals, are we really rewarding the behavior we ask of the workforce? Or are we too blandly enduring poor performance or excusing ineffectiveness on the grounds of inexperience, inadequate training, or some personal circumstance? In short, a review of the organization's rules may sharpen management's awareness of which rules need better implementation, which are really passé, which need updating or revision, and which are effective as they stand.

3. *Review the Procedures.* A review of specific actions that are taken to express the organization's philosophy and implement its policies also can be useful. Procedures are like habits, both good and bad, which become "the way we do things around here" and subtly become so entrenched they may be automatically thought of as correct. Thus procedures can easily be impervious to changing circumstances simply because "we've always done it this way." Actually, to change a procedure to which the organization long has beeen accustomed may be almost as difficult as it is for an individual to quit smoking—and often as necessary. To study all procedures of the organization by asking Why, especially if a policy has been modified or some moot part of the philosophy has been clarified, is to risk running into resistance but also perhaps to relieve people of the burden of an outmoded system. Either way, a clarification of "why we do things the

way we do around here" can only have beneficial results in the long run as the organization keeps pace with the times.

What to do—Specific Considerations

1. *Know the person*. This requirement involves a thorough knowledge of the person as a person, not just as a member of the organization. To know his skills and capabilities, even his capacity for greater responsibility, is routine in most effective organizations; but now a broader awareness of the individual will likely be needed: knowledge of motives, attitudes, aspirations, and total life situation. Such knowledge goes well beyond the standard information about a person provided by the admission forms, entrance tests, and casual performance reviews and manager reports.[7]

2. *Manage with skill*. The probabilities are fairly great that the individual of the decades ahead cannot be managed authoritatively and arbitrarily. He will resent being ordered around, but he can be led, even inspired, by skillful managers who know how to get the job done through others. Using the knowledge is of course essential: skill in listening, in questioning, in reacting, in knowing when to talk and when not to. In short, the successful manager will possess such skills in interpersonal relations that his managing of subordinates will indeed be artful.

3. *Compensate creatively*. It could well be that the old adage, "Everyone has a price," will no longer be true. Furthermore, the assumption that the dollar amount of compensation for a job is the most significant status symbol may no longer be valid. In other words, the probabilities in the 80s are that compensation as a prime basis for attracting a newcomer to the organization, rewarding a jobholder for work well done, or signifying a ranking among peers, will disappear and be replaced by other, more relevant, motivators. And rearrangement of functions, perhaps; an injection of new responsibilities into a standardized job (Could the quality control manager be additionally assigned to a product development task force?)—these and other unique variations might serve the workforce of the future as "golden handcuffs."

---

[7]See Chapter II, "The Individual in the Job," and Chapter III, "Performance Appraisals—Yesterday, Today, and Tomorrow," for detailed explanations of how to understand the individual in some depth.

What is certain is that compensation as a motivator, an inducer, or a reward will lose some of its usual potency.

4. *Manage by leading.* The skills and knowledge needed to fulfill managerial roles will be at a special premium in at least three areas, all involving masterful personal leadership capabilities: (a) matching jobs and people in a continuing search for compatibility; (b) using the performance appraisal system as a developmental tool in the constant effort to realize the subordinate's potential; (c) being aware of those specific organizational goals and objectives which proscribe and direct the activities of the group. These three functions affect the manager's personal relations with each subordinate. Depending upon the manager's capabilities, each in turn can be an opportunity for improving performance by leading, stimulating, or directing; or each can be disastrous to relations.

5. *Know the new laws and regulations.* Specifically, of course, management must be fully knowledgeable of the plethora of new laws and government regulations that affect the individual in the workforce. It will not be enough simply to know the rules for equal-opportunity employment or the equal-rights movement, the "freedom of access" laws, and so on; management needs to know the dynamics surrounding these prescriptions: why they exist, their history, and their probable permanence, their current impact, and their possible effects on society, the economy, and the nature of organizational life in the decades ahead.

4. CONCLUSION

The foregoing may imply a crisis in management's relation to the workforce; and to those who yearn to replicate the past it may well be so. But to those managements that can be creative in response to changes in society as they are reflected in the individual, there are undoubtedly great challenges and great opportunities ahead.

The desire for influence, changes in the work ethic and in status symbols, changes in ideology, the emergence of the new "ruling class"—all are today's facets of an everchanging society. To understand them is necessary; to ignore them is perilous; to assume they are unalterable or universal is fatuous; to capitalize upon them by ingenious adaptations to the real world is good management.

Even though we have stressed the fact of changes in the individual, what does not change is important too. Obviously certain factors, principles, and concepts never change. The concept of the individual's rights (and obligations), for example, or the principles of the free enterprise system in a democratic society, or the fact of management's final responsibility to manage—these are fixed. The challenge to managements is to view the changes in the individual in a relative perspective.

Finally, as one member of top management in the RHR survey said, voicing the opinion held by many, "A big challenge today is to be flexible," meaning thereby to avoid pat solutions, to learn from the past, and to be intellectually discriminating and alert enough to recognize good new ideas. Probably several of the top managers who cited their need for engendering flexibility were also challenging themselves to be ideologically entrepreneurial. Such a spirit and perception by capable people can surely result in a revitalized, people-centered, highly viable economy. In fact, an awareness of the value changes in the workplace may mean more than a good economy. As one RHR manager puts it, "The fundamental condition for survival of the human race is interdependence." In the past, people perhaps have been too dependent on the system, too willing to fit in and do what they thought was expected of them. Now the increasing assertion of rights probably means a strong movement toward interdependence. Such a shift is not only healthy in our society, but is necessary for survival. Interdependence is an opportunity and a challenge for management.

CHAPTER II.
The Individual in the Job

1. INTRODUCTION

A subtle but significant change in the world of management is the intensified need to match person to job. There has always been of course some degree of soundness of fit between the jobholder and the job or there never could have been any organized effort. Recent developments, however, conspire to make the obvious, almost routine matching a sensitive, crucial task.

There are several forces at work to create this shift in importance. One (discussed at length in Chapter I) is the increasing demand by employees at all levels that assigned activities in the workplace be fulfilling. Such insistence goes beyond merely doing things one is capable of doing. Employees say, in effect, "I want to be stimulated by the job; I want to realize my potential; my job must be a part of my way of life."

Another force that presses, again subtly, for a good match is the increased sophistication of performance appraisal and training systems. Since providing training and development on the job are becoming routine responsibilities of management, more precise identification of any jobholder's interests, goals, abilities, and potential is also required. When such ele-

18

ments of the individual's make-up are identified, it necessarily follows that something be done with them. There would be little point in saying, "You have considerable creativity," without also saying, "Here's a job that requires creativity." Only frustration could follow if a restless, action-minded, and gregarious person was chained to a desk alone in a room on the job. Thus as performance appraisal systems become more and more effective in developing self-awareness and as training programs are increasingly pinpointed to meet the person's specific needs for better skills or greater knowledge, the problem of matching grows in significance.

A third force is the necessity of insuring organizational effectiveness in the 80s and beyond by getting a tighter fit between the person and the requirements of the job. There are likely to be heavy penalties against organizations that waste manpower, not by having too many people on the payroll, but by having too many people with wasted abilities. In short, the organization of the future, in order to survive, will need to use all of the abilities and capitalize on all of the interests and goals of all its members.

In the effort to effect good compatability, it is obvious there are two matters that must be thoroughly understood— the person and the job. What is not so obvious is that the usual understanding of both the job and the person is inadequate to insure compatability. A job description may look like this:

Position: Field Sales Manager, Simpson Division, Holt Company

General Mission: Responsible for the sales of the company's products through the branch sales offices

Reporting Relations: Reports to the Vice-President, Marketing; has reporting to him four Regional Sales Managers

The capabilities of a candidate for field sales manager are often equally general and are usually determined subjectively in studying the references from former employers and others selected by the candidate, sometimes by the psychological evaluation by the company's consultant, and of course by an examination of the candidate's work history.

Small wonder then that a close matching of person and job

is more likely to be fortuitous than planned, more general than exact. It comes as no surprise, therefore, that the problem of compatibility will need working on in the changing world of management. This chapter proposes some considerations in understanding both the person and the job in order to assure better soundness of fit.

2. UNDERSTANDING THE PERSON

There are at least five aspects of the job candidate's personality that should be understood: intellectual effectiveness, emotional maturity, skill in human relations, insight, and ability to organize and direct others. Understanding these categories of behavior makes judgment of a person's compatability with a job reasonably sound. Some organizations may need additional understandings because of their unique activities.

The five categories may be defined briefly. Each is illustrated by a quotation from a psychologist's description of a fictitious employee whom we shall call Garth Stern, the Field Sales Manager for the Simpson Division of the Holt Company.

Intellectual effectiveness includes not only mental capacity but also how well the individual uses his capacity, since its use is more relevant to success on a job than any raw measure of intelligence such as the I.Q. Is he alert and mentally curious? Flexible? Rigid? How does he reason? Is he creative or literal? How does he handle concepts and other abstractions? Does the person think logically and analytically? Impulsively? Indecisively? Is he considered in judgment? Detail-minded? And so on and on in the many faceted area of intellectual functioning.

For the sake of determining compatability, those aspects of mental effectiveness required by a job must of course be highlighted in the appraisal of intellectual ability.

•

He thinks best about specific facts and factors. He thinks rapidly. He concentrates well on the problems at hand. He sometimes focuses narrowly, and thus excludes from his mind the interrelationships among situations or the broader implications of the immediate problem.

He is unlikely to think sharply about concepts and abstractions. He is intensely pragmatic and hence somewhat impatient with theoretical speculations or explorations of alternative solutions when one seemingly sensible one has already been broached. In fact, he is much more a doer than an idea man; he is more conventional than creative in his thinking.

He is realistic and analytical in his approach to problems. He is resourceful in applying past experiences to new problems if they are tangible and within his area of knowledge. He makes decisions soundly and quickly.

Emotional maturity refers primarily to stability and soundness of mental health. How does he cope with frustration or disappointment? How does he face reality—directly or distortedly? Is he purposive? Does he have a mature set of values? How does he handle inner tension? How tense is he, and about what? Does he habitually suppress his feelings? Or does he wholesomely express them? Or does he lack controls and live at an uninhibited emotional level most of the time?

•

He is highly self-controlled. He compartmentalizes his feelings and often represses them, so that the full emotional impact of events on him is unlikely to be noticed, even by him. Especially does he almost consciously put out of his mind unpleasant or irritating matters, rather than dealing with them directly and realistically.

He is very strongly motivated to succeed. He has a very high level of drive and stamina. He works consistently to reach clear-cut objectives. He shuns ambiguity and either puts it out of his mind or rationalizes his way around it. He is a competitive person with a strong need to demonstrate his competence and ability.

He lives with considerable inner tension, which he characteristically suppresses or tries to. He is certainly a high achiever—perhaps an over-achiever who strives for objectives that seem a bit beyond his reach unless he strains as hard as he does to reach them.

He has well-tested values of honesty, integrity, self-respect, and self-discipline.

Skill in human relations refers to the obvious; how and in what characteristic way does he relate to others? And why? Is he characteristically dominant or submissive? Is he a leader or a follower? How well does he "see into" others—i.e., how well does he size them up? How about his sensitivity to others? Does he usually move toward others psychologically or away from them or against them? Is he emotionally secure with others? Does he have strong feelings of inferiority? Of superiority in a compensatory way?

•

He is usually friendly, warm, and open in his relations with others when he feels accepted. Otherwise, his basic social style is subdued and moderate.

He especially relates quickly and effectively to those who, like himself, are goal-oriented, hard-striving doers. With such he may become almost overinvolved and thereby narrow the range of personalities he relates to well. He is reserved and thus keeps others at a kind of arm's length until he feels comfortable with them.

He is seemingly self-confident. He moves rapidly to a dominant position with his self-assured, controlled, and determined manner with those involved in his areas of experience and expertise. He is capable of leading others when the objectives of the group are concrete and visible. When the objectives are abstract and long range, he is unlikely to assert himself or attempt to take charge.

Insight, perhaps the most difficult area of personality to describe and judge, is the category of behavior that has to do with the person's knowledge of and attitude toward himself and others. The question is whether he sees himself realistically and can accept what he sees good-humoredly. Can he profit from constructive criticism; can he laugh at himself without loss of self-respect? Is he quickly defensive? Is he strongly self-critical?

•

He is aware of most of his strengths and some of his major limitations. He is unlikely to be consistently or conscientiously introspective; thus his more obvious qualities and capabilities he sees; the less obvious escape his attention.

He makes himself behave in ways that are appropriate to the goals he is trying to reach. In this sense, he is a growing, self-developing person. He tends to intellectualize his developmental needs instead of striving for an "Oh, I see" insight.

He takes criticism somewhat as an insult to his own understanding of the behavior that he thinks is best for a given situation. He is sometimes argumentative and defensive; at other times he reacts to overt or implied criticism with silence.

Ability to organize and direct the work of others is not a personality area; rather, it is the functional area of management which the personality characteristics influence. Thus a person's mental effectiveness will be expressed in the clarity of his orders as a manager; or a person's skills in human relations will be reflected in his ability to lead subordinates.

•

He directs others with emphasis on clearly defined procedures, specific objectives, and a high expectation of results or productivity. He is frustrated as a manager by ambiguous policies, ill-defined procedures, and vague expectations.

He generally leads those best who, like him, are committed to a work ethic; he is then congenial and concerned about the welfare and performance of others. He is uncharacteristically authoritative and demanding toward those who tend to be indifferent, shiftless, or negligent.

He responds well to a supervisory style that is firm and explicit in its instructions. He functions best when he is permitted independence in developing operational plans, setting priorities, and determining procedures. He accepts responsibility readily.

A breakdown of personal qualities as in this illustration enables management to match the person to the requirements of the job more realistically, but only when the job is similarly analyzed into its specific elements.

3. UNDERSTANDING THE JOB

For purposes of matching person to job, the usual job description is patently inadequate. Traditionally, it merely defines general mission, states the reporting relations, and lists the general responsibilities of the jobholder. It rarely specifies how the job is to be done, how the job's objectives fit into the organization's plans, what the person is accountable for, the nature and scope of the jobholder's authority, the quality of communication required, and, finally, the standards of performance by which the person will be judged.

An illustrative but partial job description for the field sales manager demonstrates what kinds of things about a job need to be considered if compatibility between job and jobholder is to be achieved. (See Figure 1.)

4. MATCHING PERSON AND JOB

By such a detailed study of Garth Stern (as illustrated) and by such a detailed job description (as illustrated), a greater possibility now exists for matching Stern to the field sales manager job. Perhaps "matching" is too static, too fixed a concept; probably management can better understand now not only whether Stern has what it takes to do the job, but also what he is likely to do with the job: that is, if he will fit himself into the company requirements and plans, if he will need support at any point; and what kind of growth can be expected (what potential realized) from Stern, provided he has what kind of experiences.

If the capabilities required by the field sales manager's position are specified and are compared with Stern's specific capabilities and deficiencies, the matching becomes realistic and the answers to the questions management might ask become possible. (See Figure 2.)

A sharper picture emerges when management develops a *Management Responsibility Matrix* (MRM) for the field sales manager's position as it would ideally like to see the job defined (see Figure 3). In practice, the MRM fleshes out the job description skeleton and provides a standard against which management can compare the ideal division of responsibilities versus what it would feel comfortable in assigning candidate Garth Stern.

A close examination of Garth's areas of strength and developmental needs showed that a number of responsibilities that ideally should be in Column I should be moved, at least for his initial six months, to Column II. As a result, the V.P.

FIGURE 1

Partial Job Description, Field Sales Manager

General Mission: The Field Sales Manager is responsible for the sales of the Holt Division products through the sixteen sales branch offices.

Reporting Relations: The F.S.M. reports to the Vice-President, Marketing. Reporting to the F.S.M. are the Regional Sales Managers to whom the Branch Sales Managers report.

RESPONSIBILITIES

ACCOUNTABILITY	AUTHORITY	COMMUNICATION	STANDARDS OF PERFORMANCE
1. Establishes annual sales plan	1. Shared with V.P., marketing	1. (a) Regional Sales Mgrs; (b) V.P.'s and Mgrs., Mfg., Eng., etc.	1. Timeliness; breadth of coverage; integration with corporate business plan
2. Establishes regional, branch, and individual quotas	2. Shared with Regional Mgrs.	2. V.P., Mktg.	2. Quotas represent "stretch" — i.e., growth in penetration
3. Monitors progress toward objectives as set by sales plan	3. Final	3. V.P., Mktg.	3. Takes action when deviation from plan
4. Provides leadership to sales force	4. Final	4. Regional Sales Mgrs., Branch Sales Mgrs.	4. Has ideas on new targets/approaches; stimulates additional effort

FIGURE 2

Comparison of Garth Stern and Job Requirements

ACCOUNTABILITY	KNOWLEDGE AND CAPABILITIES REQUIRED	STERN'S CAPABILITIES
1. Establishes the annual sales plan	1a. Analysis of prior sales results 1b. Understanding of company's goals and strategies 1c. Recognizes strengths and limitations of sales force 1d. Writes and speaks clearly	a. Realistic, analytical, concrete b. Impatient with theoretical tack; tends to exclude in his thinking the interrelationship of ideas c. Lacks understanding of those who differ from him in background or expertise d. Is a doer more than a thinker; has a somewhat narrow focus; hates paperwork
2. Provides leadership	2a. Personal commitment 2b. Ability to stimulate others 2c. Know-how and technical competence 2d. Creative	a. Strongly motivated to succeed; competitive b. Represses his feelings; relates well to achievers who are like himself c. Self-confident; has high degree of product knowledge d. Lacks innovative skills; relies almost exclusively on past personal experience

of marketing defined the field sales manager's position for Garth Stern as indicated in Figure 4.

A comparison of the ideal MRM for the field sales manager's position (Figure 3) and the MRM that appeared to be more appropriate for Garth Stern, at least for the first six months on the job (Figure 4), provides additional in-depth insights into his compatability with the requirements of the position and shows the V.P. of marketing's willingness to compromise with the established job requirements.

The Search for Compatability

Matching a person to a job is thus a matter of compatibility, not ability. In fact, a jobholder with reasonable ability may even perform the duties of a job passably well while being dissatisfied and unfulfilled—at least for a time. But lasting genuinely effective performance, the kind that not only fully uses the potential of the person but also adds viability to the organization, can be expected only when compatability is achieved.

From the organization's point of view, the needs of the organization may demand certain behaviors from the jobholder. For example, ABC Company is expanding rapidly and may require of its general sales manager a different quality of aggressiveness and ingenuity to establish new district offices and meet high-volume targets than XYZ Company, a slower-growth, old-line firm requires of its sales manager. Even though the job descriptions of the sales manager in both companies could well be identical, the patterns of behavior required by the jobs could well be noticeably different. If a jobholder is right for XYZ (in terms of compatibility), he won't be for ABC, and vice versa.

To pinpoint the required personality characteristics is not an easy, casual task. In the first place, the needs of the organization must be ascertained, not an easy, casual matter either. In addition, the degree of the needs—from absolutely essential, to useful but not necessary—must also be defined. In the second place, the importance of the quality of the job performance must also be established. And third, on top of all this, there is a real difficulty in identifying the personal characteristics that the job presumably requires; for characteristics also exist in degrees, are variables, and fluctuate from

FIGURE 3

Ideal Management Responsibility Matrix, Field Sales Manager

COLUMN I Can do and should do without discussion or consultation with anyone	COLUMN II Can recommend; must discuss with boss (V.P., Mktg.) before decision or action	COLUMN III Can recommend; must discuss with others in company (not boss) before decision or action
1. Analyzes sales results on an ongoing basis 2. With regional mgrs. establishes regional and branch quotas to achieve annual sales plan 3. Interprets co.'s goals and objectives to sales force 4. Evaluates performance of regional and branch mgrs. 5. Monitors adherence to established quality standards 6. Trains and develops branch and sales mgrs. 7. Approves starting salaries for sales reps. 8. Communicates regularly with regions and branches on relevant info, needs, policies, procedures	1. Establishes annual sales plan 2. Gives final approval of regional and branch objectives and goals 3. Hires or fires regional mgrs. 4. Promotes from within to regional and branch mgr. positions 5. Conducts major physical changes to branch facilities (i.e., above normal approval levels) 6. Makes changes in operating procedures which may	1. Establishes regional, branch or individual quotas 2. Handles EEO and insurance claims 3. Responds to gov't agency inquiries, legal documents, etc. 4. Be a member of professional or business executive group 5. Provides media interviews and/or information

(Continued)

FIGURE 3 (Continued)

Ideal Management Responsibility Matrix, Field Sales Manager

COLUMN I	COLUMN II	COLUMN III
Can do and should do without discussion or consultation with anyone	Can recommend; must discuss with boss (V.P., Mktg.) before decision or action	Can recommend; must discuss with others in company (not boss) before decision or action
9. Provides leadership, stimulation, and motivation to field sales force 10. Recommends changes in sales territories, branch, and regional areas 11. Acts as spokesman for co. in areas of general public interest 12. Approves or denies special personnel requests such as transfers, advance payments, etc. 13. Negotiates contracts with vendors and suppliers 14. Approves auto lease contracts for sales personnel 15. Approves hiring or firing of branch mgrs.	affect marketing or sales strategies (i.e., vendor relations, credit policies, etc. 7. Approves salary change recommendations 8. Establishes starting salaries for sales reps. in excess of established policy 9. Approves recommended sales area changes by branch and regional mgrs.	

FIGURE 4

Management Responsibility Matrix For Garth Stern's First Six Months

COLUMN I	COLUMN II	COLUMN III	COLUMN IV
Can do and should do without discussion or consultation with anyone	Assignments not clear—will change with experience & circumstances	Can recommend; must discuss with boss (V.P., Mktg.) before decision or action	Can recommend; must discuss with others in company (not boss) before decision or action
1. Trains and develops branch and sales mgrs.	1. With regional mgrs. establishes regional and branch quotas to achieve annual sales plan	1. Establishes annual sales plan	1. Establishes regional branch or individual quotas
2. Approves starting salaries for sales reps. within established policies	2. Interprets co.'s goals and objectives to sales force	2. Gives final approval of regional and branch objectives and goals	2. Handles EEO and insurance claims
3. Recommends changes in sales territories, branch, and regional areas	3. Provides leadership, stimulation, and motivation to field sales force	3. Hires or fires regional mgrs.	3. Responds to gov't agency inquiries, legal documents, etc.
4. Acts as spokesman for co. in areas of (Cont.)		4. Promotes from within to regional and branch mgr. positions	4. Belongs to professional or business executive group
		5. Conducts major (Cont.)	

(Continued)

FIGURE 4 (Continued)

Management Responsibility Matrix For Garth Stern's First Six Months

COLUMN I	COLUMN II	COLUMN III	COLUMN IV
Can do and should do without discussion or consultation with anyone	Assignments not clear—will change with experience & circumstances	Can recommend; must discuss with boss (V.P., Mktg.) before decision or action	Can recommend; must discuss with others in company (not boss) before decision or action
general public interest 5. Approves or denies special personnel requests such as transfers, advance payments, etc. 6. Negotiates contracts with vendors and suppliers 7. Approves auto lease contracts for sales personnel 8. Approves hiring or firing of branch mgrs.		physical changes to branch facilities (i.e. above normal approval levels) 6. Establishes starting salaries for sales reps. in excess of established policy	5. Provides media interviews and/or information

minor to major factors in personality depending on a host of psychological factors.

All this sounds as if the identification of necessary personal traits for any job is not only difficult but virtually impossible. Difficult it may be, but it is possible and also tremendously rewarding. To make such understanding possible calls for a pattern in the organization of continual, conscientious study of the human factor. Part of the pattern is a usable system of performance appraisals as discussed in Chapter III; part is a keen awareness of the everchanging needs of the organization; part is a scrupulous search for the organization's effectiveness in reaching its goals, following the guidelines of Chapter IX. In short, the knowledge of what it takes to do a job well in a given circumstance cannot be gained by spurts of effort in isolation from a comprehensive understanding.

Furthermore, the basic purpose in analyzing each job in order to characterize it will inevitably plow new ground for the planting of some insightful seeds of learning. Such an analysis calls for questions. Must a sales manager be aggressive? If so, how aggressive? What goes with aggressiveness? Ensuing discussions pay off in greater insight and broadened perspective as the job is related to the jobholder and the needs of the organization.

Communication of Needs

A significant factor in sizing up how a job should be done to meet the needs of the organization is the quality of communication about those needs. The jobholder, whether executive, manager, or member of the workforce, must know what the job is expected to do for the organization. Is it to be steady in its influence (like consistent, reliable production)? Is it to be inventive and creative (like product development)? Is it to be sensitive to the human factor and avert trouble as well as create high morale (like the leadership of personnel)?

Who is responsible for seeing to it that each jobholder is aware of the organization's needs and expectations? Any immediate supervisor. Theoretically, communication follows a chain of command (if there is one) from the chairman to the most recently employed, unskilled worker. If there is no chain of command, then certainly the organization pattern must create opportunities for discussion of needs and expectations at all levels.

The biggest problem in this area of communication is what either misinformation or lack of information may do to job performance. If a person has been erroneously told by his supervisor to keep job information to himself when the organization actually expects dissemination of knowledge and judgments but has failed to make its expectations known to the jobholder's supervisor, then such misinformation leads to needless criticism of the jobholder and a poorer performance. Besides, if the jobholder has no information as to expectations and needs, there is too great a likelihood of projection; that is, of filling the void with one's own wishes. Thus the jobholder who plays his cards close to his vest because he is naturally reserved can easily think that what he does naturally is what is expected of him. And thus poorer performance also results.

However, in spite of this encomium of compatability, a reservation or counterpoint should be made. It is not realistic to assume that all organizational problems are necessarily solved by perfect compatability between each jobholder and his job. Actually, there may well be situations where incompatability has a payoff. It is a truism that conflict and strain are often prerequisite to needed change. Thus a person's very unfitness for doing what is blandly expected of him opens the door to his having a personal impact on the job that forces desirable changes.

Such a reservation that this consideration imposes on the desirability of compatability, however, should not be construed as a carte blanche ticket to vitiate the search for compatability.

It's the Law

Finally, the point must be made that compatibility is now a legal requirement. To match a person's interests and abilities with the job is now a demand of the law. In other words, a minority person or a female cannot be hired just because an organization's affirmative action plans require it. The minority person or the female must qualify for the job. Thus, in this instance at least, the law is compelling organizations to do what should be done anyway—to work toward compatability for everyone.

5. CONCLUSION

Compatibility, like a ladder, stands on two legs, the two entities of the individual and the organization. Both, it is clear, must be understood; for, also as in a ladder, they gain their strength and usefulness through their interrelations which, like rungs, connect them. Without the rungs, no ladder; without interrelations between the needs of the jobholder and the needs of the organization, no compatability.

One rather startling conclusion to be reached from this exploration of compatability is that in the 80s and even later the demand for soundness of fit will be tremendous. This demand will pressure any organization to know its needs and its people and to be skillful in communicating. The old days are gone wherein the traditional size-up of the individual's abilities, experience, and potential is satisfactory. Gone too are the days when top management's inner sanctum discussions spell out for the top few where the organization should be going and what is blocking progress, keeping these ideas and expectations sacred to the boardroom. Involvement by the employee (as discussed in Chapter I) combined with overt purpose and consistent style of management (as discussed in Chapter VIII) are already beginning to dissolve the barriers to compatability. In fact, changes in management are creating a stronger and stronger base for compatability. The challenge to find soundness of fit for everyone in the organization is unending but is so rewarding in the feeling of a quality of life by the individual and in the increasing effectiveness of the organization that the enduring challenge is cause for optimism.

CHAPTER III.
Performance Appraisals—Yesterday,
Today, and Tomorrow

1. INTRODUCTION

A significant challenge for management is contained in the system of performance appraisals. As pointed out in Chapters I and IX, the changing individual in the organization today is the object of unusual management attention. The focal point for such attention is the performance appraisal system. It can almost be said that of all the changes that confront and sometimes bedevil management, the current requirements for effective appraising are highest on the list. In this chapter, therefore, we will examine the nature of these changes and what progressive managements are doing about them.

2. PERSPECTIVE: FOUR STAGES OF DEVELOPMENT

Performance appraisals, formerly called annual reviews or ratings, have evolved from being a chore, reluctantly performed by the manager at the behest of the personnel department, to an effective tool in employee development. What used to be too often a once-a-year rating by the boss of an unresponsive subordinate is now more likely to be a joint exploration of how to improve performance. Furthermore, the lordly evaluation by the manager of the subordinate's personality (how honest? how loyal? how creative?) has changed to a particularized look at the employee's performance and what the manager and the subordinate can do together to improve. These changes in both theory and practice occurred subtly and slowly through four stages. A quick retrospective look at them not only highlights the meaning of the transitions but also provides some predictive insights into the next stage of performance appraisals.

Stage One—The Static Evaluation

Ratings were probably first used by management to provide at least some objectivity in approving pay increases. "How can we judge whether a superior's recommendation for his subordinate's pay increase is justified?" management probably said. "Let's take subjectivity out and require each superior to write out his rating of each subordinate. What kind of person is the employee? What potential is there? Is the employee cooperative? Loyal? In short, is he a good enough person to merit an increase?" Thus the employee's personality characteristics were often quantified. On a scale from 1 (low) to 10 (high), the boss rated the employee's loyalty (7), cooperativeness (9), reliability (3), and so on. Finally Employee A was rated at a total of 87 out of a possible 100 points. Now, since his "score" of 87 was better than Employee B's score of 83, surely the former must be a better person on the job.

Usually the rating forms in Stage One were devised by "experts," given to managers to fill out on all of their subordinates, and required to be returned to personnel by a due-date. Sometimes a recommended pay raise for an employee would not be approved if a superior had failed to file the rating on time.

This is, of course, an oversimplified description of the usual Stage One appraisals. Nevertheless, these early rating systems established a few basic ideas, some good, some bad. Certainly the effort to be objective in evaluating an employee, a theme that obtains even today, was a good idea. But mostly the first ratings had bad ideas; maybe their very badness helped succeeding systems to be better. At first, for example, the ratee never knew how he was rated and hence lived with constant niggling fears and antagonisms—a bad idea. Also, the whole emphasis in the early appraisal was on rating the performer as a person, rarely on his performance. Who the employee was or was thought to be overshadowed the employee's performance on the job that the company paid for—another bad idea.

Stage Two—Appraisal of Potential and Growth Needs

Not surprisingly, the more progressive and insightful managements soon modified the rating system to include the superior's judgments of two more important factors: (1) the employee's potential, thus beginning manpower planning, and (2) the employee's needs for growth in order better to realize that potential. True, many superiors fudged in their judgments by making fatuous statements, such as "he needs more experience" or "he can go as far up the ladder as his ability will permit." But the seed nevertheless had been planted: an organization will increase in effectiveness as its personnel increase in effectiveness. Training programs with definite objectives reflected the stated needs for growth as given by the appraisals. Furthermore, the new emphasis on the performance of the employee coupled into one ideological unit an obvious but often neglected idea: the person and the job are inextricably tied together. So began the perception that has led to more meaningful job specifications and descriptions— What abilities are required for this function? What skills? What personal characteristics? How will effective performance be determined? Added to this was a more objective gauging of the organizations's human resources.

But Stage Two appraisals were still a one-way street. The employee rarely knew the content of the appraisal, although almost certainly the superior would now tell the subordinate, tactfully or otherwise, what were the employee's "needs for growth."

Interestingly enough, in Stage Two superiors often began to be held responsible for the subordinate's realization of potential. Suddenly, this expectation changed the nature of appraising. The superior now began necessarily to be very much personally involved in what potential his subordinate was believed to have and, more important, in how he himself might foster his subordinate's growth. Now at least one of the two became active, even though the appraisee remained largely passive or unknowing.

Stage Three—Development

Finally, the passivity of the appraisee began to disappear. He was now often asked to sign the completed appraisal form, indicating knowledge of its content, although not necessarily agreement. The superior began to stress the need for specific improvements in the appraisee's performance and/or behavior. On top of that, it followed naturally that the superior would suggest specific procedures, training, reading, or observing to the subordinate. The superior still controlled the appraisal experience. He told the subordinate what was needed to improve on the job; the superior didn't ask. Instead, the superior evaluated the performance in terms of his own standards and demands. The appraisee was thus still essentially passive, even though participating enough to sign the form and feel freer than before to discuss, even perhaps to argue with, the superior's recommendations.

Stage Four—Goal Setting

In recent years, the appraisal systems, at least of enlightened organizations, have taken a long leap forward, perhaps capitalizing upon the considerations discussed in Chapter I. Several significant characteristics of Stage Four appraisals can be listed in a somewhat idealized form, as follows:

1. The purpose of the appraisal system now is to involve both superiors and subordinates in personal growth on the job in order to enhance the effectiveness of the total organization; in short, the development of the organization's human resources to carry out the plans of the organization.

2. The superior and the subordinate agree on specific targets for the coming year, plus some detailing of new knowledge and improved skills required to reach them. How to get the new knowledge or develop improved skills may also be specified.

3. The superior and subordinate agree in advance on the criteria to be used to determine how much progress has been made, as well as what evidences will indicate the degree of attainment of the objective. Some criteria are easy to establish; if, for instance, the objective is to increase sales by x

percent, the increase in percent of sales is evidence enough. Some criteria are more difficult to establish. By what yardstick, for example, can progress toward improved morale be measured? Or, how can improvement in communication be measured? Even though such questions are difficult to answer, the very discussion of them will inadvertently, maybe even inevitably, alert both parties to the need for identifying in advance what will be considered as evidences of progress toward the specific targets.

4. The performance appraisal has finally become almost exclusively that—an appraisal of performance, with little or no attention to personality characteristics. This is a matter of focus and emphasis. Although the personal patterns of the employee color *how* the job is done, the intent of the appraisal is primarily to examine *what* is done.

5. Throughout the appraisal discussion two significant factors are now explicit in Stage Four appraisals: one, the organization's needs and goals, (i.e., the results of its efforts, especially those that give specific relevance, even urgency, to the subordinate's job objectives); and two, the appraisee's personal needs and expectations. These two considerations are vital. If what the organization needs from the jobholder and what the jobholder needs from the job are aligned, all is well—expectations are justified and realizable, performance is objectified, and potential conflicts are avoided. This is indeed compatability as discussed in Chapter II. However, if the organization is demanding accelerated growth, for example, but the appraisee is inclined to look instead for the security of a "fur-lined rut," there may be obvious difficulties ahead. By the same token, if the appraisee's personal career objectives demand a life of exciting creativity and rapid, if not frenetic, growth, but the company is more slow moving and stable, there may be trouble ahead. The point is that Stage Four appraisals may identify any disparities between the company's goals and the individual's needs, thereby clarifying the issues of "Is this the right organization for me?" and the counter question, "Is this individual right for the organization?"

3. WHY PERFORMANCE APPRAISAL IS ESPECIALLY IMPORTANT TODAY

Today the theoretical niceties of Stage Four performance appraisals are in fact enforced by law. The "freedom of access" law permits any interested employee to see his personnel records if he wants to. The customary wraps of secrecy are off. No longer can a manager write out evaluative judgments, documented or not, without risk of disclosure. He may be compelled to support those judgments with facts, observations, and the yardsticks against which the subordinate was measured. Thus disclosure, even though repugnant to some, is not too bad. It simply forces the appraiser and the appraisee to do a joint performance appraisal.

Furthermore, Stage Four appraisals are psychologically sound for several reasons *if* the organization's purpose is to increase the employee's effectiveness on the job as well as to enhance personal growth. First of all, it is psychologically healthful for the appraisee to know where he stands with the superior and why. Such an open, candid relation is surely a long step forward in enabling a manager to fulfill his responsibility, committed as he must be to developing subordinates' resources. Playing games, double talk, fencing, politicking, many of the little deceits and shams that tend to make a relation superficial or even hypocritical, are thus greatly reduced, if not eliminated. The appraisee no longer needs to fear that his tenure depends on the shaky ground of a superior's undisclosed judgments. The appraisee is psychologically free to focus instead on improving performance.

Second, goal setting is motivational. It is a truism that all human behavior is consciously or unconsciously purposive, serving the person's needs in some way. For an appraisee to know (and to accept) the specific goals, objectives, or purposes (whatever they may be called) inevitably focuses drive by making it more conscious. The appraisee's reasons for behaving in a certain way are pinpointed. He knows why he's doing what he's doing.

Third, Stage Four appraisals focus on the organization's needs and thereby the performance requirements of the appraisee's job. The job targets are meaningful, relevant, and specific, though depersonalized. For example, an organization must cut costs and the appraisee, a sales manager, is a congenial but a spendthrift leader of men. During the appraisal, the target of controlling costs is determined by the organization's soaring expenses. The discussion is not centered on the personal lifestyle of thoughtless spending; only the specific goal to cut costs by x percent is detailed—how can we do it together? The appraiser need not, therefore, threaten, persuade, or criticize the sales manager, but instead challenges him to meet a target of reduced costs, a challenge created not by the superior's personal predilection, but by the organizational situation both the appraiser and appraisee are in.

Finally, even though Stage Four appraisals are objective and performance oriented, they are not coldly computerized. Of course, the relation based on candor and openness between the manager and the subordinate, with a minimum of dissimulation and ceremony, is psychologically essential. After all, these are two human beings, each with prejudices, blind spots, and emotional preferences. But if their intention is to look objectively at the appraisee's performance and achievement of results, their open relation will produce clear communication, easy understanding of targets, and cooperation in reaching them.

Besides being psychologically sound, the Stage Four joint appraisal expresses the mood of the times. Everywhere, action is taken *with* people, not *on* people. Perry Rohrer, one of the founders of Rohrer, Hibler & Replogle, Inc., venerated the leader who "exercised power with others, not over others." Lawrence Appley, long-time head of the American Management Association, often defined managing as "getting things done through others." So it is not at all surprising that the performance appraisal system is increasingly a joint effort.

Thus both the current law and today's values combine to make the performance appraisal system into a developmental tool for management. To develop subordinates and to enhance their abilities have of course long been objectives of management. It is indeed a rare organization that doesn't provide in-house skills-development training programs and seminars. Courses by trade associations, universities, consultants, and individual experts have recently proliferated. But lurking in the background of all of this development and training has been the awareness that in the final analysis only the individual learns. "Mark Hopkins on one end of the log and the student on the other" has long been the ideal teacher-student relation, one to one—individualized learning. Transferred to the organizational circumstance, this one-to-one concept idealizes the manager-subordinate relation and is made effective by the Stage Four appraisal system. At long last the performance appraisal system may become the focal point of employee development. That it is also enhanced by the "freedom of access" law is irrelevant to the basic soundness of a one-to-one developmental effort; but the law certainly compels organizations to move more rapidly toward individualizing their developmental programs.

4. CONDITIONS FOR EFFECTIVE PERFORMANCE APPRAISALS

On the Part of the Appraiser

What must the appraiser know? First, the organization's philosophy and goals and how these affect the job of the appraisee must be clear. In the case of the spendthrift sales manager who must cut costs, is the expectation of the company one of strong demand, or is it easygoing, or even *ad hoc*, in its inconsistency? In what stage of growth is the organization? Knowing the organization's philosophy and goals enables the appraiser, and of course the appraisee as well, to know by how much the sales manager must cut costs and, more importantly, why. Knowing the climate of the organization—"We're in this together" or "You'd better shape up or else" or "Let's be careful in our analysis of the problem before we take action"—the appraiser can then move with certainty and with appropriate action. Without such knowledge, the appraiser's judgments and observations will be only his own and not representative of the organization.

Second, the appraiser needs to know something about human behavior. He needn't be a lifetime student of human behavior; but there are a few basic premises that an appraiser must know. For example, he must know that

• all behavior has causes

• all behavior meets some needs of the individual

- each individual is unique in some respects and the same as all others in some respects

- each individual's behavior at any moment is the result of the interaction within him of his biological make-up (genetic inheritance) and his culture (parental and social milieu, values, philosophy, etc.)

- generalizations about behavior are false: for example, all redheads have tempers; all Dutchmen are stubborn; all fat people are happy-go-lucky

Without such elementary knowledge, the appraiser can make serious errors in defining targets for the appraisee. The superior might erroneously urge upon the subordinate a job target that requires imagination when the appraisee is literal-minded and pedantic. A more knowledgeable appraiser knows that imagination is unlikely to be acquired. In short, it it is clear that to conduct a competent appraisal some knowledge of human behavior is essential, the more the better.

But knowledge is not all that a good appraiser must have; skill in applying that knowledge is equally necessary. Listening skills, articulating skills, questioning skills, decision-making skills: the list is long. It is probably inappropriate in the present context to detail all of the skills required to use one's knowledge competently. Certainly to have great knowledge used in foolhardy, bumbling ways is worse than ignorance. However, in all probability, as knowledge is acquired so is the skill to use it. How could one be acutely aware that all behavior has causes without developing some skill in ascertaining, through questioning and listening, what is causing the sales manager's spendthriftness?

Finally, there is the third basic requirement of an appraiser: an appropriate attitude. Let us assume that attitude is an emotionalized mind-set, a feeling tone, a point of view, made up of the appraiser's interests, desires, needs, and experience. If the appraiser, for example, sees appraisal as a chore, the appraisal will be performed perfunctorily. But if the appraiser sees appraisal as an opportunity to contribute to the appraisee's development, his attitude will be different. The appraiser must feel (and communicate) a total commitment to the success of the subordinate. If deficiencies and shortcomings show up during the appraisal procedure, then the appraiser's attitude should say, "You and I have a problem here"; it should not say, "Here's a problem area you need to work on." Thus, if the appraiser really means what he says—and it is part of appraising effectiveness to mean it—then the subordinate is much less likely to resent criticism and to see the boss as one who genuinely cares.

In addition to the appraiser's knowledge, skill, and attitude, there is the obvious requirement for an understanding of the appraisee as a person. Since a major objective of appraisal is to improve performance and to achieve desired results, the personal resources of the appraisee must logically be understood if the targets for growth are to be either challenging or attainable.

How well a superior understands the subordinate is fairly easily determined by applying a simple criterion: Can he predict the subordinate's behavior? That is, given any known circumstance coming up, can he foresee the subordinate's general reactions and behavior? If Charlie the salesman generally has an alibi for his late weekly reports, the superior, knowing Charlie fairly well, can predict that Charlie will have another excuse this week.

The good appraiser should also be an astute observer of human behavior. This means more than casual observation; it means instead a close study of how and why the subordinate behaves as he does. Is Charlie always late with weekly reports? If not, what kinds of reports is he late with? The good appraiser objectively studies the subordinate, avoids quick generalizations, and consistently tries to understand the complex causes of behavior.

Furthermore, the good appraiser knows how to individualize a program of learning and growth in order to improve performance. Doing something with one's understanding of a subordinate as a person and with one's knowledge of a subordinate's job is the essence of Stage Four appraisals. Here is where the good appraiser's ingenuity and insight create a custom-built training/development program, a one-to-one, specific, understandable effort to improve performance.

The effective appraiser knows how to encourage the subordinate. A technical term for encouragement is reinforcement. When an appraiser's progress toward specific goals is reinforced by evidence, he is inevitably encouraged and spurred on. He can then feel comfortable at knowing how he is doing. The significance of such reinforcement lies in the fact that almost everyone needs an answer to the question, "How am I doing?"

Finally, the good appraiser views the performance appraisal as a formal recording of his relationship with the subordinate. It is not a summary of a once-a-year, required confrontation. In fact, the appraisal forms, listing performance objectives and evidence of progress toward them, may often be referred to by both superior and subordinate. The documents are simply a running record of the subordinate's progress. Such a system, conducted with such an attitude, goes a long way toward vitalizing the appraisal system as a developmental tool.

Requirements of the Appraisee

There are requirements, too, for the appraisee. First of all, the appraisee, it must be assumed, is motivated to improve his performance. If he is indifferent, complacent, lethargic, or resistant—in short, unmotivated to improve—then his attitude and expectation should be the appraiser's concern.

It is worth digressing to point out, however, that a human being is never actually unmotivated. As indicated earlier, all behavior has causes and all behavior serves to meet the individual's needs. Therefore, the so-called unmotivated, indifferent jobholder may be an employee with needs that are not being met by the job, let alone by a need to improve in performance. The employee may have needs that conflict with the requirements of the job such as family worries that transcend his interests in the job; or there may be needs that are met outside the job that preempt any causes for wanting to improve in performance, such as a desire to have one's own business that is so strong that the job is merely a means for earning the cash with which to start it.

An example drawn from our experience makes this point clear. The manager of a large department of clerical employees complained: "Look at those people; it's a quarter to five and already they're clearing their desks, waiting for the five o'clock quitting bell to ring. They're simply not motivated." When the bell rang at five, all sixty dashed for the elevator. Obviously, they were motivated—to get home, maybe, or to do some last-minute shopping. Their purposes were simply not aligned with their jobs. They were motivated all right, had in fact lots of drive, but not for their positions, and not for improved performance.

Another requirement of the appraisee, one shared with the appraiser, of course, is to be candid and open about the jointly determined, specific targets as the search is made for ways to improve performance. Obviously, defensiveness is inappropriate and stifling. But candor and objectivity in discussing performance (not the performer, let's not forget) is vital to the process.

5. CONCLUSION—THE FUTURE OF APPRAISALS

In all probability, Stage Four appraisal systems will endure unless our society radically changes. The bases for endurance can be briefly summarized.

1. Responsible managements, especially of larger organizations, will always need to know how each employee performs, what potential is available, and how to guarantee effectiveness of the total work force. Appraisal systems help to meet these needs.

2. Participation (involvement) of the subordinate in the appraisal process is psychologically sound.

3. In some ways, appraisal systems foster career planning, by which the employee's needs for a satisfying way of life and the organization's needs for effective job performance are both met. Appraisals seem to be one excellent way to control judiciously the stability of the organization. In fact, appraisals complement such traditional "golden handcuffs" as guaranteed wages, contracts, stock options, vested pension programs, and the like. An effective appraisal effort accentuates the voluntary involvement of the employee in the organization. It says to the appraisee, "You can't be bought, but you can be won over."

4. Clearly, appraisals are beneficial to both appraisee and appraiser. The process of careful examination of the subordinate's performance, the setting up of near-term objectives, and the evaluation from time to time of progress inevitably provokes self-examination. Such an observation is no quixotic leap in logic. If superior and subordinate are genuine in their discussions of these matters—how each sees himself, how each feels, how each sees the other—their discussions will

certainly produce insights. And these are the beginning of wisdom. Thus the two parties in the appraising process help each other.

Finally, as one tries to penetrate the future, one concludes that a new, less static term than "appraisal" may well emerge. Perhaps something like "developmental guide" or "improvement planning guide" or some happy phrase can be found that more distinctly identifies the purpose and use of a continual record of performance.

PART TWO
The Manager

CHAPTER IV.
The Roles of the Manager

1. INTRODUCTION

The changes in the individual within the organization as discussed in Part One—changes in expectations, values, interests—compel changes in his manager. This chapter examines the nature and significance of these changes in the role of the manager and identifies the major forces that will almost certainly affect that role in the foreseeable future.

The concept of role and its implications are matters of growing importance in today's culture. It is the next step in the search of the 60s for identity. Now people are asking not "Who am I?" but rather "How do I fit in?"—in other words, "What is my role?"

It is not surprising that this concern for role and for supporting role concepts has become more pronounced in the study of business organizations as well as in the current theories of the science of management. The emphasis on role, however, is not well articulated. There are frequent oblique references to the role of management or to the role of managers, but there is little direct attention to the definition of and the exploration of role concepts per se. As a result, it has remained an illusive and undefined concept, wandering in and

out of discussions ostensibly devoted to other more easily defined topics.

In the past, studies of management have displayed a preoccupation with the "how to" kinds of things. "How to" can be
specific, well articulated, and quite structured. It is not surprising, therefore, that it has received an initial emphasis in
the science of management. By contrast, "role" deals with
less structured but more fundamental questions such as, "For
what purpose do we need to have management?" Thus,
"role" attempts to deal with less general and more broadly
applied principles. For any situation, roles can be as individualized and diversified as personality itself. In analyzing role,
therefore, it is not a rigidly formalized "how to" that is of
concern but rather the matter of fit of a given person to the
needs of a specific organizational situation. Consider the following:

George was stunned. He sat at his desk not knowing what
to do. Today was to have been the high point of his very successful career. He knew that Jim was due to retire in a few
months, leaving an opening at the corporate vice-president
level. George was sure that he was a leading candidate for
the position and when Harry, the chairman of the company,
had invited him to join him at his club for lunch, he
naturally assumed that it was to tell him of his promotion.

But George's hopes were crushed when over coffee Harry
brought up the matter of the corporate vice-presidency.
Harry's words ran through George's mind again and again as
he sat, hurt and confused, back in his own office.

"George, you've done a top flight job with your division.
You've turned things around and built up the business to a
solid, profitable state. You've been a real dynamo. Now I
know that you want to replace Jim in the corporate office. In
fairness to you, I wanted to tell you personally that we've decided to give the job to Bill. He's done a good job too and
he's just more of what we're looking for to fill Jim's shoes.
George, the things you've done, you do very well. But they're
not the things we need to have done at the executive office.
Frankly, we just can't see you fitting the role of a corporate
vice-president."

We have here a general manager who has performed with
excellence. He is a very capable and skilled manager. He
would seem to have earned the right to be promoted. But he

was judged not to fit the role of a corporate executive. Can there be valid reasons for this?

In this instance, Harry did have good reasons for his decision. George was a hard-driving, strong-willed manager who had turned a failing division around by using his entrepreneurial flair and his dominant will to overcome problems. He was successful because, being totally involved, he was always at the scene of the action. He solved all of the problems himself. His people were good performers but strictly implementers with no real decision-making talent; and they were developing none because George made all the decisions. His role was that of a strong, dominant leader, an incisive decision-maker, a one-man show.

A corporate executive position required a role that George's temperament and style prevented him from fulfilling. It required the ability to manage from a distance and to maintain control without being in the thick of things. It was a role of guiding other Georges to find the best answers themselves, not to decide for them. George was a success dealing with today and with a near-term future. The corporate job was for a long-range thinker and a good analyst, not a shrewd, intuitive thinker. The risk that George would become a Peter Principle[1] statistic was too great in Harry's eyes, so he decided to promote a man with less flair who had demonstrated the qualities that were needed for the executive job.

2. THE DEFINITION OF ROLE

What is meant by the role of the manager? The dictionary defines role as "a part which has to be played." But the indiscriminate use of the term with regard to management, together with the lack of a specific, defined body of knowledge about it, confuses role with other concepts. To define role it is helpful first to point out what role is not.

Role Versus Function
Functions of management refer to the tasks and responsi-

[1] Lawrence J. Peter and Raymond Hall, *The Peter Principle*, New York, Morrow, 1969.

bilities of the manager such as planning, organizing, controlling and evaluating. Functions may help to determine what is needed in the role of the manager, but the functions are not the role itself. Functions deal with what is done and are more task oriented than role and more tightly defined. Controlling, for example, is a basic function in management; but how control is exercised may not be basic to the specific situation. For instance, a manager is almost always accountable for control in his area of responsibility. The exercise of that control, however, may be taken care of by systems and procedures or may be delegated as a responsibility to others. In that case, to control is not central to the required role of that manager. Functions tend to grow out the division of labor and are most often expressed in the position description. Role, on the other hand, is determined by the total context of the situation.

Role Versus Style

A style is an integrated and consistent set of behaviors characterized by an identifiable perspective. As an example, leadership is usually a role requirement for most managers. The individual manager may choose to exercise that leadership in a manner that would be described as authoritarian, or he may choose to exercise the leadership role in a manner that would be described as participative. The terms authoritarian and participative refer to styles of managing, but the role is leadership and that remains the same regardless of the style that is used to fulfill the role. Styles tend to be determined by the make-up of the person and by previous successful experiences. Role, by contrast, is determined by the needs of the situation. While style may have either a facilitative or a limiting effect on the capability of the manager to fulfill a required role, it does not determine what the required role is. On the contrary, the most effective style is best determined by the role requirement.

Role Versus Technique

Techniques are specific ways of doing things. They are action oriented and implemental in nature. Techniques are selected on the basis of the task to be accomplished while role requirements are determined by the context of the total situation. To use a management-by-objectives approach would be an example of choosing a particular technique that might serve to fulfill several roles. Furthermore, techniques tend to represent choices, for there are usually a number of different techniques that could be applied to a given task. On the other hand, a specific context is likely to produce only one constellation of role requirements.

The Role of the Manager Defined

Both "role need" and "role requirement" will be used interchangeably in defining a manager's role, for it is always a complex constellation of different role needs that must be fulfilled at the proper time. This is one way of saying that managers exist for purposes and the purposes vary according to changing conditions and the tasks to be accomplished. A specific purpose for the manager's existence creates a role need or role requirement. The constellation of role needs relevant to a given position in a given company at a given time determines the total role of the manager.

Two conceptual characteristics of role must be understood in order fully to comprehend what role is and how it functions. The first is that role is an *interactive* concept. We refer here not to interpersonal interaction even though such may be a critical part of a given role requirement; rather we refer to role needs that come about from the interaction among goals to be accomplished, among resources that exist for the accomplishment of those goals, and within the situational context in which the goals must be achieved. Goals may be short or long term and whichever they are affects the role needs required of the manager. Resources include people, equipment, systems, and whatever else might be available for the accomplishment of a goal. The context is the complex of conditions under which the goals must be met.

For example, let's assume that a product manager has been charged with the introduction of a new product. All the strategies have been set in motion and the goal is to gain a specified market share in a given period of time. The resources include the advertising programs to support the product, sales representation from the existing sales force, and, among other things, productive and distributive resources consistent with the strategic plan. The context would include general market conditions, specific competitive pressures, competing demands that limit the use of the internal resources, as well as a large number of other variables. At this point, the product manager's role may center largely around implementation and control to see that the programs come off as planned. However, a sudden change in goal, resources, or context can produce an interaction among the three that requires an urgent shift in role requirements.

Secondly, role is an *integrative* concept. In carrying out a role the manager does not simply interact with the goals, resources, and situations. It must be a manager's purpose to integrate effectively the task and the resources within the context of the situation. One specific role common to all management responsibility is the role of the manager to integrate tasks and resources.

Peter Drucker has commented that management is the organ of society charged with making resources productive. This comes very close to providing a definition of role as related to management. We could define management role as making resources productive, but this falls a bit short of the mark. If this is all that there is to the management role, then there would likely be a single constellation of specific roles that would fit practically all management situations. But this is not the case. Role constellations vary from company to company and even from position to position within a company. Two contrasting examples illustrate the point:

The XYZ Corporation was a very successful small company in the consumer product field. It had an organization of very capable people. They were all eager and energetic, but they were all implementers. They were great at carrying things through and following up to see that things got done. When it came to devising strategies, having ideas, or making plans, they were really very mediocre. They needed to be pointed in a specific direction and told what had to be done. Then they went off and did it superbly. Ted, the president, played these roles very competently. He was a good intuitive entrepreneur and liked having to come up with the ideas. Therefore he played the role of strategist and planner and directed his people skillfully to see that plans were carried out. It was a good match and the company prospered.

The ABC Corporation, on the other hand, was a different kind of company. It was approximately the same size. It also had a good management organization. They were a different sort of managers, however. They were good conceptual planners and strategists in their own right. Each showed the initiative to move out on his own and determine the best course for his area of responsibility. Tom, the president, had a different set of roles to perform. Because the managers were strong performers with good initiative, they occasionally headed in different directions. Tom's role was one of control and integration of the efforts of his subordinates so that a synergistic result was obtained. Tom guided and coached rather than directed and pushed. He made decisions when he had to but could afford to delegate decision-making responsibility because his people were capable of exercising that responsibility effectively. Tom's company also prospered.

In fulfilling any organizational responsibility, a multitude of roles must be performed. When managers are responsible for people, those people are resources for carrying out the required role. So long as the resources match role requirements, the manager's role is one of pure integration and facilitation of the productivity of his resources. This would be the embodiment of the concept of a manager as a person who gets things done through people. Or to expand upon the Drucker concept, we could define the role of a manager as facilitating the productivity of his resources.

These are only half-truths, however, for they represent the ideal which is seldom found in the real world. After matching resources to role requirements, there are usually role needs left over with no resources to cover them. But the manager is himself a resource and so it usually falls to him to fulfill those remaining role requirements.

3. THE ROLE OF THE MANAGER IN THE PAST

This definition refers to the generalized and total concept of the role of the manager, a role which in itself is a complex constellation of many roles. This constellation of roles has evolved over the years from relatively simple beginnings.

The Manager as an Expert

The oldest approach to selecting managers was to select the best doer to become the manager of other doers. The manager himself was the most knowledgeable and most prolific producer. The engineering manager was the best engineer; the sales manager, the best salesman; the controller, the best accountant. In production, the foremen, superintendents, and managers were those who were the best individual producers. The legends are countless of presidents and vice-presidents of companies, who, when things went wrong, charged into the plant themselves to fix the machinery or to make things happen on the production line.

This simple role is a function of what David Riesman referred to as the industrializing society,[2] although it influenced manager selection long after that era and is still today a frequently dominating factor in the selection of foremen in manufacturing. The major feature of the industrializing society was that public demand outstripped production. Productive capacity had not yet reached a stage where all that could easily be consumed could be produced. As a result, the company that could produce more than its competitors was more profitable. Therefore, the earliest forms of business strategies were production strategies.

In that kind of business environment the role of the manager was that of a technical or functional expert. The management of people was a matter of showing them how to do something and then directing them to do it. Expertise was respected and motivation was based on an internalized work ethic. Authoritarian approaches were therefore successful. The principal ingredients for success were technical knowledge, functional skill, and sound experience. Business acumen and skill in human relations were nice to have, but were not required for the role. The dominant roles of the manager were first, to know what to do, and second, to tell people to do it. This pattern of roles prevailed in all areas of management. The boss was expected to be more knowledgeable and more skilled than his subordinates.

The Manager as a Motivator of People

The period of the industrializing society ended with World War II. The massive war effort produced an industrial complex in North America capable of higher production levels than ever before, virtually totally supporting the war effort of the allied nations. With the end of the war, as this industrial complex turned to producing for the consumer, supply began

[2]David Riesman, *The Lonely Crowd*, New Haven, Yale University Press, 1950.

to exceed demand, and competition among producers became stronger. This ushered in Riesman's "industrialized society" of the 1950s. Manufacturing began to lose its dominance; the importance of sales and, later, marketing grew. A switch from a total reliance on technical competence to psychological skills was begun. Within a short period of time, the primary role of the manager became that of managing people rather than that of managing things. Concomitant changes in cultural values made workers less willing to accept authoritarian approaches and less respectful of pure expertise. Increased emphasis on secondary and higher education made more people experts in their own right. Along with these developments, the concept of motivation gained ascendancy. Being able to stimulate and challenge people became a greater requirement for the manager than being merely a functional expert.

The behavioral sciences began to have an impact as "Theory X" and "Theory Y,"[3] the Blake and Mouton managerial grid,[4] and the original studies on job satisfaction provided some basis for learning how to manage people. Managers realized that people were not all alike and that recognition of individual differences was necessary in order to manage them effectively. By the end of the 1950s, the most effective manager was not the technical or functional expert but the one who knew how to get productivity from people no matter what their functional area. This role was more complex than the one of the earlier period. Managing people involved fulfilling many roles—directing, counseling, coaching, or whatever the situation demanded. Moreover, the necessity of influencing people outside one's own organization placed a demand on the manager to sell ideas as well as a product. Finally, the manager was no longer just an expert; he was a leader. Those managers who could not make this transition drifted into more specialized technical roles, or else simply became ineffective managers.

The Manager as a Professional

Business continued to grow more complex and new role

[3]Douglas McGregor, *The Human Side of the Enterprise*, New York, McGraw-Hill Book Co., 1964.
[4]Robert R. Blake and James S. Mouton, *The Managerial Grid*, Houston, Texas Gulf Publications, 1964.

needs evolved. No longer was managing a matter of responding just to technical requirements or just to the needs of
people. A constellation of needs that had to do with the
business as a business began to evolve. In the industrializing
period, a period of undersupply, the company that could produce well was automatically profitable. As the business world
moved into the era of the industrialized society, a period of
oversupply, the company that could sell its product effectively
was automatically profitable. In the later industrialized
period, this was not sufficient. To be profitable, the company
had to be effective as a total business. As a result, the concept
of professional manager evolved, centering around this new
constellation of role needs such as planning, controlling, evaluating, and organizing, which existed regardless of whether
the management position was in manufacturing, marketing,
or personnel.

With this common group of core roles that applied to all
functions, management began to move from the realm of an
art toward that of a science. This produced the first generalized and broadened role of management. The manager became an expert not on technical or functional matters or on
people alone, but rather an expert on the process of management. For the first time these specific roles were carefully defined, differentiated, and categorized. The manager was a
planner, regardless of whether he was at the executive or
middle-management level. The emphasis on planning differed
according to the situation, but planning as a role was a constant. The manager was also an evaluator, an organizer, and
many other things. As the science of management evolved,
specific techniques were identified for use in accomplishing
each of the management roles. Management by objectives,
participative management, and management by exception are
examples. As additional and alternative techniques were identified, defined, and described, the process of management became more formalized. Managers, or at least good managers,
were seen as professionals and more as generalists than
specialists. This led to some problems, for the emphasis now
was on process more than on the results produced by the
process. Managers began to view the role of management as
a unitary function. The way things were done became more
important than what was accomplished.

This focus on process rather than on results dominated the
concept of management role into the late 60s and still colors

the perspective of many managers. Many seem to be preoccupied with a single right way to do things, neglecting the results that they are able to accomplish. Nowhere does it show more strongly than in the perspective that many managers have of the role of leadership. Unfortunately, those managers who overemphasize process and cling to a sterotyped concept of professional management see only one way to exercise the management roles. They cannot (or will not) examine the goals and the situation to determine which roles and therefore which tools are required to accomplish effective results.

The more successful professional managers, of course, do not fall into this trap. They see professional management techniques and styles for what they really are, tools for accomplishing worthwhile goals and results. As business moved through the late 60s and into the 70s, the more results-oriented managers brought the professional management style closer to a full realization of its potential. As alternative methods and approaches were developed, the professional manager added these to his capability and was thus in a better position to facilitate the productivity of his resources by personally supplementing those resources when necessary. The less effective managers were those who selected the tools according to their likes and their habits rather than to fit the role that was needed.

4. THE EFFECT ON ROLE OF ORGANIZATION EVOLUTION

Chapter VIII traces the evolution of organization structure from its beginning in the entrepreneurial stage through various stages to the final stage, the complex matrix form. The role of the manager has very closely paralleled this organizational evolution. There are many organizations today in the entrepreneurial stage wherein the role of management is quite different from that in organizations that have reached the bureaucratic or even the matrix stage. Consider George, the successful division manager who was not selected as a corporate vice-president. George was successful because he fulfilled the roles required by an entrepreneurial organization. However the corporation of which the division was a part was making the transition from the personal to the professional stages of management. Not having demonstrated any of the capabilities necessary to fulfill the executive role under those conditions, George would indeed have been an excessively high-risk candidate for the position of vice-president.

The most trying periods for identifying and fulfilling the role needs in an organization are those periods of transition from one organizational phase to the next. The role requirements for managers change very quickly and many managers are not able to perceive the need for such required changes. When they do, they can be successful in either avoiding or minimizing the effect of the crisis periods that propel an organization from one stage of evolutionary development to the next.

5. THE EVOLVING ROLES OF MANAGER

Within the general role, as we have defined it, there are a multitude of specific roles that the manager must handle according to the situation. The role of the manager today is never simple; nor is it static. The forces of change cause shifts and modifications of the role needs and, therefore, of the general role itself. Because of the interactive nature of a role, a change in goals, objectives, context, or the available resources requires a shifting of the manager's role. A new product may be launched, budgets may be revised, a new law or regulation may be passed, or a key team member may be lost. Each event might force a shift in the many roles that the manager must fulfill. The emergence from the period of organizational crisis that accompanies the shift from one stage of development to another may so drastically alter the manager's role that he is unable to move with his organization from one stage to another. This is a disease that frequently has no cure; it can only be prevented. This is why the preparation of managers for assuming new roles must be such a vital part of ongoing management development.

It would be impossible to list and describe all of the roles that a manager might have to fulfill in carrying out his responsibilities. However, we can point out a few of the roles that are common to most management situations. Many specific roles are easy to fulfill and require almost no conscious attention on the part of the manager. But there are tougher roles, such as being a leader, businessman, strategist, and interface, which are of such importance that a failure to fulfill them adequately may place the whole managerial effort in jeopardy.

The Manager as a Leader

Whenever people are a part of the resources available for meeting objectives, the manager must be a leader. This is no different from the earlier entrepreneurial and industrializing periods. The entrepreneur and the authoritarian managers were also leaders, and effective ones. Their effectiveness was based on a suitability of leadership style to the role required in their situations. What is different today is the combination of goals, circumstances, and resources which gives an entirely different role requirement to leadership.

In the earlier periods, the leader himself was the important factor. What he could do effectively determined the best way for him to lead others. Today, however, those being led are at least equally as important, particularly when the complexity of tasks and goals are considered. It is of crucial importance that each team member make his fullest contribution. Today, a leadership style will be effective, therefore, when it fits not only the leader but also those being led. People are quite diverse and therefore styles of leadership can also be diverse and still be effective. Consider Ted and Tom, the presidents of the two companies cited earlier. Each had an entirely different way of leading his organization, yet each was effective.

Leadership style may even have to vary within the approaches used by a single manager. He may find that he must provide firm, unambiguous, and clearly authoritarian forms of leadership to one member of his team while another may be led most effectively by a loose, permissive, and participative style. Attempts to vary his own style of leadership produce additional problems for the manager as well as for the managed, and must be accomplished without disintegration of the manager's overall style and without obvious inconsistency. It is this kind of complexity that makes the leadership role a challenge.

The Manager as a Businessman

Today most managers are required to fulfill to some degree

the role of businessman. Not only at the executive level but also in the functional management areas, it is necessary to look at what is being done as a matter of business rather than just as production, sales, or accounting. Even the purely staff areas must think in business terms about the services they supply. Each functional area is a sub-business within the total business with its own particular form of bottom line. Being a businessman in addition to being a functional manager is an unavoidable role in almost all situations.

The Manager as a Strategist

The decade of the 70s will probably go down as the decade of the strategist. The ability to devise and implement the strategies of marketing, finance, as well as the total business, has set off the strategist in management from those who lack that ability. Strategic management appears to have developed with the birth of "marketing" as a concept separate from the supportive services that originally were grouped together under that term. Today, all functional areas are considered amenable to strategic management. There are strategies for manufacturing, for employee relations, and even strategies for research and development. Since strategies determine what will be done in a business, those who are capable of devising good strategies have an advantage over their competition for top level management positions.

Strategic thinking, the foundation of strategy development, is a difficult thing to describe because there is still much to be learned about it as a phenomenon. The physical sciences frequently identify the existence of physical realities long before they can accurately analyze their make-up; and so it is in the behavioral sciences. Strategic thinking can be identified, it can be evaluated as to its quality as a whole; but all the components that go to make it up are not known nor is it known exactly how they relate to each other.

Nevertheless, some of the key components of strategic thinking have been identified and managers can develop skills in their use. For instance, good strategies are directed at the attainment of clearly identified goals. This may seem oversimplified, but it is not. Many companies and their executives include tactics in their planning that have no identifiable bearing upon the goals that they are trying to achieve. Rather, these activities are directed at emotional goals that are quite different from the rational goals that have been set. We also know that strategic thinking places heavy emphasis on options. The better strategists keep their options open as long as they can do so without losing options by default. The strategist also tends to place more emphasis on contingency planning as one form of dealing with options.

Other and better understood concepts undoubtedly play a role in strategic thinking as well. Problem identification is an example. The strategist will want to know the exact dimensions of a problem and also what a problem is not.[5] Strategy formulation is possible not only across all functions but also often at relatively low levels in an organization. Overall, the ability to play the role of the strategist is likely to be the most valuable role concept in the manager's repertoire of capabilities.

The Manager as an Interface with the Outside World

In the past, contact with the world outside of the organization was limited to a few areas of the business. The salesman, of course, was the primary contact with the customers. Higher-level executives carried out external relations of a different sort such as negotiations with the financial community or with governmental regulatory bodies. Most other managers, on the other hand, were required only to relate to people within the organization. However, the concept of customer service began to bring research and development people out of their laboratories and engineers away from their drawing boards in order to contact the world of the customer. In the late 60s and early 70s the importance of financing began to take people in the accounting and treasury functions away from their ledgers to interact with financial institutions and the investment community. Increased governmental regulation forced managers in many functional areas to be concerned with a variety of effective interactive roles with their local communities.

Furthermore, a higher percentage of companies now actively encourage their people to take part in civic activities, professional associations, and other forms of public participation beyond the requirements of their day-to-day work. In

[5]Charles H. Kepner and Benjamin B. Tregoe, *The Rational Manager*, New York, McGraw-Hill Book Company, 1965.

taking part in these activities, the manager contributes, not only in his own name, but also as a representative of his company.

The manager of today simply does not have the luxury of being able to isolate himself within the boundaries of his own specific area of responsibility. It is no longer unusual to have first-line production supervisors visit customer installations in order to understand the requirements for special processing or to go to a supplier's plant so as to be involved firsthand in the purchase of new equipment or new supplies.

Today's requirement is therefore for a person who deals not only with the people who report to him and those to whom he reports but also one who interacts with the outside world in whatever capacity is required by his particular responsibilities. This obviously increases the requirement for sound interpersonal capability of managers. The "bull of the woods" and the back-room analyst have limited usefulness in today's management structure (and even greater limitations in opportunity for advancement). When management was originally described as getting things done through people, the reference was to the people who reported to the manager. Today's meaning is broader. The manager still gets things done through people, not just his own but through whomever he must interact with in his own company, in someone else's company, or in government. The interface role is firmly estabished among the role needs that require significant attention from effective managers.

6. MANAGEMENT ROLES OF THE FUTURE

What changes can be predicted in the role requirements of managers in the future? In the development of management role there has been a growing complexity of role requirement. Is this likely to continue? At what point will complexity become so great that coping with the situation will be impossible? It is likely that the growth and complexity will continue. If role requirements do not become more complex, they certainly will be different. If complexity becomes too great, the past tells us that new forms of organization and division of responsibility are likely to occur. This in turn affects management role, assuring us that the requirements will be different in the future. The requirements will vary according to the new interactions between situations, goals, and resources.

We cannot predict exactly how these changes will occur; but we can look carefully at the factors that will influence them in order to get a general feel for their trends.

Cultural Changes

The changes that occur as a part of the evolutionary process of cultural growth will have a significant impact on business in the future and, therefore, upon the role requirements of managers. We exist in an era of extreme cultural unrest. Cultural values and mores, which today are in a constant state of reassessment, will have a powerful impact on future managers.

For example, the present stress in our society on human rights, the pressure to secure quality of life on the job, and the insistence by an increasing number of people in the workforce that they be involved in policy decisions—aspects of the cultural revolution such as these certainly will affect the job of the manager. As cultural needs are altered, the context in which organizations function, do business, or provide services also changes. The human rights needs as they have evolved in the last ten to twenty years are an example; they are now recognized and acknowledged, and the pressures of society, both moral and legal, have altered the context within which the manager must manage people. Recruitment, selection, supervision, training, development and promotion are affected and either create new role needs for the manager or significantly alter those of the past.[6]

Contextual Influences

We have discussed a change in context as a result of today's cultural revolution. Context as well is subject to change as a result of its own influences. Technical advances, new approaches to doing business, innovative ideas that get widespread application—these all represent variables in the context within which the manager must achieve his specific objectives. In Chapter VIII, the evolution of organization's

[6]Chapter X reports the results of an RHR survey of top management's concerns, which include the effects on the business climate of societal changes.

structure is traced, with each phase of organization development representing a different context and calling for different roles to be met by the manager.

Organizational Influences

Various organizational factors will exert both singly and in combination an everchanging influence on the role of management. The people who make up organizations change, and those changes affect what must be done in order to manage them.[7] The increasing professionalism of managers will require quite different roles in the future. The role of the expert will become even less crucial and other roles involving more effective kinds of leadership and strategic emphasis will take over the top priority. Managers and those who are managed are already better educated and more sophisticated in their knowledge and perceptiveness. This trend will continue and, perhaps, even escalate. Greater competence will permit increased decision-making responsibility at lower levels. The capability to make these decisions will, in turn, increase pressure for the right to make decisions. One of the major tasks for both the present and the future will be to push decision-making responsibility down to the lowest practical level without abdicating accountability or control.

A second internal organizational influence will be a continuing pressure for both effectiveness and efficiency of management. Accountability will be more clearly and more stringently defined. The management structure will be as lean as effectiveness permits. The changing structure of an organization as it moves through various stages of development will itself place new requirements on the manager, as the organization progresses (as discussed in Chapter VIII) through the entrepreneurial, personal, professional, bureaucratic, and possibly the matrix stages of development. As new needs arise, even more advanced approaches to organization structure may evolve, bringing a new set of contextual conditions affecting role needs.

The Measures of Success

Managers are constantly reminded that profit or the "bottom line" is a measure of success, sometimes even considered

[7]See Chapter I, "The Individual in the Organization."

the only measure. Such an emphasis on profit will continue, but what may change are the values that determine how much profit is considered necessary and how that amount may be measured. Profit as the principal measure of success is thus only a half-truth. There are other measures.

Even though it is seldom explicity stated, most businessmen would readily accept the fact that *viability* represents an equally important measure of success. Viability is the condition of ongoingness and potential through internal organizational capability that almost guarantees continuation of the business. Profitability without viability is unthinkable. Viability comes about because of many factors. Financial viability is always a requirement since profitability and viability are inextricably linked. There is also business viability: a business organization must be prepared to stay with the times in terms of product development, new forms of service, and efficiency of operation. Organizational viability is a critical area often overlooked, for an organization should have within itself the means of renewal through orderly succession and management development.

Will there be other measures of success that will join profitability and viability to complicate the picture of management role? Yes, it is likely that there will be. Although exact prediction is impossible, there appears to be at least one in the embryonic stage—namely, political and social influences that seem to threaten the American free enterprise system. These influences are ideological pressures to take the social responsibility of businesses, the role of "good citizen" that so many organizations have dutifully played, and entrench it so that contributing to the welfare of society is a major requirement, not a voluntary matter at all.

But if such an extreme is not reached, it is quite certain that the context in which profitability and viability will be judged will change. The use of profits may be more stringently judged than will be the amount of the profits. And management may well need to play the role of advocate and apostle for the free enterprise system if some of these influences continue to be rampant.

7. CONCLUSION—IMPLICATIONS OF CHANGES IN THE ROLE OF THE MANAGER

1. *Role-playing.* The quintessential fact about the manager's job in the 80s is that it will be multi-faceted. The traditional concept of the manager's functions is unaltered, perhaps by definition, unalterable. He still will be responsible to fulfill Fayol's 1916 analyses—i.e., to plan, organize, staff, direct, coordinate, report and budget.[8] But the AMA and others notwithstanding, the 80s manager will do these things in many different ways, depending on the circumstances and the people who are managed. In other words, managing is not today, nor will it be tomorrow, a unitary function, a universal formula to be followed, a duty to be performed according to set rules regardless of the situation. The effective manager will be skillful in adapting his managerial activities, his role, to the needs of the moment. He cannot only authorize, direct, and order as means of securing action. The future manager must be, in truth, a person of many parts.

2. *Exerting less overt authority.* The mood of the times will probably reject as amateurish a constant reliance by a manager upon the inherent authority of the position. Those who are managed will probably dislike any show of authority and will either rebel against it or walk away from it. The old-style boss whose word was law and whose orders were unquestioned is outmoded. Instead, the more substantial reliance in managing upon knowledge, communication skills, clarity of objectives, and even that subtle charisma in a personality that stimulates and inspires will be effective—and may be demanded by subordinates. Credibility will outweigh command as a way of securing cooperation from subordinates. This style of exercising power with, rather than over, people is not a new technique or an adjustment to the individual of the present day. Rather, it is a managerial philosophy that respects the capacity of others to contribute to the enterprise and actively solicits their ideas.

3. *Using present personnel.* In the future there may be fewer changes in personnel, thereby compelling managers to

[8]H. Fayol, *Administration industrielle et générale*, Paris, Dunod, 1916.

secure effective performance without shuffling the players or
bringing in new talent from outside. The best managers always have been skillful, like a Casey Stengel or a Vince Lom-
bardi, in developing winning teams without filling their
benches only with superstars. But if the trends in today's social legislation continue, managers will have to be increasingly resourceful in finding ways to lead available personnel
to be effective performers.

4. *Integrating goals.* The manager of the future will be
like his predecessors in knowing his own goals and objectives;
what he wants to accomplish will always be clearly before
him. But he will differ from most of them in his clear perception of how what he's striving to accomplish fits into the
goals of the whole organization. His goals actually may be
determined as he participates with colleagues—other managers, staff people, officers—in setting the organization's
goals. As this is done, strategies for reaching them may also
be discussed. And such strategic matters will shape each manager's procedures and plans. In short, the manager will not be
isolated in a cocoon with his own group, he will be part of a
total group effort.

5. *Practical and custom-built training.* Another implication
is that the training of managers will be practical, not theoretical; and it will be custom-built, not generalized. For one
thing, the materials for seminars, for group experiences, and
for skills-training programs will come from researchers who
have made extensive, on-the-spot studies of what managers
actually do. Consequently, managers will more and more be
trained to practice with skill the actual activities of managers, not the activities that a nonmanaging academician may
think managers should be engaged in.

Furthermore, the training will enable the manager to accomplish his own goals in his own way. This custom-built or
individualized learning is necessitated by the many roles of a
manager as he lives with many different situations and circumstances. In other words, the old way of training managers
by instructing them in a "one best way" is gone. The new day
calls for a broader span of both understanding and skills
which will enable the manager to manage effectively in any
circumstance.

6. *Education: More is better.* The increase in the educational level of the workforce, which is predicted to continue,
will have several effects: communicating should be easier and

more frequent; understanding of goals and objectives will be improved; the rationales for integrating all aspects of the organization (that is, the reason for teamwork) will be better understood and accepted; the abstractions of the organization's philosophy will be more readily understood and believed. Finally it is obvious that a better-educated workforce will require better-educated managers who understand the complexities of philosophy, of policy changes, and of goal setting, and, most importantly, can clearly articulate their understanding. Mangers will get more questions and suggestions from subordinates who are using their education to do more independent thinking. And to these each manager must be open and responsive and must not automatically read the subordinates' behavior as disloyality or a challenge to his authority.

CHAPTER V.
The Skills and Training of the Manager

1. INTRODUCTION

The understanding of the manager's skills and how they are
obtained has evolved over many centuries. Over two thousand
years ago Plato described the best selection and training for
the guardians of the state. The education of princes for the
task of governing was concisely described by Machiavelli.
Nineteenth-century military and colonial organizations made
their own additions and refinements. Concern over the distinctive abilities of those who lead has probably been with us
since the time humans first came together in groups.

Modern day ideas about the manager's job requirements go
back about half a century. In 1916, Fayol, in France, writing
on the functional analysis of administration, provided the first
systematic description of what managers ought to do. He
stated that they should plan, organize, staff, direct, coordinate, report, and budget. These seven activities, rooted in
logic, history, and experience, became the foundation for the
traditional thinking about management which persists to the
present. Structures of industry, government, the military, and
universities were established using these categories. Schools of
business administration formed programs of study around
them. Their presence was verified by research, and the con-

temporary tools of management added an element of precision.

Before World War II these ideas about management were the concern of specialists, consultants, and university professors. But with significant exceptions, such as Standard Oil and General Motors, few practicing managers paid any attention to the thinking and writing about management. Even in universities the subject was taught either as part of a commerce course or as a specific functional skill, such as production management or financial management. However, after 1941 the tremendous pressure for effective wartime production brought about an explosion in the development and use of both management science and management tools. What had been the practices of the few became the methods of the many. Because of, or in spite of, these new approaches, organizations were assembled, managers chosen, and systems of operating designed with beneficial results; industry manufactured and delivered huge amounts of goods, and both public and private organizations selected and trained great numbers of people for unfamiliar roles and new skills.

This massive, concentrated application of management concepts and methods had a profound impact. Managements came to see them not as academic pastimes but as practical devices for securing effective performance. Schools of business administration and commerce were never the same again in methods, status, or funding. Where before the war there had been but three schools of advanced management training, hundreds now flourished. Their graduates were sought after and their researchers accepted, if not welcomed.

Postwar patterns of business education and writing have paralleled Fayol's seven functional activities. The manager is perceived as a rational planner. His basic tools are extensions of mathematics—for example, accounting, financial analysis, and linear programming, and logic—such as the case method, decision making, and organizational structure. He must be trained to apply those tools skillfully to the basic business functions. Conventional wisdom supposes that the manager would perform better if he knew more about how to plan, organize, and direct. A casual glance at current brochures for management courses will show that they are aimed at building functional knowledge and skills. The courses listed are in mathematics, statistics, computers, finance, accounting, managerial policy, managing human resources, and marketing. It would appear that we have not moved very far from Fayol's concept of the manager.

One condition complicates the application of traditional ideas to the practice of management: both the professors of business administration and the designers of management courses live in an academic environment. To persist and prosper they must be accepted by their superiors and counterparts in other academic fields. Consequently, they have a genuine need to make their subject matter and their research compatible with the university environment. It was naturally desirable to base management science firmly in mathematics and logic. Research and writing reinforced and reconfirmed traditional management thinking. Until very recently the whole structure of management training was based upon the assumption that the skills attributed to managers by theorists, writers, and academicians are actually those that managers displayed on the job. But managers are, in reality, somewhat different from the theorists' preconceived assumptions about them. Although managers ought to plan, for example, perhaps the constraints and pressure of job activity keep them from planning to the extent which nonmanagers believe necessary. This kind of circumstance might help to explain why managers complain that so much of management education and training is unrelated to the demands of their work. Similarly, students, coming from their graduate training in business, discover that their hard-won knowledge and skills are often held in low esteem by experienced managers.

Consider the following telephone conversation:

"Hello, Harry. I want to apologize for the three-year plan being late, but the production problems have been such that I couldn't spare the time or the people to finish it. The main thing is getting the production out, and we've done that on time. Yes, I know I'm in budget trouble. But the oil crisis and currency fluctuations on raw materials have made a joke out of those figures. Don't tell me you're still going to hold me to that?"

Every operating manager recognizes how commonplace are these conflicts between what should and what does happen. On the other hand, if traditional concepts of the manager's activities and skills are to be accepted, such conflicts should be minimal. As this gap between theory and practice has become more obvious, many managers have accepted it as an irritating fact of life. They recognize the face validity of the need for planning, control, and coordination. Indeed the expectations for their performance are set on this rational level. Although they accept the virtue of the principles, they are unable to apply them effectively to their jobs.

2. NEW APPROACHES

Researchers recognized this dilemma and in recent years began to move from armchair, academic theorizing toward direct contact with managers at work. Initial attempts, using conventional survey methods, tended to reconfirm traditional concepts. However, closer examination revealed that both the researchers and the managers were reflecting established ideas. These surveys were constructed and analyzed using categories based on conventional management thinking. Managers themselves provided answers that proved to be very general and to reflect the expected. Social research found what it expected to find.

Such unsatisfactory methods continued until researchers began to observe the day-to-day behavior of managers in their workplaces. Studies of manager skills evolved from theory and speculation to the other extreme of direct observation. This movement began in the 1950s with Carlson[1] who persuaded Swedish company executives to maintain diaries of their activities. Stewart[2] did similar work in Great Britain with middle managers. However, a more exact picture of manager activity was not obtained until Mintzberg[3] persuaded North American senior managers to be observed in their day-to-day activities by researchers.

There have been by now a wide variety of studies from chief executive to foreman that tell us what managers actually do on the job.[4] This research concludes that a manager's

[1]S. Carlson, *Executive Behavior: A study of the workload and the working methods of managing directors*, (Stockholm: Strombergs, 1951).
[2]R. Stewart, *Managers and their jobs: A study of the similarities and differences in the way managers spend their time*, (London: McMillan, 1967).
[3]H. Mintzberg, *The Nature of Managerial Work*, New York, Harper and Row, 1973.
[4]M.W. McCall, Jr., A.M. Morrison, and R.L. Hannan, *Studies of Managerial Work: Results and Methods*, Tech. Rep. No. 9, Greensboro, N.C., Center for Creative Leadership, 1978.

activities are markedly different from the usual assumptions about what managers do. First, managers are not reflective planners. Most of them are continually busy with interpersonal contacts. Owing to the frequency of interruption, the time they can allot to any one task is brief. Much of the manager's time is spent in obtaining information, the basic ingredient of his work. A greater proportion of time is spent in this activity than in decision making. The information is secured or relayed primarily orally. Most managers spend little time writing because it reduces the amount of time available for information gathering. If the manager must spend time documenting information, less time is available for staying in touch. To keep current, the manager maintains a network of contacts within the organization which may not reflect the formal structure, for frequently the manager is forced into fire-fighting. For most managers the problems in delegating are often inherent in the work itself rather than resulting from the intentional neglect of subordinates. A manager's activities reflect the demands of the job rather than expressing his personal qualities or preferences. A large part of his performance is controlled by other individuals and groups.

From these observations Mintzberg developed a model of manager skill which differs sharply from the traditional model and supports in detail the results of the research. Managers work at an unrelenting pace. They perform a wide variety of tasks in short, unrelated segments. They flourish in a network of interpersonal contacts that keeps them supplied with information gathered primarily by word of mouth. They are surrounded by live action and have little time for reflection. But most important, Mintzberg sees the manager as more controlled by events than controlling them.

One might conclude that the skills required of a manager would be significantly different from those taught in business schools or conventional manager training programs. For example, planning amid chaos and making judgments on oral information appear to be significant. The manager also needs to be able to negotiate with people outside his direct authority for needed resources. He also must have interactive skill with people in order to build a network of relationships to support his needs for information.

These two models of the manager are not mutually exclusive. The frantic activity on a building site does not deny the existence of carefully prepared blueprints and cost estimates. However, the analysis of the behavior of managers requires a change in thinking about the skills of managers and the training appropriate for these skills.

Because managers do not plan or organize to the extent that traditional writers thought they did does not mean that such activities are not needed or do not take place. Mintzberg's model of frantic activity and Fayol's model of rationality and deliberation can be seen to operate concurrently in many present-day organizations. It is possible that managers operate on two separate planes and in two separate time frames. Building contractors, for example, customarily move from a stage of planning, design, and estimating into the commotion of a major construction project. Similarly, many organizations engage in planning sessions at designated times away from company premises in order to escape the limitations of the rapid pace and fragmented time imposed upon them by day-to-day activities.

Importance of Both Old and New

The manager very likely needs two sets of skills. One set would apply to those activities which require deliberation and which have a long time frame. These skills would be patterned after the traditional business school programs. The other skills would apply to day-to-day behaviors and would pertain to interacting with people on a short-term basis and acquiring information for direct action. To this date little attempt has been made to integrate these two ways of describing what managers do. Currently there appears to be more pressure for business schools to conform to a more traditional academic model. The behavior analysts have become increasingly concerned with very specific outcomes and their results may lack general use. Certainly the traditionalists need to study the environment of the manager more closely. At the same time, the more recent researchers need to understand clearly the aims of the behavior they observe.

If our understanding of managerial skills is undergoing a revision, the training of managers is undergoing similar complex changes. An increased understanding of the ways people learn and the impact of communications technology have combined to bring about a revolution in training and educational methods. An age gap exists in how people have learned to learn. Managers in senior positions today were educated managers. In fact the creation and generation of new in- under different principles from those used to train younger formation and methods is so rapid that the providers of train- ing themselves are soon out of date.

3. MISTAKES IN TRAINING

In spite of its presumed importance to the effectiveness of an organization, manager training has often had a bad repu- tation. This poor record often came from a misuse of training by the organizations themselves.

Imitation
Consider the following conversation:

"Say, Harry, Acme is using assertive condescension en- counters for their sales managers. It sounds very good to me. Why don't you see if you can line it up for our people at next month's sales meeting?"

Training by imitation is one of the most common misuses of organizational time and money. What may be right for Company X could be misleading or have no meaning at all for Company Y.

Diversion
Some organizations might use training to divert the atten- tion of managers from a real problem:

"Performance is really down in the development engineer- ing department, Marcia. Why don't you see if we can get them a seminar on creativity?"

Reward
Training is often used as a form of reward:

"Phil, you've done an outstanding job. We're sending you away to Harvard for 13 weeks. Peter will run things while you're gone."

Substitution
Sometimes training is substituted for the building of a sound working relationship:

"I can't understand it. Bill has had the human relations

course and people are still leaving his department. I guess it
didn't take."

Gimmickry

Most misuse of training is rooted in a fascination with
training methods and a disregard for training needs. The
hardware, techniques, and content of many present-day training programs are intriguing and entertaining. Anyone who
has participated in a complex management game recognizes
its challenge and has been stimulated by it.

4. REQUIREMENTS FOR GOOD TRAINING

The problem for organizations is not obtaining participation in training, but determining what kind of training will
improve performance and prepare the manager for greater
responsibility.

Understanding Needs

The starting point of any training is a clear understanding
of organizational needs. Most organizations fail to integrate
training with their long-term manpower plans. This results in
expenditure for training related to present-day demands but
not to those of the future. Corporations which would not
neglect the maintenance of their capital equipment give little
consideration to maintaining their human resources. Most
training departments have not achieved the status of being
considered in long-term planning.

The options identified by assessing organizational needs are
not what sort of seminars to choose, but what new behaviors
or skills the organization requires. Appropriate training can
be selected to fit the individual as well. Consequently, training ought to be linked to performance appraisal. The organization then must decide how it is to integrate this new
behavior or skill into the organization. It may be that, even
after careful analysis, training and job performance are in-
compatible. Such situations, when identified, permit training
courses to be corrected. Fundamentally trainers need to agree
with top management about the results desired from training.
Without this agreement any program to improve skills will

wander from its intended goal and will lose relevance to both the organization and its managers.

Agreement between trainers and top management is an ideal which is not often obtained in many organizations. The two groups do not meet regularly enough for trainers to establish influence. Consequently, when problems arise or plans are made, training is not thought of as a resource. Until there is a strong link between plans and training, programs will be provided that relate only by chance to what is needed. Rarely do we see a combination of corporate need and the powerful, present-day methods of training.

Conditions for Learning

What is it that trainers have to offer to increase the manager's ability to do his job? Galileo said, "You cannot teach a man anything; you can only help him find it within himself." Since Galileo's time, we have discovered significant things about how people learn. Only recently have these findings come out of the laboratory and into practical use. Schools were slow to employ the benefits of this new knowledge, preferring to rely on traditional methods. This is not surprising. The scientific study of learning is less than a century old and has been characterized more by conflicting ideas than by clarity. Nevertheless, certain results stand out to aid our understanding and knowledge of how learning occurs.

If training is to take place, the basic conditions for learning must be present. Drive or motivation must be present in the individual to arouse him to take action. We are motivated by biological drives, needs such as hunger or thirst. We are also motivated by social factors such as recognition and status. The question is frequently raised, "How can I motivate people?" Motives, however, are inside people and always present. Consequently, we cannot motivate them. What we can do is to find reinforcers to satisfy the drives that people have.

In the process of searching for the satisfaction of motives, the individual encounters a variety of objects and situations to which he responds. Some responses result in the motivation being satisfied. Such responses tend to be repeated and to become connected to the object or event that brought about the response. This process which connects drive, stimulus, response and reinforcer is fundamental to learning.

The learning process is seldom considered when training is provided within organizations. It is taken for granted. In earlier times the manager in a training situation was seen to be the passive recipient of facts, an empty container to be filled with new knowledge. Learning-based models see the manager as an active, motivated searcher, willing to explore to find those things which will satisfy his personal motives.

Consider the following example:

George decided that one of his department heads, Bill, did not show a ready understanding of control figures. Consequently, he decided to send him to a local three-day seminar on finance. Bill agreed that this would be a good idea and completed the course. His understanding of figures did not increase, however. If we could have seen inside Bill, we might have understood that he attended the course because he was insecure about keeping his job and wanted to please George. Once into the course he found the content uninteresting and did not respond to it. However, he did respond to his fellow students in ways that satisfied his need to build new social relationships and ease his insecurity. He returned to his company to tell George that he had enjoyed the course and would recommend it to others.

Methods of Learning

Human learning is a more involved topic than we can explore adequately here. Some basic points can be helpful, nevertheless, to the understanding of manager training.

Learning by Trial and Error

Much of learning is trial and error, the testing out of responses just to see if we can get what we want. It is a common experience to be told, "You give it a try" or "Sink or swim." By exploring the situation, the goal eventually will be reached. However, if the method was complicated, it may be difficult to find the way again. A certain number may never discover it. Some sink rather than swim. Although trial-and-error manager training may have the least investment, it has a high cost in time and in people. Its usefulness in learning management skills is limited.

Learning by the Big Picture

Learning also occurs if we are given an overall view of the task to be accomplished. If we can obtain a preliminary idea of the route to the goal, the proper sequence of actions to reach the goal can be prepared. This system helps reduce the error rate. The optimum method is more quickly apparent, saving time and effort. Manager orientation and familiarization courses can help the individual by organizing his understanding of what is to be learned and identifying the characteristics of the learning situation.

Learning by Modeling

We also learn by modeling the performance of others, following the example of someone more experienced or more skilled. Apprentices and mentors are examples of this process. Through observation the learner avoids the mistakes of the one he is modeling. However, this assumes the two have similar motivation, and it loses suitability as the needs of the learner change. Although modeling is restricted by the experience of the one being modeled, it is especially useful in the early stages of learning interactive skills.

Modeling is a strong element in learning the traditions and standards of an organization. By observing how the boss conducts himself, younger managers can identify those responses the organization rewards. The "assistant to————" position is an example of training by modeling. Bad practices may also be modeled, which often poses a drawback.

Learning by Communicating

A large proportion of a manager's skill learning takes place through communication with others. He listens, he responds, he reads, he studies examples, he observes diagrams and tables. Much of present day management training from books, seminars or university training, exemplifies this process.

Most management training is too complex to follow any single method. Some trainers conclude with Galileo that all learning is self-learning and that, consequently, managers should not learn highly specific skills but should learn how to learn. In the complicated and changing business world, isolated problem-solving methods are no longer applicable. The image of the Lone Ranger firing off decisions is a romantic fiction. Instead the manager needs to be closely integrated with his co-workers and with the ebb and flow of information. Present circumstances suggest that the manager needs tools that help him to learn. Reading rapidly and efficiently, listening effectively, using resource material, analyzing information, and finding the right questions should be the start of a manager's training. They do not, however, substitute for the skills required to perform management tasks.

5. CATEGORIES OF TRAINING

Methods of training managers can be divided into three broad categories. The first centers around transferring the knowledge, experience, and judgment of the trainer to the learner. The second is concerned with increasing the learner's understanding of group interactions through the experience by the learner of participation in a group. The third concerns changing the actual behavior of the learner using methods based on behavior analysis.

One: Increase in Knowledge

The first method—increasing the manager's knowledge—assumes that new knowledge will improve performance. The practices of this method include reading, lectures, discussion, and case studies. All depend to a greater or lesser degree on the information and the format provided by someone other than the person who is learning. These follow traditional patterns, paralleling those of a university or school system. Large numbers can be accommodated at reasonable cost; concepts and facts can be explained in detail. To these approaches most managers are accustomed.

However, information can become rapidly obsolete if not regularly renewed. Because the manager has little direct involvement, his motivation may be weak; and the content may be unrelated to the tasks he has to perform on his job. In this category of training the manager is usually learning principles to cover a broad class of situations. Ideally this requires the trainer to understand the surrounding in which these principles will be applied. For example, teaching technical experts to be managers may be a waste of time if the two sets of skills conflict with the demands of the workplace.

Programs of training that only increase knowledge of the ideal or theoretical add little to managerial skill. The worth of the principles taught, of course, cannot be denied. However, as with any ideal, there is extreme difficulty in putting them into practice on the job. For example, some research shows that much of leadership training has actually done little to increase leadership on the job. In fast-moving, high-stress situations, emphasis on good human relations and consideration for subordinates may hinder getting results.

Two: Experiential Training

The second training category centers on the learner's involvement and is often referred to as experiential. The trainer provides only minimal rules or devices to maintain the involvement of the learner and stays in the background except, from time to time, to interpret what the group is doing. The main content of such training is how people work together in groups. Individuals learn about their own reactions and those of the group by participating in the process of learning, of change, or of group interaction. The group explores how it reaches agreement, establishes tasks, methods, and leadership, and settles disagreements. Feedback from the trainer provides greater understanding of the individual's role in the group and the dynamics of change within the group.

In contrast to the methods of training based on business functions, experiential training is rooted in sociology and social psychology. Learning principles and research results from these two fields are used to support the learning that occurs by increased motivation as well as careful use of reinforcement. Understandings acquired under such circumstances can transfer to the workplace in the form of improved insights about how departments work together, how to prepare for change, and how to involve others in defining and solving problems.

However, according to follow-up research of experiential training, not all these activities build skills that increase manager performance. Laboratory training, or the T Group, as it is popularly called, is a method for developing both self-understanding and understanding of how groups function. Although still useful for promoting personal growth, it has passed from the scene as a means of building managerial skills.

In management-team building, experiential training is used to improve performance of small groups. A group chosen from within an organization is given a task or series of short exercises, each of which demonstrates to the group some aspect of its own inner workings. Current organizational issues can be used as material with experienced groups to learn not only about the process of problem solving but also how to identify an optimum solution.

But experiential training makes some managers uncomfortable. Brought up in the knowledge-based tradition, they are ill at ease with the comparatively unstructured format of team training, with leaderless groups, and with instructors who do not appear to do anything. The apparent lack of relation between the content of the training and the activity of the organization may also be discouraging. These concerns are not unfounded. The assumptions underlying experiential training, including the trainer's notions of how people ought to work together, may be inconsistent with the realities of the workplace or a specific organization's philosophy.

Three: Behavior Analysis

The third approach applies behavior analysis methods to the training of managers in skills tailored to specific job activities.[6] In any skill area, such as negotiating, some managers show more success than others. By identifying the specific behaviors that account for the level of success, a behavior profile can be designed which compares a given manager's behavior with that of high performers. The manager's training can then be specified in a program that emphasizes simulation of real life situations. Thus the individual manager's performance in negotiation is observed, measured and the results fed back to him; new goals are set to bring the skill profile more in line with that of highly skilled negotiators; unproductive actions are replaced by more efficient ones; and performance success increases.

Training through behavior analysis has the advantage of allowing the simulations and other course content to be tailored to a specific organization or task. In addition, the content is described in the familiar language of the job rather than in business school or psychological jargon. While the applications of behavior analysis to manager training are few, there are many managerial skills which might be investigated: per-

[6]A. W. Martin and D. A. Hawver, "Behavior Analysis: A Productive Approach to Management Skills Development." *Management Review*, AMACOM, 1979.

suasion applied within organizations, the advocacy and presentation of ideas, and the assembling of large amounts of fragmentary information.

Behavior analysis methods have been used widely to improve the skills of sales supervisors. Every other sort of training has been applied to this job with indifferent results. Behavior analysis compared the performance of highly skilled and less skilled sales supervisors and discovered marked differences between the conventional wisdom about what supervisors should do and about what they actually did. For example, the traditional emphasis on the need for closing a sale actually reduces in practice the likelihood of making a sale, except on low-priced items. Unintentionally, people have been trained to fail.

Behavior analysis has also been applied to interviewing, performance appraisal, negotiation, and the conducting of meetings. In general the results of training based on behavior analysis are marked improvements in performance against specified criteria. As in other methods of training, the choice of method is still determined by desired outcome. The use of behavior analysis rests on the assumption that the behaviors identified are critical to a manager's performance in a given organization, actually accounting for the differences in success among managers. The risk of irrelevance to the organization is reduced; the likelihood is enhanced that the manager will be able to apply what he has learned. It should be pointed out, however, that the validity of the assumption that a given specific behavior may account for effective performance is indeed difficult to establish. Its proof comes only from practical and relevant experience.

The behavioral trainer, unlike other trainers, seems to perform with neutral values. Up to this point in the application of these methods, little concern has been given to the purposes for which these techniques are used. For instance, if such powerful skill-building methods are not available to both sides of negotiation, is the untrained side at an unfair disadvantage? Assuming that such methods are available to any who want them, could they be put to socially damaging ends? It is, perhaps, too early for these questions to be real issues; nevertheless, trainers using these or other methods to induce change in behavior need to consider the ethical and social impact of their procedures. Given present rates of change, these issues will soon have to be faced.

6. THE FUTURE OF MANAGER TRAINING

Understanding the manager's skills through activity analysis
and the analysis of manager behavior seems to be the most
productive approach for future training. While it gives no instant answer to training questions, it provides a method of
identifying what skills should change as well as the means for
changing them. More research is needed on the persistence of
the new skills and what retraining is required. The focus on
individual behavior is a drawback. Much of management interaction takes place in group settings where individual skills
may be submerged. Concentrating exclusively on the building
of individual competence may lessen the effectiveness of team
performance. Nevertheless, there is a clear indication that be-
haviorally oriented training products measurable improvement in specific manager skills.

One might correctly conclude from these descriptions of
training methods that educators, researchers, consultants, and
trainers have had the most influence on the nature and content of manager skill training. For the most part, managers
have accepted what these groups have offered, even though
they have not been completely satisfied. What feedback there
has been from managers to the academic community has itself followed traditional lines. Suggestions from management
have met resistance from the academic establishment if they
deviated from conventional scholarly programs.

However, some industries are making progress. Cooperative programs are one way those who aspire to management
can obtain practical experience in business and exposure to
the environment of managers. In Canada, major retailers, in
cooperation with the community college system, have built
programs of marketing and merchandising courses designed
by managers and taught by managers. The students are provided concurrent practical experience. Although such training
remains along functional lines, the involvement of managers
from the work place is an encouraging step. The educators
have had to accept more flexible entrance qualifications,
prerequisites, course content, and instructor training in order
to make manager training relevant to the needs of business
and industry.

Ideas about a manager's skills and training have come from diverse sources. Often the holders of these ideas have competed actively for adherents in the marketplace. One underlying area of conflict is between the advocates of individual competition and those who favor collaboration as the means of producing results. The image of the manager as a rugged individualist who makes his way on his own achievement is fading. This has been brought about by the very complexity of organizations, the demands placed upon them, and the multiple responsibilities they have within the community. The impact of any single individual is difficult to identify. The achievement of one person may be dependent upon a host of others, and appraisal of past performance for compensation purposes becomes puzzling.

Much of manager skill training is aimed at improving individual skills. Organizations have been slower to adopt training which improves group effectiveness or builds skill in collaborating with others. Such courses were viewed as wooly-minded and impractical. However, business and industry, with increased frequency, use matrix management, task forces, project teams, and problem-solving groups. It is obvious that managers will need to build their skills in working cooperatively while holding individual competition constructively in check. Organizations will continue to compete within the present system, but individuals need to develop more effective ways of working together.

The traditional and the work-analysis conclusions about manager skills have also been in conflict. Educational institutions have a strong investment in following the traditional patterns of business functions. However, analysis has shown that managers spend very little time performing the classic business functions, but rather exist in a frantic environment of short-term contracts. Nevertheless, plans do get made, budgets are formed, organizations are structured and staffed, all in the traditional way that has been taught for decades.

These two delineations of the skills of a manager do not conflict but are parts of a whole. Both views are reasonable; each is of a different aspect of managerial activity. How these perceptions interact is more important than which one of them may be more true of the manager.

If the concept of manager skills has broadened, the ideas about training have also changed. We have moved from the nineteenth-century notion that a liberal arts degree from a

good university would fit one for most anything. Business
schools established professional programs in management following classical patterns. Social psychology and sociology
added the dimension of understanding group dynamics to
training long dominated by economics, accounting, and engineering. More recently behavioral psychology has added another dimension. Using programs tailored to build specific
skills, managers have made measurable and durable improvement in activities critical to performance.

Faced with this complexity, one wonders whether within
practical limits any manager can ever be fully trained. The
situation demonstrates the importance of organizations defining for themselves a general policy for training. Such a basic
policy should include:

1. A periodic inventory of the skills that will be required
   to meet the organization's medium and long-term plans.
2. The specification of training options in preparing managers to meet these requirements.
3. The integration of performance appraisal outcomes with
   training plans both for the individual and for the organization.

In practice, no manager should be provided training of any
sort without a clear set of goals which are relevant to both
the person's growth and the needs of the organization. Upon
completion of training the goals should be followed up by the
superior. The results need to be evaluated to correct or adapt
the training program. Further, consistent with the original
goals, the new skill, knowledge, or behavior should be integrated into the life of the organization.

The skills which managers need will continue to evolve.
Consequently, training must also change. Managers whose
main medium of communication is oral rather than electronic,[7] for instance, may not survive unless they are trained
in the new techniques of using information.

World events and shortened lines of travel and communication require the manager to develop not only interactive
skills but the capacity to apply these skills to a wide range of
people in different cultures and among different language
groups. Negotiation and persuasion will take place more often in a cross-cultural context. North American managers

[7]See Chapter VII, "Management in the Computer Age."

should equip themselves to keep pace with their counterparts in other countries.

Managers will need to develop the ability to handle rapid change. Fast rising crises in oil, foreign exchange, and politics have had direct impact on managers who might have been insulated from such happenings in the past. Organizations can be exposed to risk quickly unless managers can develop skill in preparing for the unexpected.

With increasing frequency, powerful groups take actions which impinge on the manager. Governments, cartels, industry associations, and labor unions will increase in size and impact. The manager will become less a man of action and decision. He will be seen more often as a negotiator, and his skills must be equal to those on the other side of the table. In the future, the organization will be able to take fewer and fewer actions on its own initiative. The freedom to act at all may be a function of the management group's skill in negotiation.

If the trends in social legislation continue, the manager will be limited in the capacity to terminate any employee. When combined with the present limitations placed on selection, it suggests that the manager will need skill in building high performance teams from available personnel. The manager will need to integrate his understanding of learning, of group interaction, and of behavior change in order to find ways to bring about needed results where group membership may be relatively constant.

7. CONCLUSION

Discussions of what it takes to be a good manager can become quite heated. If one listens to the points of view expressed among managers, most of them follow traditional lines, supporting lists of functions or personal traits which the armchair philosophers, writers, and consultants have said were present. Recent research findings, however, have provided different conclusions about managers; but the conventional wisdom about manager skills has not caught up with empirical results. If their activities are taken for granted, or if all persons with the label "manager" are considered alike in skill and circumstance, there can be no practical training at all. By continually testing assumptions, both managers and researchers will contribute in ways equal to the needs of the future.

CHAPTER VI.
Negotiation and Managing

1. INTRODUCTION

The common denominator of organizational life is negotiation: there are interpersonal relations to be developed and maintained, the inevitable conflicts to be resolved, the trades to be made, and the people to be persuaded. But oddly enough, this critical negotiator role, as well as the process of negotiation, has often been neglected by skills trainers and other students of management.

Recently, however, with the growth of behavior analysis as a method for scientifically studying human activity, both the process of negotiation—its frequency, its skill requirements, the causes of its failures and successes—and the negotiator himself are being carefully examined. There now is a rather substantial body of negotiation research literature on which trainers can draw. The staff of the RHR Institute, building on these initial contributions,[1] has studied negotiators in several parts of the world in their prenegotiation planning, during negotiation, and in postnegotiation reviews. Three years of intensive study have produced some major findings that are

[1]N. Rackham and J. Carlisle, "The Effective Negotiator," *Journal of European Training*, Vol. 2, No. 6 (1978) and Vol. 2, No. 7 (1978).

given in this chapter, demonstrating a method by which, in time, all roles of management can be fruitfully examined and illustrating how improved skill in negotiating can be taught when its specific skills are understood.

2. THE NEGOTIATION PROCESS

Characteristics of Skilled Negotiators?

There are five distinct and significant differences between skilled and less skilled negotiators. The skillful are distinguished by

1. Their practical understanding of the negotiation process and the behaviors which are appropriate to the issues involved
2. Their characteristic use of certain communication behaviors to facilitate the flow of negotiation and arrive at satisfactory agreements that can be successfully implemented
3. Their ability to manage negotiations by process and content control
4. Their capacity to prepare resourcefully for negotiations, to implement their strategies effectively, and to adjust their expectations and assumptions in the light of actual experience
5. Their ability to recognize tactics employed by the other party and to use counter-tactics which will promote productive cooperation, reduce conflicts, and protect their own interests

Bargaining versus Negotiating

Until recently, the understanding of the negotiation process had been retarded by confusing bargaining with other types of negotiation. Skilled negotiators avoid this confusion by recognizing that negotiations are always a combination of co-operation and conflict. Without any common interest there would be no reason to come together. In spite of this common interest, however, there are conflicting interests on both sides; otherwise instant agreement would be reached and no negotiation would be necessary. Furthermore, cooperation and conflict are rarely in balance; but as long as each element is present to some degree, there remains the possibility of coming to terms. Relative emphasis on either cooperation or conflict will vary not only from negotiation to negotiation but quite often within the same negotiation. Figure 1 diagrams the negotiation spectrum, showing conflict as dominant at one end and cooperation at the other (see Figure 1).

FIGURE 1

The Negotiation Spectrum

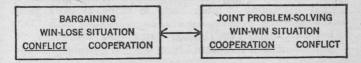

At the bargaining end of this spectrum there is enough cooperation present to keep the parties talking to each other even though conflict predominates. Negotiating for a used automobile is a classic example: this negotiation is characteristically a short-term relationship in which there is one simple issue: price. The higher the price is, the greater the gain for the seller and the greater the loss for the buyer. This is a win–lose situation.

If we divide a cake into two parts, a larger portion for me means a smaller portion for you. An alternative would be to cooperate in baking a larger cake. Then, even if we kept our original relative shares, each would be larger than before. In contrast to our bargaining example, this is a win–win situation. We have both gained. In business negotiations there are often opportunities to work together to increase the sum available to both parties. For example, if I negotiate an agreement with one of my distributors that enables him to capture a larger market share, he will gain and so will I.

So parties can often cooperate to bake larger cakes, but even then there may be conflict to be resolved by negotiation. Who pays for the increased ingredients and who is entitled to the larger slice of the larger cake? The disposal of the joint product of our cooperation is still a matter for negotiation.

Business relations, especially within but also between organizations, are frequently long-term. The parties must live with each other in mutual accommodation over the years. Engaging in short-term, win–lose behavior in these circumstances invites retaliation and breeds more conflict and reduces productivity.

Opportunities for negotiating in the joint problem-solving mode are not always easy to find.[2] There may be a number of constraints. For example, some issues lend themselves only to win–lose bargaining, such as a wage increase without a commitment to increased productivity. Joint problem solving takes time because it essentially involves fact-finding and searching for new, more creative alternatives. So when time is limited, bargaining is more likely to ensue. If one's plane leaves on Friday evening, habitual bargainers are more likely to begin negotiations on Thursday rather than on Monday.

The attitudes of the parties involved in the negotiation and the nature of their past relations with regard to cooperation-conflict are likely to influence the mode of negotiation. Also, some individuals are dyed-in-the-wool bargainers whatever the circumstances; they are takers, not give-and-takers. In addition, it can be difficult to reduce traditional conflict such as often exists between marketing and manufacturing.

Sometimes, unskilled negotiators get involved in joint problem-solving when they should be bargaining. But more often they engage in a lower order of bargaining when a higher order of joint problem-solving is both feasible and appropriate. Baseball and soccer are both team sports involving cooperation and conflict. They call, however, for very different behaviors. Skilled negotiators are much more able to identify the particular ballgame in which they are currently playing and to behave accordingly.

Facilitating the Flow of Negotiation

If we understand the nature of negotiation, we can then develop an insight into the specific behaviors that are involved in negotiation. Skilled negotiators much prefer to deal with skilled negotiators, just as tennis pros prefer playing against other pros instead of amateurs. Less skilled negotiators are usually more unsure of themselves in selecting appro-

[2]R. E. Walton and R. B. McKersie, *A Behavioral Theory of Labor Negotiations: An Analysis of a Social Interaction System,* New York, McGraw-Hill, 1965.

priate behaviors and hence are apt to be more unpredictable. As one skilled negotiator likes to say, "You don't know what they are going to do because they don't know what they are going to do."

Skilled business negotiators influence would-be bargainers, when it is appropriate, to move toward more productive problem-solving. They do so first by setting an example and then by encouraging behaviors favorable to productive negotiation and discouraging those which are counterproductive. They employ such stratagems because they have a strong self-interest in producing an agreement which can be implemented without continuing conflict.

Less skilled negotiators are often so hypnotized by the necessity for getting an agreement that they are content to live with vagueness or sweep issues under the rug, postponing conflict rather than resolving it.

When possible, a climate favorable to problem-solving needs to be created. But there is no virtue in showing good will by making initial concessions, for it only invites an escalation of demands.

Skilled negotiators set the stage for productive interaction by indicating the potential benefit of cooperation, not so much by a direct statement as by a skillful review from time to time of common ground between the parties. Reinforcing common interests, identities, experiences, and goals mitigates the stresses and strains of subsequent differences.

Trust tends to produce trust, expressed animosity generates reciprocal animosity. Indeed a spiraling effect has long been noted by students of communication.[3] Reciprocated agreement or support tends to produce a positive upward spiral. Skilled negotiators effectively reinforce these upward cooperation spirals; less skilled negotiators often become trapped in a tailspin of increasing disagreement.

Disagreement is necessary, of course, to give shape and direction to negotiations. Although cooperation does not rule out disagreement, successful negotiation calls for an overall balance between agreement and disagreement. Less skilled negotiators favor disagreement at the expense of agreement, thus reinforcing conflict. Skilled negotiators are more apt to postpone disagreeing until they have listened thoroughly to

[3]T. M. Scheidel and L. Crowel, "Idea Development in Small Discussion Groups," *Quarterly Journal of Speech*, 50, 1964, pp. 140-145.

the proposals and arguments of the other side in the hope
that disagreement may not be necessary after all. Premature
disagreement reduces the forward flow of negotiation.

Skilled negotiators may occasionally escalate disagreement
to an *ad hominem* attack: "Look, you have questioned our
integrity three times this morning and if you do it one more
time . . ." This tactic is especially appropriate when the
other side is consistently counterproductive. To retain its impact, however, skilled negotiators do not overemploy or pro-
long confrontation.

Counterproposing, another necessary tactic, depends for its
effectiveness on content and timing. When disagreeing, skilled
negotiators are more likely to withhold their counterproposals
until, having heard the other party out, they have obtained
sufficient information for a full understanding of the other's
proposal. Premature counterproposing frustrates the other
party and is as likely to be as ineffective as "blocking"—a
disagreeing without giving reasons. Blocking behavior, quite
frequent in labor negotiations, does much to push the negotiating down to the bargaining end of the spectrum. Although
blocking as a show of strength is favored by less skilled negotiators, it can significantly reduce the flow of negotiation.

Negotiations depend upon a give and take of information.
Giving information is the skilled negotiator's most frequent
single behavior, although it rarely accounts for more than
half of the total behaviors in any negotiation. Seeking information by asking questions is typically the next most frequent behavior. Less skilled negotiators are likely to overemphasize the giving and underemphasize the seeking of
information, leading not to a dialogue, but to a duologue
with two parties talking past each other.

The quantity of exchanged information is not the only important variable. Skilled negotiators try harder to secure quality information. Less skilled negotiators are likely to repeat
endlessly the same information, confusing presentation with
persuasion, apparently presuming that the sheer logic of their
case must prevail if only sufficient attention is given to it.
Thus, in a misdirected attempt to add weight to their arguments, they overstate them, stating opinions as facts and estimates as hard data. Such gratuitous dogmatism is easily
recognized by a sophisticated negotiator and can be used not
only to demolish any particular number or position which is

patently in error but also to undermine the credibility of the other side.

Skilled negotiators are less inclined to presume understanding either on their own part or on that of the other party. They are more likely to test their own understanding by questions which are designed to clarify the information they have received. Simple questions—"Do I understand correctly then that you are opposed to the last part of our proposal?"—can do much to avoid misunderstandings. In addition, skilled negotiators more frequently summarize understandings of agreements apparently reached. "We have so far agreed on issues A, B, and C." This allows a negotiator to test the understanding of the other party and to maintain a focus on cooperation. Negotiations are complex interactions in which it is only too easy to presume understanding or agreement when neither exists. Actually, when the emphasis upon clarification is lacking, we found many "agreements" that were more apparent than real and, worse still, could not be implemented.

Managing the Negotiation By Process and Content Control

If a negotiation is to flow reasonably smoothly toward agreement, it must be under control. Control is facilitated by asking questions. Skilled negotiators ask significantly more questions not only to obtain information but also to gain the attention of the other party, to move the negotiation into new areas, and, on occasion, to give themselves time to think ahead. As a skilled German negotiator puts it, "Wer fragt, fuhrt." ("Who asks, leads.")

Skilled negotiators also frequently make use of proposals relating not to the content but to the process of the negotiation itself. If the negotiation has reached a temporary impasse, a proposal such as "Why don't we come back to this later after we have discussed the marketing plan?" can maintain momentum.

Knowing how to time the introduction of new issues demands great skill. The fact that most negotiations contain more than a single issue can complicate negotiations but can also facilitate them by providing more options. Dealing with issues as separate entities tends to encourage bargaining. Joint problem-solving is often made more feasible by breaking down issues into subissues or by linking them to other issues.

Skilled negotiators pay attention to the possibility of tie-ins and trade-offs and think in terms of packages.

An issue of lesser importance to one party may be of greater importance to the other. One side may be willing to yield some ground on an issue if more ground can be gained on another—"We let them have their advertising budget because we really needed that price increase." Skilled negotiators have a realistic grasp of what is possible at a given time. "We'll get that next year" can be a rationalization for failure, but it can also indicate a shrewd and long-term perspective.

Skilled negotiators generally introduce easier issues early in order to initiate a climate of agreement before tackling the more difficult issues (although this stratagem can go awry if the "easy" issues turn out to be not so easy). It can also be useful to have easy issues as throw-aways for use later on. Skilled negotiators have a sure sense of when to depart from customary issue management.

As Disraeli pointed out, the next best thing to knowing when to take an advantage is knowing when to forego one. Taking advantage of every weakness of the other party is a characteristic of the less skilled negotiator. At times it may not pay to back the other party into a corner; allowing the other party to make a graceful retreat can be advantageous. When parties have overcommitted themselves, the negotiation flow may easily disappear. It is not surprising to find skilled negotiators, therefore, at pains to prevent the other party from publicly taking an untenable position from which it may find it difficult if not impossible to back down without losing face. If prevention does not work, there are a number of other techniques which skilled negotiators use that enable the other party to rationalize a concession or revise expectations downward.

There is a current vogue which emphasizes the role of nonverbal communication in negotiation, postulating that physical postures or gestures indicate states of mind. "When he leaned back in the chair and folded his arms, we knew he was negative." Such analysis, however, is similar to graphology: it has enough validity to make it intriguing but not enough for sound judgments, particularly in cross-cultural situations where the same gesture can vary diametrically in meaning from culture to culture.

In evaluating both the verbal and nonverbal behaviors of the other party, skilled negotiators strictly control the temptation to interpret behaviors too quickly, since misinterpretation can detail negotiations. Less skilled negotiators perceive disagreement more frequently, often clutching at straws and relying on misinterpretations instead of asking questions to establish agreement or disagreement.

To reduce the risk of reasonableness being interpreted as capitulation, skilled negotiators find it useful to establish that both parties are willing to make concessions before they actually make specific comments. Coordination of expectations is achieved by signs or signals, which may or may not be verbal in nature, but are tactics for limiting commitment. A toe is put in the water, and if the temperature is not right, its withdrawal leaves little or no trace.

Skilled negotiators use a variety of signals or tacit communications. These are most effective when the other party is also skilled and when the parties are used to dealing with each other. Skilled negotiators therefore use them with caution until they feel that they know the other party. Tacit communication is a subtle art because it has to use ambiguity quite deliberately. It is easier for less skilled negotiators to misinterpret a signal or not perceive it at all. "Is this a smoke signal or a smoke screen?" may be a difficult decision to make. Not responding to an issue when it is introduced, for example, may indicate a rejection of that issue; but it may also leave the door open for future discussion. The other party can say to himself, "At least they didn't say no."

Directly postponing the discussion of an issue may also indicate an open-ended flexibility. The sign of potential willingness to revise a position becomes stronger with more specificity, especially when the statement becomes conditional:

- "Let's not discuss that."

- "Let's not talk about that now."

- "Let's deal with that later. It shouldn't be much of a problem."

- "We would be willing to consider that if you would be willing to consider this."

What is not said can be as important as that which is. For instance, an issue which is being raised less frequently or given other signs of lesser prominence may be a hint that now a compromise is possible.

Less skilled negotiators are prone to use the counterproductive tactic of ambiguity to confuse the other party. A popular negotiation "skills" training program actually advocates the stratagem of confusing your opponent. Skilled negotiators, however, use ambiguity to limit commitment. They also are more aware that tacit as well as explicit communications have their ethical implications. To renege on even a limited commitment can be cited as negotiating in bad faith. An issue that is postponed and labeled as minor but that is later reintroduced and labeled as major is likely to be negatively received, thereby diminishing trust.

The use of tacit communication is a fine art, reserved for those occasions where ambiguity is a plus. Ordinarily, skilled negotiators reduce ambiguity by seeking more information, testing, understanding, and summarizing.

The Importance of Planning

Skilled negotiators do their homework. While this is also true of most of the less skilled negotiators, there is a significant difference in the quality of preparation. The hallmarks of skilled negotiators are resourceful preparation for negotiations, effective implementation of their strategies, and willing adjustment of assumptions in the light of actual experience.

Planning for negotiation has two main objectives:

• To provide a roadmap for use during negotiations.

• To avoid surprises wherever possible.

When you ask a negotiator after the sessions are over what did not go according to plan, you inevitably hear that "We expected them to ask for one thing and were surprised when they asked for another." While there is no way to avoid all surprises during negotiations, it is regrettably true that surprised negotiators are rarely at their best—"We looked at each other and called a coffee break as soon as we could." Successful outcomes may be jeopardized by surprises. The protesting of assumptions, although not an easy matter, is therefore a key ingredient in negotiation planning. It is no accident that less skilled negotiators run into more surprises.

The great military strategist Clausewitz said that in the first ten minutes of battle, every general changes his plan. It is an impressive observation. Please note, however, that the emphasis is on changing the plan, not abandoning it. More importantly, there is a plan which can be changed. Less skilled negotiators not only may not have much of a real plan to start with, but they may lose confidence in it within the first five minutes after listening to the initial demands of the other party. Or they may stay with their plan come hell or high water even though its value is patently diminishing.

The danger of such rigidity increases when a negotiation plan is the result of team effort. The final plan may be the result of much internal negotiation, and even when circumstances change significantly, there may be a strong reluctance to begin internal negotiations all over again.

To be an asset rather than a liability, a negotiation plan should be a guide, not a straitjacket. Although spontaneity has its place in negotiations, improvisation should be an alternative rather than a strategy in itself.

Thoroughgoing consideration of one's own options must be complemented by systematic attention to the options available to the other party. What can be done is often dependent upon what the other party will allow. The other party may or may not engage in explicit planning. It would be rare, however, to find a party across the table without at least an implicit concept of what they want and how they are going to obtain it. Skilled negotiators generally have a clearer grasp of the probable thinking of the other side and are less dependent on a rational model. "Surely it must be in their best interest to do X" becomes "It would pay them to do X, but knowing those characters, I think they are quite likely to try Y and Z."

It is not uncommon to find less skilled negotiators concentrating on developing their own plans without enough consideration of the range of possibilities available to the other side. Indeed, in developing their own plan, they may not become aware of all the options open even to themselves. There is room in creative negotiation to use brainstorming or other imaginative techniques before being critically evaluative. Resourcefulness in implementation is certainly more likely when resourcefulness has been exercised in planning.

. Explicitly or implicitly, skilled negotiators develop a strategy; more frequently it is explicit because it is then easier to review, to revise, and to communicate to other team members. A planning form may vary in complexity from a back-of-an-envelope format to a very detailed document. Systematically prepared plans allow negotiators to compare methodically their predictions with negotiation realities.

In regard to the basic elements of strategy planning, skilled negotiators

1. Give more thought to the interrelatedness of issues, rather than seeing them as necessarily separate or independent.
2. Set general objectives and specific goals, with appropriate priorities.
3. Give themselves a range in which to maneuver with freedom rather than restricting themselves to fixed positions.
4. Allow themselves room to make concessions downwards but do not begin with absurdly large demands.
5. Emphasize common ground and plan to build on it rather than overemphasizing differences.
6. Plan realistically when to joint problem-solve and when to bargain.
7. Have a preferred agenda and order of issue introduction but are flexible in gearing their presentations to actual circumstances during negotiations.

A strategy which cannot be readily implemented is of little practical value and may require modification in the light of a tactical review. (See Figure 2.)

FIGURE 2

The Dynamics of Strategy and Tactics

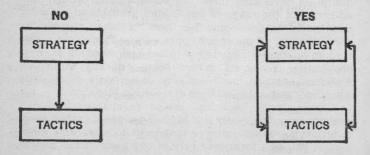

Tactics and Countertactics

Until recently, little research has been devoted to the tactics and countertactics of negotiation. The popular literature abounds of course with personal, often contradictory, prescriptions. One unfortunately typical pundit advises buyers always to demand cost information from sellers and urges sellers always to decline to give such information. This is really a prescription for deadlock rather than agreement.

The RHR Institute research examined the differences between skilled negotiators and less skilled negotiators in the ability to perceive the tactics of the other side and to employ appropriate countertactics. "Tactics of the other side" is an accurate statement because most of the identifiable tactics are ploys (which is not synonymous, incidentally, with dirty tricks) and are used by habitual bargainers rather than by joint problem-solvers. Although some tactics are used sparingly by skilled negotiators, our research has identified, defined, and recorded twenty basic tactics and twenty-six countertactics employed in negotiations.

Skilled negotiators perceive more quickly the tactics being employed by the other party. This is especially important when the tactics are less blatant:

- "We realized that if we kept granting all those little concessions, we would finally wake up and find that we had given away the whole store."

- "Their offer was very attractive, but I thought I'd better find out if there were any hidden strings attached. Thank heavens that I did."

- "Sure they said it was their 'final' offer, but we just knew it wasn't. We didn't take the bait."

The more blatant tactics are even more quickly recognized by skilled negotiators. They are much less likely to give concessions to the "good guy" because the "bad guy" on the other team is playing his role with gusto. Their prenegotiation planning and teamwork makes them less vulnerable to being divided and conquered.

Skilled negotiators anticipate tactics more effectively than less skilled negotiators. They expect their opponents to attempt to control the agenda, including some items which they

do not want to negotiate and excluding some items which
they do. Skilled negotiators also anticipate that the opponent
will cite limits on authority, budget, etc., as constraints to
making concessions. Skilled negotiators are also more
prepared for the last minute demand, which too frequently
surprises less skilled negotiators.

Skilled negotiators are more likely to feel unthreatened by
the other party and therefore are able to discredit threats in a
lighter manner—"We just laughed." They also demonstrate a
lighter touch in ignoring some tactics, refusing to charge every time that a red flag is waved. They are more inclined to
hear the opposition out, to ask questions, to test their understanding, and to stress common ground. They reserve the
right to attack only when the situation is really getting out of
hand. Then they move quickly into other behaviors that will
get the negotiation back on course.

All of this is not to imply that skilled negotiators are mas-
ters at parrying every tactic used against them. They on occasion may be too ready to accept the lure of round numbers
or to split the difference or to accept a new demand which in
contrast to previous demands is more modest but is yet too
high.

Cross-Cultural Negotiations

Skilled negotiators use the same basic behaviors when they
are negotiating between cultures as they do when negotiating
within their native cultures, but with a different quantitative
and qualitative emphasis.

Worldwide, skilled negotiators employ more clarification
behaviors than those who are less skilled. But in situations
where there are many opportunities for misunderstanding because of differences in language, patterns of thinking, or use
of logic, the specific behaviors of testing understanding and
of summarizing have an even greater usefulness. Questioning
is especially effective in cross-cultural negotiations.

Skilled negotiators maintain a balance between agreeing
and disagreeing rather than giving a disproportionate emphasis to either of these two behaviors. Blocking—the use of
flat disagreement without giving the reasons for it—is also
kept under greater control by skilled negotiators in cross-cultural situations. In short, skilled negotiators maintain their
quantitative behavioral profile across cultures, but the ex-

pression of these behaviors is qualitatively different. It was surprising to find, for example, that Japanese negotiators were apparently using few if any disagreeing behaviors. Primarily by asking polite questions, they subtly signaled disagreement to avoid more open and direct disagreement. The American negotiator in Japan also has to be able to differentiate between "agreeing" statements which merely indicate that something has been understood and those statements which show actual agreement.

Skilled negotiators relate their behaviors more quickly to the local cultural context and, being aware of "culture shock," anticipate revising their expectations and assumptions in new cultural settings. Anthropological models of culture are hardly applicable to the business negotiation situation. However, hundreds of critical incidents analyzed in the RHR Institute research have provided a sound basis for another, more useful model. Those critical incidents are negotiators' observations that identify a feature of a foreign culture which caused culture shock either during negotiations or in the post-negotiation review period. (See Figure 3.)

FIGURE 3

Negotiating Across Cultures

CRITICAL FEATURES OF CULTURES AFFECTING NEGOTIATION	
Social Systems: 1. Position and Role 2. Status 3. Family	*Value Systems:* 1. Laws 2. Religion 3. Protocol 4. Ethics 5. Time/Space
Learning Systems: 1. Education 2. Language 3. Thinking 4. Decision—Making 5. Negotiation	*Economic and Political Systems:* 1. Government Role 2. Government Attitudes 3. Government Operations 4. Economic Situation

The relative impact on negotiations of these seventeen features varies from culture to culture. Americans negotiating in England, for example, will not find religion to be an important cultural variable. In Indonesia, however, they may have to wait for an astrologer to schedule their meetings. In Saudi Arabia, the Islamic legal code has a definite influence on business and hence on negotiations.

Some cultural features will be a likely source of complication in almost any cross-cultural negotiation. Mechanical time is universal: there are 60 seconds in a minute and 60 minutes in an hour in any business culture. However, every culture has its own time system. Concepts of "soon" or even "tomorrow" can be quite radically different across cultures.

Analysis of cross-cultural sensitivity and its effect on negotiation flow and outcomes is valuable because of its implications for negotiation training. Reducing the time involved in learning to be sensitive to the cultural differences that impact negotiations is one obvious advantage. Continuing research into the impact of cultural differences should provide finer nuances for current cultural models and establish models for other cultures. As far as the major cultures are concerned, there is no longer any reason when transferring managers to another country to throw them into the deep end of the pool hoping that in time they will learn to swim.

3. CONCLUSION—NEGOTIATION TRAINING

Can managers be trained to negotiate more effectively?

Now that there is a research-based model of the skilled negotiator, the question can be answered affirmatively.[4] In fact, applications of initial training have provided positive results even for experienced negotiators. An objective model of a skilled negotiator not only permits the identification of certain weaknesses but provides a practical means whereby individuals can modify and extend their negotiating skills.

For less experienced negotiators, the results of negotiation training can be dramatic. Skill training in negotiation now

[4]Anthony W. Martin and Dennis A. Haver, "Behavior Analysis: A Productive Approach to Management Skills Development," *Management Review*, (1979), pp. 22-25.

can provide sound conceptual inputs, combined with practice plus objective, quantified feedback. In addition, when individuals can set their own goals for skill development, receive the feedback they require, and experience objectively measured improvement, their motivation is reinforced.

The last words on negotiation have yet to be written, but the application of scientific methodology has made a significant advance in uncovering—to paraphrase Gilbert and Sullivan—the very model of a model negotiator.

PART THREE
The Organization

CHAPTER VII.
Management in the Computer Age

1. INTRODUCTION

We are all aware of it. We have all tried, some more success-fully than others, to interact with it. We have all heard jokes about those who try to argue with the computer. And who of us hasn't tried to get the computer to correct an error on a bill?

On TV, in the movies, and in novels, we see and read about computers and their role in fantasies of the future, in medical analysis, and in the space program, guiding moon landings and, more recently, interpreting data received from Mars, Jupiter, and Saturn.

Managers at all levels are more or less familiar with how computers generate the masses of printouts that land on their desks. And most managers also know the computer as an aid to writing history and producing reports and records that can be studied as next moves are planned.

To most managers, however, computers exist in a separate department, cared for and fussed over by operators and pro-grammers who speak a language that few managers under-stand. They think of computers as requiring vast infusions of time and money to keep them up to date. Few managers real-ize that the "total computer system" includes not only the large main frame equipment found in corporations, but also word-processing systems, small distributed intelligent terminals in such places as retail stores, banks, and insurance offices, as well as the small systems used in geographically dispersed company facilities such as warehouses, remote sales offices, and distribution centers. Just ahead of us lies the age of personal computers and home terminals, already in production and steadily decreasing in cost. We have already moved from the white-coated-expert approach to real-time, natural language systems that every manager can, if he so desires, use to command data, call up information, manipulate and test various possibilities, and communicate instantly with another manager in the next room or half a world away.

Here is a list of Computer Age terms with which managers are already becoming familiar.

Call up—Refers to the process of retrieving information stored within the computer in a variety of ways, i.e., usually on a console screen graphically, or in hard copy

Console—Uusually refers to the keyboard and visual display screen associated with computer terminals, and adapted for desktop use.

Distributed Processing—The use of small, stand-alone systems, either in a network of such systems or in conjunction with a large centralized computer

Intelligent Terminal—Usually refers to a stand-alone system to which a communications capability has been added to give it the capability of communicating on a line with a large, central computer system or in a large distributed processing network.

Interrogate—Refers to the ability to question, search, and examine the data base, possibly including exploring for other relevant data, etc.

Main frame equipment—Usually refers to the large central computer found in most large corporations

Microcomputers—Microprocessors to which memory, timing, input-output logic, cabinet, and power supply have been added

Microprocessors—A single silicone semiconductor chip (or possibly two or three semiconductor chips) on which control, logic, and arithmetic units have been fabricated; first developed in the late 1950s and introduced commercially in the 1970s

Minicomputers—Smaller and lower priced than the conventional main frame computers; usually characterized by short word lengths

Model—Refers to the ability to test and try out by simulation techniques, using computer-based data handling and data processing capabilities

Natural Language Systems—Systems that operate in basic English, rather than using the programming languages such as FORTRAN, COBOL, etc.

Real-Time Systems—Refers to on-line functions that are conducted as needed, at any point in time

Small Business Systems—Generally considered (today) to to be those systems priced under $100,000 that have a system configuration as well as application programs particularly tailored to the needs of business; example: an appropriately programmed minicomputer or microcomputer with a disc memory, printer, and a video (CRT) terminal

Stand-Alone Systems—Small business systems, generally costing between $10,000 and $100,000, used by companies in individual plants, departments, or offices

Word-Processing Systems—Usually refers to the ability to enter, process, format, edit, and transmit or reproduce data, either directly or from preproduced tapes, etc.

2. SOME BASIC ASSUMPTIONS

1. The Computer Age is here. The "computer-management-interface" in which decision-making executives will interact with data centers and data processors is coming much closer each day. The equipment and software necessary to

achieve such an interface is now available and is rapidly becoming less expensive and more widely accepted.

2. Education in many high schools and colleges is ahead of general management in the acceptance, use, and training of young people to interact comfortably and effectively with the computer in all its forms. As these trained, younger professionals move into business and industry's lower and middle management ranks, they will of course push for more widespread application of data-processing capabilities. Inevitably this will lead to a widening gap between themselves and the older generation of management people who do not have this background and training.

3. Technological advancements may be ahead of management's understanding of the use and potential of the computer system's equipment and its accompanying software. Word-processing systems, added to advanced communication capability, are moving rapidly in the direction of electronic mail. Records, data, correspondence, and drawings can be recorded, stored, retrieved, distributed, and reproduced almost instantaneously over telephone lines in widely dispersed locations. Executives with terminals at their desks can have access to a plethora of information about their company's divisions or units in as many different formats as they desire, either on their own console screens or on handcopies. Using their console keyboards, they can manipulate the data, can insert decisions, and can transmit directions to associates and subordinates anywhere.

4. Sociological and psychological changes in our society, concurrent with the onrush of the Computer Age, will have a significant effect on the structure and organization of the management decision-making systems of the company of the future. These include changes in values basic to our society, the work ethic, the importance of lifestyle, the relocatability of both employees and management, the attitudes toward fellow employees and management, and the social responsibility of organizations.[1]

5. Government regulation and influence, in all of its pervasive forms, has and will continue to affect the way in which management functions. And with the already widespread use of data-processing equipment by government, it is not in-

---

[1]See Chapter I, "The Changing Individual" and Chapter X, "The Concerns of Top Management."

conceivable that in time government computers will be linked directly to a company's data-processing facilities in order to monitor compliance with government regulations, collect data, and even issue regulations. Thus the whole matter of confidentiality and security of information for both planning and reporting purposes must be carefully reviewed to prevent misuse by government.

3. CONCERNS FOR MANAGEMENT PLANNERS IN THE COMPUTER AGE

For the purpose of this discussion, we can conceive of significant issues in the Computer Age falling into two broad categories:

A. Those that will directly affect the individual executive or indirectly affect his relations within the organization

B. Those that will affect the organization—how it is structured and how people within it will interact

In real life the distinction between the effects of the computer on the individual and on the organization is not as clear as our dichotomy above would suggest; nevertheless, it is a useful framework for a more thorough exploration of the relevant issues.

A. Issues That Will Affect the Individual

1. *The chief executive's role*. We must begin by understanding the executive's decision-making role in the management process. In practice the active executive spends only a very small portion of his time analyzing data—whether new or processed. He spends most of his operating day in oral communication, gathering information, balancing options based on the analyses and recommendations of others, and reacting or responding to the needs of others for direction and guidance, for arbitration, or, more frequently, for approval of actions already taken. Large amounts of time are devoted to reviews, both regular and irregular, of progress against plan or budget, of plans for the next period, etc. And a significant part of any review is devoted to discussions that arise from the plans and data presented by others.

In other words, the decision-making executive is not data

centered but instead is shaped and influenced by the results of data-based analyses prepared or required by others.[2] Therefore, direct interaction between the top echelons of management and the computer in any of its forms is likely to be minimal and the effect on significant decisions minor.

True, many executives may insist (and probably will) on having consoles in their offices, if not on their desks. But, apart from the novelty of playing with the keyboard and watching results on the tube, the most serious use of the equipment will be to monitor the data being produced by the system as well as the decisions taken by those whose role it is to interact and respond directly.

Some serious, analytically-oriented managers might well take advantage of the modeling potential of the information-processing system to test out alternative decisions in order to see what impact each would have on other areas of the company and on the overall plan. Once the necessary computer programs have been produced and built into the system, the potential for such modeling is enormous. However, we believe that this will be for the next generation of top executives to exploit. Today most senior executives probably will accommodate the Computer Age with only minimal changes in their way of handling management's decision-making process.

2. *Coping with computer-generated information and demands.* The enormous quantity of data that can be generated and disseminated by modern computer systems and the extraordinary variety of ways in which it can be presented, treated, and analyzed, poses a serious challenge to management.

In the past, and even today, executives can be less than incisive in their thinking and in their requests for information. Requests for data and for analyses are frequently couched in global terms that rely on the understanding and expertise of a subordinate who is asked to refine and sharpen what really is needed or expected. Frequently executives will ask for a re-

---

[2]The distinction between *data-centered* and *data-based* can best be explained by reference to the distinction between the bookkeeper's or accountant's position where the primary focus is the proper manipulation and classification of data without responsibility for its implications, versus the air controller's job where the data presented is used to control and direct aircraft on the assumption that the data presented is valid and accurate.

view of a problem without knowing exactly what they expect to find, depending instead on their experience and business knowledge for help in identifying and resolving any problems.

The process of working with computer-based data systems requires executives to think through the questions and to formulate them more precisely because a global question can produce such a variety of responses that a critical issue with its relevant data may be concealed by a welter of irrelevant information.

Of course, it is always possible that today's executive will continue to frame his needs or questions as he always has, but rely on a competent, experienced subordinate who interacts with the computer on the executive's behalf to understand what is really wanted or needed.

3. *The rise of the "analyst class"—Data-centered versus decision-making roles.* Both of the issues described above suggest the need for an intermediary or assistant, a computer analyst whose role is to operate as "interpreter-buffer" between the executive and the computer data base. In the best of all possible worlds there will be a clear understanding of the distinction between the "data-centered" roles of the analyst, the accountant, the computer programmer, the computer operator, etc., and the "decision-making" role of the executive. However, the executive's time constraints and workload can easily blur the roles. The ambitious, aggressive, and capable analyst cannot only influence the executive's decisions but can take advantage of the analyst position to exercise some of the executive's authority. The very significance of his role as interpreter-buffer, furthermore, allows the analyst, if so inclined, even to select and influence the data presented to the executive in such ways as to suggest the alternatives which the analyst may favor. The analyst can also pinpoint significant factors in the mass of computerized data that otherwise might be overlooked.

More than likely the analyst will be computer oriented if not computer trained as a result of both general and professional training. For instance, an M.B.A. educational background together with skill in using computer-based data-processing systems would make an analyst an effective assistant to an experienced senior executive. In the future, as the advantages of such a combination of modern-age knowledge and skills and experience-forged management practice be-

comes evident, the role of the analyst may assume ever greater importance.

4. *Sharpening the focus of decision-making.* The development of data-processing capability for handling management
data, together with the opportunity to treat masses of information rapidly in a great number of ways, will probably
narrow the range of decision making by removing many of
the variables that formerly affected the executive's thinking.
Data processing allows the executive to examine and dispose
rapidly of variables that affect a problem and thus narrow the
range of issues to consider. At the same time, the executive
can focus on only the critical elements that require his attention.

The data-processing system in this instance has become the
means of disposing efficiently of extraneous issues that might
otherwise distract both the executive and his staff from the
main issues. Of course this implies self-discipline in learning
to avoid the distractions raised by these peripheral issues and
the opportunities they provide for avoiding decisions that
may not be easy to make.

5. *Impact on middle and lower level managers.* So far we
have been considering for the most part the effect of the
Computer Age on members of senior management. But in the
Computer Age middle or lower level managers will also be
expected to handle terminals on their desks, "call up" and analyze available data, and make decisions at their levels in response to computer-based information.

The most significant impact of the Computer Age, initially
at least, may well be at these middle and lower levels of management. They may be among the first to see the opportunities and advantages of the computer and may also be among
the first to acquire the necessary skills and training to use it.

These middle and lower level managers will be expected to
deal with masses of data, respond rapidly to changing information and situations, and communicate their decisions via
computer links to other middle-level managers in affected areas of the business. Where necessary, they will have the
means to interrogate the data base, perform appropriate analyses, change the resultant data, and, in general, keep in close
touch with rapidly changing situations. They also will have
access to stored information and records and to means of
querying sources and transmissions of directions throughout
the organization. Not only will they have the means of per-

forming these functions, but they also will be *expected* to operate effectively in close interface with the computer data base and the information-processing system.

Those in middle and lower management ranks who are unable to adjust to such a way of operating or who find the associated pressures too great will undoubtedly be relegated to less important positions, the future back benches of management.

6. *Speed of decision-making and the executive's readiness.* Computed-based management means more rapid decision-making. The ready availability of any desired and necessary data, together with the need to respond in a timely manner to queries from others, does not allow for the luxury of committee discussions or consultations. The manager on whose console appears a request for information, direction, or decision is expected to respond on the basis of his own experience and knowledge. While there is nothing in the system to prevent him from indicating that he is unable to do so without further thought or discussion, there is something in the nature of a computer-originated message that makes deferring it harder than deferring a letter or memo that can be left in the in-basket.

Computer-based systems have a time-urgency immediacy about them in the same way that a telegram seems to demand opening before a letter. The executive facing a console screen seems impelled to respond then and there, as though he were operating in full view of the outside world.

Many of today's decision-makers are not accustomed to such pressure. More widespread computer usage in management decision-making will only increase the level of stress, particularly on the older generation of managers who are less familiar with computers.

Managerial readiness for decision making implies a degree of self-confidence about one's readiness to deal with particular questions or problems. Today's managers who encounter questions or problems outside their experience are accustomed to tabling an item until enough information from associates or subordinates can be assembled to provide the sense of security needed for decision-making. The need to respond in a timely fashion to a computer-generated request places a person's insecurities right in front of him in rather inescapable terms; and without the opportunity for consultation and data collection, this can be exceedingly stressful, if not traumatic. Moreover, reluctance to change one's response patterns can be deeply ingrained.

One alternative, obviously, will be to narrow the field of potential decision making to that in which the executive feels secure, although this may be neither practical nor desirable from economic or organizational standpoints. The dilemma remains to be resolved by management at each level of decision-making.

7. *Decisions will be immediately visible to all.* The extension of management decision-making via computer-based systems means that decisions ingested into the input system via an executive's console will be immediately visible throughout the system. And, unless specific protective measures are built into the system, those decisions will be available to anyone with the means for requesting or retrieving the pertinent information or data on his own console. For the self-confident manager who is not at all dismayed by a high level of visibility, the concern is minimal. For those lacking self-confidence or who are concerned by how their actions may be viewed by others, the threat posed by the system can be very real.

Undoubtedly, the same sense of self-confidence that is involved in the speed of decision-making applies here and is coupled with the awareness that one's decision will be instantaneously visible to one's boss, who, if he feels so inclined, can intervene in the data- or decision-entering process in full view of others within the system.

A considerable degree of error-consciousness may result, particularly within the lower or less experienced management ranks. Management will have to learn to exercise a high degree of self-discipline in this area to avoid creating this problem, or at the least to minimize it.

8. *Depersonalization of executive contacts.* The need for face-to-face meetings in management today is usually justified by saying that this is the only way for all involved managers to review the same data simultaneously, to exchange ideas as to the implications or outcomes suggested, and to share in developing appropriate strategies and decisions. In the Computer Age, all of these functions can be performed via computer-linked systems, which can also model situations, project potential results or outcomes, manipulate the data base rapidly and effortlessly, and communicate decisions instantaneously to remote locations.

The frequently heard comment that meetings are needed to

"get to know one another better" remains a valid concern of management, but most businesses will find it hard to justify more than the occasional meeting for this sole purpose. This, combined with the ability to operate effectively at a distance, may well lead to a drastic reduction in executive travel, which for many involves a great deal of wasted time and energy. Almost certainly it will result, in time, in depersonalizing contacts within the organization.

9. *Differences in age groupings.* Throughout this discussion we have referred to the potential differences that may appear between those who have been educated in the Computer Age and have developed familiarity with the computer's potential and use, as well as with its problems, and those who completed their education in earlier years and to whom computer and data-processing systems are somehow alien and at best only superficially understood.

Obviously then, as the whole organization moves into the Computer Age, some means of helping the older age group become familiar with data-based systems will be necessary in order to make maximum use of their accumulated expertise. Special training will be necessary. The ways in which managers and executives work both alone and with others will have to be reexamined. Heavy dependence on staff and secretaries may give way to greater involvement with the analysts and greater personal interaction with the data base and information pools. The automated office will take some getting used to.

10. *Individual relationships in the Computer Age.* One possible casualty of the Computer Age may well be the unique set of relations that managers build over time with their peers and associates. The type of close interdependence which enables executives to know one another so well that they can frequently predict how the other is likely to respond under various circumstances may give way to a more impersonal set of relations when executives communicate via the computer and their consoles instead of face to face.

It is likely that data analysis, data trends, and analyst-produced interpretations will take the place of the opinions and suggestions of peers. The informed coffee session, away from the desk and console, rather than informal work sessions, will be an opportunity to get away from the computer's decision-making demands and analyses.

Relations will develop between those who have reason to

communicate via their computer networks rather than between those who may happen to work in close physical proximity. Work-related interactions will be much more clearly the focus of interpersonal contacts than at present. Time and distance barriers will become less significant. It is entirely possible that new loyalty groups may result. Very often today programmers and other computer personnel may have a greater sense of loyalty to their profession than to their employers.

11. *Data and information self-control.* With the vast resource of information that can be retrieved and made available to management decision makers, an important aspect of a manager's training will be to develop self-control and restraint in the amount of data that he feels is necessary for objective decisions. Here we move into an area that may be called the individual's "security zone," that is, the sense of self-confidence that defines the amount of information actually needed for decision-making versus the amount requested or reviewed before the manager feels sufficiently secure to make decisions. Thus, in addition to experience and familiarity, self-confidence with the subject area plays a large part in determining the size of a person's security zone.

The sheer availability of large masses of information and the potential for manipulating the data in an almost endless variety of ways continue to form a trap for the unwary manager. Only an analysis of the key elements of a problem and the determination of the data required for its solution can provide an answer. The training that is needed is nothing more than training in analytical thinking in order to define the actual problem as well as to know the amount and kind of information that is needed for a solution.

B. Issues Affecting the Organization

The second broad area of concern for management planners is the impact of the computer on the organization itself—how it is structured and how people within it interact.

1. *Role of the analyst group.* A group of analysts can affect the life of the organization if they strengthen their positions at the right hand of the key decision-makers by combining their familiarty with the data processing and handling systems with their business knowledge and good judgment.

Such persons may head a small, highly qualified staff who are trained to analyze data, identify trends, check out alternatives, and present findings in a meaningful and conclusive way. They themselves may occupy senior staff positions which give them access to all parts of the organization and to the information that each part needs to function effectively.

Because of the importance of their missions and the respect that capable analysts may gain from key executives within the company, they can wield considerable influence. A measure of their own judgment is the way in which they exercise such influence; and a measure of their stature is how they react to the same pressures other executives experience. The overall knowledge of the business that they acquire as analysts makes them prime candidates for senior line management positions—if they are so inclined and if they develop the necessary people-management skills.

The difficulty then will be in their transition from the analyst-consultant role to the manager-executive role. An analyst may become too closely identified with a particular executive or with the development of a particular policy, thereby limiting both his usefulness and his potential career path within the organization.

It is possible that, as the role and value of analysts becomes better understood, each segment of a company will require its own analyst, much as individual divisions or units today have their own controllers. However, just as today's controllers usually have both line responsibility to a unit manager as well as functional responsibility to the corporate controller, so the analysts also may have dual reporting relations with strong functional relations to a corporate analyst group to whom they will owe ultimate responsibility.

2. *Team-building and identity*. Both popular and professional literature about management realistically extol the virtues of team-building, for people need others within the organization to whom, if necessary, they can turn for support or counsel as well as for the interpersonal relations that make them feel a part of a group. This desire to belong will still be present in the Computer Age because it is a human need, although the interpersonal relations required by team-building may be less easy to establish. Team-building implies face-to-face interaction, the free exchange of ideas and opinions, and the development of mutual respect and acceptance in an open social framework. Data-centered decision making and the

ability to work relatively independently and physically apart from one another would seem, therefore, to raise barriers to team-building.

In this area where professional identity may be viewed as being of greater value than company loyalty, management planners will have to give serious thought to how to nurture group identity.

3. *Performance appraisal versus monitoring.* Performance appraisal is a difficult and sensitive area for today's management group. Although many books have been written and courses and seminars given on this subject, managers still feel uncomfortable when they have to play the role of appraiser. Few do it well; fewer still do it well on a consistent basis. One difficulty that often plagues the appraiser is the lack of good documentation and other data that illustrate the quality of the appraiser's performance. But now the Computer Age provides the means of maintaining an automatic tally on an individual's box score versus his goals and also gives managers the means of retrieving the exact experience or decision they want to refer to when they discuss performance with the individual.

More important from the point of view of growth and learning through experience, however, is the opportunity for the manager to monitor the performance of a subordinate by means of a personal console. If the manager so desires, every action and response of a subordinate, as well as the resulting effects on other parts of the organization, may be observed. In fact, a manager may have to restrain his impulse to take overriding action—that is, from intruding into the subordinate's computered activities (unless such intrusion is absolutely necessary) because the override action would be visible to others throughout the system and could have a negative effect on the subordinate. However, continued monitoring, together with proper feedback and counseling by the manager, gives the individual excellent opportunity for growth experiences that could be more valuable than today's annual or semiannual reviews.

4. *Quality assurance in the Computer Age.* Because of time constraints and the plethora of computerized information, decisions will be taken and transmitted and the resulting actions will be processed even before the manager or executive can review them. So quality assurance, at least insofar as management decisions and reactions are concerned, will de-

pend on ensuring that actions and results lie within acceptable limits or boundaries, rather than on individual right or wrong.

"Management-by-exception" may well have to become the rule because of the enforced pace of decision-making and subsequent reactions. Results and reactions that lie within planned, predetermined limits will be presumed to provide the desired quality assurance, while those outside the predetermined limits will sound built-in alarms, calling managers' attention to themselves. Systems such as these already exist and are in daily operation in automated plants and aboard aircraft. Expanding them to the management function should not be difficult.

5. *Need-to-know and protection of privileged data.* The concern for ensuring privacy and establishing "need-to-know"[3] is almost as old as the Computer Age itself, yet it remains a significant problem. Managers today control "need-to-know" through the distribution of vital documents, through the use of various "restricted" stamps, and other means of identifying key data and controlling access to them.

However, in the Computer Age this will become a difficult area to manage. Experienced data processors can have access to any information they want. It would be exceedingly difficult to try to foresee what data an executive or analyst may actually need in order to perform his task properly and to restrict his access only to these data. It is possible to key certain data to control its availability, but even this is no sure protection. There is little an organization can do to prevent managers with appropriate "needs-to-know" from obtaining total information on a company's performance and then making improper use of the data.

We also have referred to the possibility of government computers tying in directly to a company's data base and then obtaining whatever information, whether confidential or public, is wanted about the organization. The question of "privileged" data thus becomes more important than ever. Today's increasing government intrusion into the management process suggests that such a scenario is not as farfetched as it may appear to be initially.

Additionally, managers may want to build "self-destruct"

---

[3]Refers to the job-related need to have access to a particular body of information in order to carry out a responsibility.

modes into collections of data, particularly personnel performance records, to avoid the syndrome of past history forever hanging over a person's head. The failure to have such a "self-destruct" mode creates another potential problem for the human resource manager in the Computer Age.

6. *Office automation, word processing, transmission, etc.* The office of the 80s is with us today. The automated office, including storage of records and correspondence, their retrieval capability, word-processing systems with the capability of entering and editing data combined with hard copy printers, automatic electronic transmission systems to allow reports prepared in one location to be sent and reproduced in other locations, and executive desk terminals that provide access to any or all data within the company data base—these all are available today.

Executives' reliance on secretaries, secretarial pools, and the like will give way to greater self-reliance, greater freedom of action, and greater independence. The executive decision maker can probably operate just as effectively away from an automated office as in it, provided there are the necessary lines of communication with the computer in the office.

7. *Role of staff meetings.* Staff meetings, executive committee meetings, operating group meetings—all have become routine in today's business world. The usual rationale for these meetings is that they provide opportunities for executives to improve mutual understanding and communication. However, this rationale loses its validity in the Computer Age. Instead, these meetings may be used for other purposes: discussions of policy and of strategy; philosophic discussions about future directions; and other matters too global or elaborate to be considered via the computer network.

From the foregoing it is clear that some computer users will continue to require direct interactions such as meeting with decision-makers so each can judge the information presented. Interaction with peers as to the correctness of these judgments could take place with or without a staff support person (i.e., an analyst), and provide appropriate checks and balances within the executive function.

4. CONCLUSION

The relentless advance of the computer threatens tradition-al management processes. The decision-making executive is now influenced by the results of data-based analyses pre-pared or required by others. Computer-generated informa-tion and demands require an incisiveness in decision-making that creates totally new pressures. In addition, computer-based management means a process of more rapid decision-making that can be completely visible (everyone who wants to can see the same underlying data). So an executive's deci-sion, possibly hertofore delayed by some reluctance to face a reality or by a carefully concealed indecisiveness, now, by a plethora of data, is forced, whether he is ready or not. Fur-thermore, interpersonal relations are likely to be effectively depersonalized by the substitution of computerized systems for personal contact. And the organization will feel the im-pact of a new group, the analysts, those skilled interpreters of computer data who speak in strange tongues and reach con-clusions in mysterious ways. If deceitful or power hungry, the analysts may even deliberately misinterpret data to their own advantage without the less sophisticated users realizing it. Fi-nally, the highly extolled virtues of team-building may like-wise be threatened by the impersonal, robotlike features of the computer. But like it or not, the computer is here to stay; and management must learn not only to live with it but to use it to their advantage.

CHAPTER VIII.
The Life Cycle of the Organization

1. INTRODUCTION

Most of us see organizations as impersonal, faceless, even threatening. In spite of their being structured according to well-ordered principles, we see them as amorphous. And, what's worse, we tend to lump together their vast diversity in size, demography, and purpose into one generic term, the "organization."

Actually, organizations are much more than legal entities. They are as individual and unique as human beings, and as complex. They are indeed organisms, with an identity and nature that is the result at any given moment of life's forces and factors, just as a human being's condition at any given moment is also the result of life's forces and factors.

To perceive any organization as an organism is natural when one realizes that it consists of an assortment of human beings who are tied together in some structured fashion to accomplish something that no one of them could do alone.

The structure determines the relations among the members of the organization; it assigns control over and responsibility for a subordinate; it defines duties; it lays down the rules that the members live by (policies) and it determines how
126

they should work (procedures). A subsociety is thus created with a pattern and a structure that abides by well-tested rules in governing the interrelations of its members. Together the members constitute an entity; and the structure they live in and the fact of their humanness combine to create a unique organism that cannot be exactly duplicated anywhere else.

Perhaps only managers and those who work intimately with them understand how completely human is any organization. In the early entrepreneurial stages of a business, the individuals making up the enterprises are more visible and are easier to deal with on a personal basis. But as the organization grows in size, complexity, and power, a heavy cloud seems to descend, obscuring and isolating its people. This chapter is an effort to dissipate that cloud. We will try to catch a glimpse of the human nature of the organization. In addition, we will illustrate the premise that for organizations, just as for individuals, the whole is a great deal more than the sum of its parts. As the human elements of an organization adopt roles that are subservient to a corporate purpose, molding their identities into organizationally determined functions, the individual personalities interact to produce a corporate entity that as a whole fulfills its economic or public mission. Such wholes have limitless diversity. They are living, developing, maturing social organisms, made up of human beings. It is not too fanciful to ascribe human properties to them. Like an individual, an organization has its own internal environment, and it is this internal organizational environment that comprises the organism's personality.

To illustrate: we visit the clean, well-groomed, and muted offices of a small financial institution. Its conservative and well-controlled nature is in no way a mere matter of its decor or public image. It is made up of people who live consistently according to uncompromising and detailed standards and procedures. They were hired for low-paying jobs and moved with painful slowness but with great security in slow succession to executive positions. No single individual is allowed the autonomy to make very important decisions because decisions involve the public's money and are made slowly; in fact, all change comes about slowly. This bank is just what it ought to be—solid, stable, strong in character and distrustful of impulsiveness or ill-considered risk.

Next, we visit a national chain of fashion-oriented retail clothing stores, a young, rapidly growing business with a very different personality. One observer described it as "a very tough cookie." Impressive is the youth of the managers and their sheer load of activity. But one may also be appalled at their hip-shooting reactivity. This personality is not a matter of purposeful public image; rather, its characteristic comes from its people who are newly hired and who must perform quickly or be left behind. They have confidence, drive, and energy. They live without much structure of systems or policies or traditions because those have not yet developed.

Next we visit a manufacturing plant which turns out parts for the automotive industry. A visitor is kept waiting by the plant manager who is in a meeting. The atmosphere is tense, purposeful, controlled. It doesn't take long to discover that the people are professional, competent, and task oriented. The visitor feels swept along as if in a current. People seem to listen with one ear for the next crisis or to keep a sharp eye out for an impediment which must be removed quickly before it delays progress. It is businesslike and under control and very professional, but crisis always lurks just below the surface.

Finally, we visit a technology-based specialty chemical company. In a physical environment of an ultramodern office with campuslike landscaping many conversations are conceptual dialogues. No one seems to feel under pressure to come quickly to a point, nor somehow to feel competitive. This is an intelligent and technical personality, quite concerned with understanding but also quite intellectually critical and perfectionistic. There is a certain assumption of superiority with respect to its own product and expertise. One understands immediately that unseemly emotion or aggressiveness is out of place here. Problems are solved by scientific and technical approaches; deficiencies are corrected through better planning. As in the other instances, the people make up this personality but at the same time the personality of the organization is fashioning the people.

In *The Organization Man*, William Whyte[1] is contemptuous of the constraining interrelation between the individual's

[1]William H. Whyte, Jr., *The Organization Man*, New York, Simon and Schuster, 1956.

and the corporation's personality. He mostly perceived the
harmful effects of forcing individuals to conform to the organization's purpose and need. Almost forgotten, however, is
the enormous personal satisfaction and the great public good
that have come out of the investment of individual identities
in an organizational identity and purpose which transcend
anything an individual can do alone.

2. THE CONCEPT OF LIFE CYCLE

In addition to having a personality, the organism has a life
span, a beginning and an ending. As it characteristically
grows through the years, its nature changes. It enters a life
cycle and an evolutionary process that fundamentally determines its nature at each stage. Initially, this conceptualization
is a simple analogy between the organization and the individual human being. Individuals are obviously growing, living
organisms; so are organizations. Just as individuals have distinct personalities and a life cycle of maturational stages between birth and death, so do organizations. Like people,
organizations begin with a traumatic entrance into the world,
small and vulnerable, and proceed through a period of
growth wherein they establish their identity and character; finally they arrive at a period of maturity. They may then drift
off into organizational senility, marked perhaps by hardening
of the markets.

Such a life cycle is not constrained within any particular
time frame, nor does every organization necessarily always
pass through the exact same stages. However, the growth and
evolutionary processes in organizations are more than pure
analogy. There is a definite pattern determined by its growth
in size and by its relative position in the marketplace. This
idea of the evolution of organizations has been showing up in
recent literature: in the Rohrer Hibler & Replogle's *Managers
for Tomorrow*,[2] in Blake, Avis & Mouton's *Corporate Darwinism*[3] and in Greiner's *Evolution and Revolution as Orga-*

[2]Rohrer, Hibler and Replogle, *Managers for Tomorrow*, New York, The
New American Library, 1965.
[3]Blake, Avis, & Mouton, *Corporate Darwinism*, Gulf Publishing Co.,
1966.

nizations Grow.[4] A distillation of the literature[5] and of RHR experience postulates that there are five distinct stages through which an organization goes in an evolutionary manner, each characterized by a somewhat different style of management:

> **Entrepreneurial management**
> **Personal management**
> **Professional management**
> **Bureaucratic management**
> **Matrix management**

Within each of these management stages there are distinctive differences in at least four dimensions which are helpful in analyzing the evolutionary process:

Function

Each stage of management is functionally suited to the particular demands for survival and growth at that stage in its life cycle. Fundamental to this concept of function is the premise that the leadership of the organization has a very different role and responsibility in each evolutionary stage.

Management Style

The style of management is also different in each stage of organizational development, going beyond such relatively minor considerations as whether or not management is authoritative or participative to the basic nature of the management process. Fundamental to this dimension is the fact that different stages in management evolution require different kinds of managers, differing kinds of leadership, and different environments. Depending on the evolutionary stage of the organization, family-style management may be very appropriate and effective; professional, bottom-line management may be very ineffective.

Human Relations Contract

People are attracted to organizations for a variety of rea-

---

[4]Larry Greiner, "Evolution and Revolution as Organizations Grow," *Harvard Business Review,* July-August, 1972.
[5]In *Managers for Tomorrow,* David W. Merrell of the RHR staff conceptualized three stages of organizational evolution leading to bureaucracy and decline. In 1972 Greiner described the same basic evolutionary stages, treated bureaucracy as a fourth stage, and predicted that matrix organization would prove to be the fifth stage.

sons. Some individuals like big businesses; some the security of a well-established family business; others enjoy the pace of a highly competitive, sophisticated industry. Each employee comes to the organization with certain expectations. By the same token, employers also have their expectations of employees. What both expect of each other varies widely according to the stage of the organization's evolution. This human relations contract is unwritten and usually unspoken. A great deal of difficulty, however, may occur as organizations move from one stage to another, thereby changing the human relations contract, unless the employee is prepared for the change and can adjust to it. This type of difficulty is especially likely during a change from the personal management stage to the professional management stage.

Management Crisis
Larry Greiner prefers the word "revolution" to "evolution" to refer to the periods of crisis in an organization. Greiner has taken a major forward step in describing the growth of market conditions which precipitate the crises which in turn result in a revolutionary period leading to the next evolutionary step. Indeed, it is the crises that determine the evolutionary process, and (departing now from the human analogy) no evolution or maturation is possible if such crises of growth and marketplace do not develop.

3. ENTREPRENEURIAL MANAGEMENT

Function

The entrepreneurial phase of management obviously encompasses the birth of an organization. Organizations are spawned in a variety of ways, but the birth of each is in its own way as traumatic and miraculous as the birth of a baby. The mortality rate is fantastically high, ranging from 80 to 90 percent. Sheer survival, therefore, is the overwhelmingly important objective for the entrepreneurial management. A new market or at least a new place in an old market must be found. In order to survive, entrepreneurs must be extremely flexible. Their general advantage is that being small, they can exploit any opportunity immediately and decisively. They have the advantage of not being restricted by traditions, pre-conceptions, organizational systems, structures, policies, or procedures.

Management Style

The entrepreneurial organization is almost always dominated by one person, probably an essential condition for survival in this early stage. That one person, if he is knowledgeable, resourceful, and decisive, as well as controlling, pilots the organization safely in those early vulnerable years through a jungle where customer, consumer, or constituent may hold the power of life and death.

The entrepreneur builds an organization that in effect is an extension of himself—his eyes and his voice, his hands and feet. He essentially makes all decisions. He is almost always the kind of person who wants to know what is going on at all times in all parts of the organization.

The entrepreneur runs the organization according to personal needs, feelings, and judgments. On such a basis are duties and responsibilities assigned and decisions made on salaries and bonuses. The entrepreneur leans heavily on those people who are useful, with a fine disregard for organizational structure and systematic definition of responsibility or careful delegation of authority. Crises are reacted to immediately. Solutions are *ad hoc*. Detailed, long-range analysis and planning are neglected. In short, the entrepreneurial organization phase represents a paternalistic, highly reactive, but yet resourceful period in every organization's life.

The Human Relations Contract

In the entrepreneurial phase the individual is far more important to the organization than its system or structure. The basic relation between the employer and employee is simply that of leader–follower; anyone wanting to join the team must fit that relation.

The program for successful human relations in the entre-preneurial organization is simple, for it depends solely upon the strong personal appeal and impact of the entrepreneur and upon his accessibility to employees at all levels. The entrepreneur will likely know every employee by his first name, will know his family and his problems. If the organization is a business, there often may be promises to the favored em-

ployee of financial participation sometime in the future, even
to the point of ownership. Troublemakers are quickly weeded
out. Whether the entrepreneur's organization survives will depend greatly on whether loyal but submissive employees can
be attracted. There is no way the entrepreneur can reward
them monetarily in the way big, established organizations
can, so the entrepreneur depends on personal appeal and on
building personal friendships and loyalties. Consequently,
people are often employed who might not be hired by a
larger organization.

The Crisis

As the entrepreneur's organization grows, it may begin to
experience human relations problems which may be beyond
the founder's capacity to handle. Although it may not be
recognized as such immediately, the entrepreneur may be entering what is called the leadership crisis. The organization
may now be too large to permit personal handling of all of
the problems. The entrepreneur may no longer be so acces-
sible. The substance of the organization's effort may now require specialized administrative and/or technical management
skills which may be beyond the founder's ability or interest.
Therefore there emerges a tendency to manage more and
more by dicta and slogans. Individual employees or supervisors who try to step up to problem-solving challenges may
end up committing the cardinal sin of challenging the entrepreneur's authority, a conflict that can lead quickly to deteri-
oration in morale. But when employees, fearful of upsetting
the entrepreneur, fail to step up to problems, they risk increasing the organization's ineffectiveness.

Capsule: Entrepreneurial Management

This organization form is structured around tasks and outcomes. Role definition is very flexible. Key personnel jump in
wherever expedient. The entrepreneur often ignores efforts by
subordinates to define jobs and establish a management hierarchy. As the organization grows, informal organization
gradually solidifies around key employees. The entrepreneur
continues to circumvent the maturing structure by going
directly to his favorites. Organizational flexibility promotes
opportunism, resourcefulness, and decisive action.

The Transition to Personal Management

The solution to a leadership crisis, of course, is the development of a management team or similar alternative to the one-man management style of the entrepreneur; if this cannot be done, the organization will soon be in deep trouble. One alternative management is a strong Number 2 person, an excellent administrator who happens as a personality not to challenge the entrepreneur's authority. Another solution is the building of a competent, second-level management team. For either alternative to occur, the entrepreneur needs to recognize the ineffectiveness of the one-man boss. If neither alternative is acceptable, a competent administrator must be brought in from the outside. But such a move seldom works if the entrepreneur continues to be present, for he inadvertently overshadows the outside manager.

4. PERSONAL MANAGEMENT

The Function

If the organization survives entrepreneurial leadership crises, it can embark on a period of sustained growth marked by a new organizational style—personal management. Having now successfully built a competitive advantage of some sort, the organization has one basic function: to maintain and exploit that advantage. If it is a business, the organization has captured a sizeable portion of a market because of technological skills, services, specific patent, or carefully guarded manufacturing techniques.

The Management Style

While still under the shadow of the entrepreneur, the new management team, who now really function as maintainers, must nevertheless and simultaneously build the company's competitive advantage while exploiting its advantageous market position. Relations among members of the team tend to be highly personal, sometimes even political, rather than determined by job description and structure. The team of managers is often put together on a trial-and-error basis, but their rise to power is largely based on their personal fit with the entrepreneur or his successor. (In a family-owned business that maintains a constant competitive advantage, the personal management phase may last for several decades as leadership-ownership is passed from father to son.) The personal management team is further characterized by deep product knowledge and outstanding expertise developed through the years. The organization is proud of its product or service, for quality tends to be more important than cost or efficiency. The chief executive officer may be quite democratic or extremely autocratic, but regardless of niceties of management style, the paternalistic attitude of his entrepreneurial predecessor is generally maintained. Traditions become sacrosanct. Seldom does the organization go to the outside for additions to the management team. There is through this period an almost adolescent egotism which assures the personal management team that they know more about their product or service than anybody else possibly could. A few new ideas, some systems, some changes in structure, a few new people, may be brought in slowly from the outside, but only when forced by the company's growth, particularly if it is rapid. Within the personal management phase, functional organization, a certain amount of system, and a great deal of standardized procedure develops; however, these develop more as a matter of habit and tradition rather than by reason of carefully prescribed study or engineered systems.

The Human Relations Contract

The basic relation between employer and employee in this period is one of loyalty—security. The employee expects to have a secure position for life; the employer, in return, by encouraging a sense of family identification, expects absolute loyalty. As long as the personal management period lasts, this unwritten security–loyalty contract works to the advantage of both, even though each may make certain sacrifices by adhering to it. For example, the employee may pass up better opportunities with other organizations; the employer may tolerate less productive people, maybe even to the annoyance of the more productive members of the organization.

All in all, this can be the happiest and most serene period of an organization's life cycle. The profit margins may be the best. The deficiencies may be hidden by the umbrella of its enduring competitive advantage.

However, this benign existence will end during the most traumatic transition within an organization's life—the transition with all of the emotional upheaval and crises of identity that characterize the typical move from adolescence to adulthood, the transition from personal management to the professional management stage.

The Crisis

During the personal management phase interpersonal relations have been good if the team has developed a family atmosphere which has successfully attracted loyal, hardworking employees. In so doing, the personal management team has controlled the organization. Within the loyalty–security relations, people are given step-by-step salary increases based on seniority; most problems are handled by arriving at some kind of personal solution with the grieving parties. Management remains heavily centralized, although with the newly developed functions have come specialized skills and capabilities. Harmony (family unity) and an efficient growth continue to dictate that there be no boat-rockers or divergent groups within the organization.

Unfortunately, this demand for conformity provokes what has been called the autonomy crisis. Traditions, subjective solutions to personnel problems, top-down control—these gradually prove ineffective. Since strong, lower-level managers are not allowed to solve their own problems, they begin to lose faith in a management that adheres to obsolete strategies. Competitors begin to pass them by. The president, recognizing such people and organizational problems, now sees the need to develop a much more professional and autonomous lower-level management, a decentralization or delegation of authority, and a new human relations trade-off with employees.

Capsule: Personal Management

This organization form is structured around key functional managers who form a close supportive team for the entrepreneur or his designate. This is a period during which expertise is developed, elaborated, and institutionalized. Functional departments are the primary structuring entities. Functional roles become clearly differentiated, although functional managers may be selected more on the basis of their fit with the entrepreneur and the team than on their management skills. For the most part, both expertise and management are home-grown. This personal–functional phase promotes the exploitation of a competitive advantage and establishes an identity, a rich body of company know-how, and a strengthening of tradition.

The Transition

The period of professional management is often ushered in as profit margins decrease. Competition has gradually eroded the company's advantage; price cuts have begun to shake up what was once a stable market, giving the competition a greater share of the market and bringing a reduction in the company's high profits.

The personally managed company may complacently disregard the danger signs for months or even years, believing wholeheartedly in the intrinsic superiority of its products or service. Management may ignore the cost of quality and fail to see how lean, hungry, and efficient the competition may have become, even blaming them for cheap substitutes or, in final self-destructiveness, blaming their customers for being deluded by such unworthy competitors.

At some point the personal management realizes that its competitive advantage will now have to come through efficiency, overall excellence of organization, and effective management functioning, rather than as in the past through some one specific area of competitive advantage. Perhaps ruefully, the company also recognizes that during the period of personal management much of its one-man entrepreneurial effort has been lost and must now be replaced by a controlled, but still creative, organizational entrepreneurial effort.

5. PROFESSIONAL MANAGEMENT

The Function

Professional management's primary function is to provide strong general managers or profit centers that are closer to where the action is. This is done in part by decentralizing authority, which generally means dividing the corporation into units to allow better profit planning and control, and in part by stimulating growth of specific products or product lines. Additionally, the professional management function is to balance all areas of the business so as to prevent domination by one, even if it may mean (as it often does) cutting back the exact area where the company's former competitive advantage lay. Perhaps there may be the first layoffs of technical people in the company's history. But in all areas of management, a balanced organizational approach is now demanded of the management team.

In the advanced stages of personal management, the organization was in crisis, unable to respond to changes, particularly in its marketplace. Traditions and standard practices had stifled managers who were close to the real problems of the organization. Now the transition to professional management is made more difficult by the fact that it usually must reward those who have become critics of the organization. Very often the maintainers of the competitive advantage that had run the organization for so long are now considered obsolete. The combination of (1) the necessity to cut back inefficient and high-cost elements of the organization and (2) the need to replace effective but maintenance-style managers with professional managers usually results in a period of disturbance and low morale.

The Management Style

Perhaps the most traumatic effect as the organization moves toward professional management is the dramatic shift in management style. The new emphasis is relatively impersonal, businesslike, and profit oriented—a sharp contrast to the former, cozier personal management style. The new breed of managers, gradually cultivated or hired from outside, are now the general managers of divisions or units, with all of the autonomy, profit responsibility, and prestige within the organization only known previously by the top functional staff, and they succeed or fail almost without support from above. This is the period when scientific management may get a strong foothold as jobs become better defined and relations become more professional. As the company grows and the new breed of managers succeed, a kind of *macho* political bravado may develop; general managers may learn to pride themselves on their tough-mindedness and their ability to take pressure and stress. In one highly decentralized company, for example, the young general managers like to refer to themselves as "gun slingers." The new breed report directly to the president of the corporation, at least up until the time that the company is large enough to support an intervening level of group vice-presidents. The managers are jealous of their autonomy and are often disdainful of staff executives and staff departments. They expect to approve and monitor any outsider's contact with their unit, and in many other ways they demonstrate an emphasis on a strong line of authority (shades of the style of the one-man entrepreneur!).

The introduction of professional management always means a hard look at costs and efficiencies. A new manager of a new professional management team, brought in to effect the transition to professional management, is generally appalled by the number of people retained, even promoted, on the basis of personal commitment rather than demonstrated competence. The professional managers thus generally see the organization as too fat with excess people; and, using the bottom line as the final criterion, they work quickly to get departments in balance.

The Human Relations Contract

In professional management, the contract between employer and employee is basically and simply performance–reward. The professional manager and those whom he attracts to the organization believe that the employee owes the employer successful performance; in return, the employer owes the employee a reward commensurate with the effectiveness of that performance. Thus, in a professionally managed organization, the employee is much more likely to leave if he feels he is not being compensated appropriately; likewise, the company feels much freer to discharge an unproductive employee.

This is a traumatic shift from the loyalty–security trade-off of the personally managed organization. The shift is often felt to be dehumanizing. It soon is evident that people are not simply one big happy family, but are rather performers on a team who are relatively expendable if, in the shifting of circumstance, they are not needed or do not perform. During the earlier periods of the organization when growth was comparatively easy and profits were good, inefficiencies were blithely ignored and excess personnel were tolerated. But as the professional management process gradually brings in better planning and budgeting, inefficiencies and excesses in personnel become visible. This engenders a great deal of insecurity among some, particularly if a simultaneous business recession telescopes cutbacks into a short but bloody episode of layoffs. In general, the highly motivated and confident employees welcome this shift in the human relations environment in spite of cutbacks; they apparently consider that those who perform well will therefore move ahead much more rapidly. The employee who sees himself as potentially excess, for whatever reason, is much alarmed at the change in the environment; and often a clique of insecure old-timers who are highly critical of the organization will emerge.

The Management Crisis

During the professional management period the successful business organization continues to grow, generally by diversification through acquisition and/or development of new products and services. As more and more organizational units come into being, they are generally layered into groups and perhaps the groups into businesses, all reporting through several steps but all in a direct line to the corporate chief executive.

The managers are generally rewarded on the basis of their division's performance. They compete with each other for corporate resources, usually good naturedly. Basically, each is concerned with his own unit's profit and growth.

At corporate senior executive levels, management is usually by exception; that is, since general or unit managers are permitted to run their own operations, top management steps in only when help is requested or when there are obvious indications that things are going wrong.

Now, as divisions or units become more scattered and more diversified, even the successful organization evolves a new crisis. Greiner[6] calls this "the control crisis" which occurs when "top executives sense they are losing control over highly diversified field operations. Autonomous field managers

[6]Greiner, op. cit.

prefer to run their own shows without coordinating their plans, money, technology, and manpower with the rest of the organization. Freedom breeds a parochial attitude."

Not only do unit heads compete for corporate resources, but they hoard both technological and human resources. The professional management stage is extremely wasteful of people because of the immediate bottom-line time frames: one year's hero can be next year's bum. A plant or a division with chronic problems will devour several unit heads and even several whole management teams before it is again healthy. Managers at various levels soon may again conflict; the chief executive must again recognize that the human relations problems are related to the developmental phase of his organization. The organization is getting out of control.

Capsule: Professional Management

Through the segmentation of markets, acquisition, or internal development of additional products, the primary structuring entity becomes the division or profit center. This often requires major reorganization: either breaking up the original functional structure or relegating it to a one-among-many divisional status. The emphasis shifts from developing technology and function to the development of general managers and the bottom-line control of all organizational units. Organizations can then continue an almost unlimited growth through the proliferation of division and subsidiaries. The profit center phase frees the company from the constraints imposed by a narrow, traditional definition of company purpose.

The Transition to Bureaucratic Management

Thus it is that top managements establish corporate staffs who at first relate to the units primarily in a service capacity. Such corporate staffs in effect are a centralizing and controlling influence.

The bureaucratic management period comes on slowly. In contrast to the trauma of the transition to professional management, bureaucracy seems to arrive unannounced, uninvited, and for the most part unwanted. It is marked by a few skirmishes between corporate staff people and line operators. It involves a huge investment in the latest computer techniques. But at least, as the crisis deepens, the corporate executives recognize that a more bureaucratic approach provides company-wide planning and control systems. Furthermore, it assists in enabling the resources of the organization to be used in meeting corporate objectives rather than the needs of individual units. At long last, the corporate staff, filling its dearth of information through new systems for gathering data, are no longer stymied in their efforts to determine corporate priorities or to allocate funds appropriately. Basic, corporation-wide financial reporting of course is in place; but, since the general managers have had their say as to what systems and procedures they want to use, other systems vary widely in their sophistication and adequacy from unit to unit. It thus has taken a bureaucratic system of corporate staffs to unify, coordinate, and control the multifaceted, sprawling organization.

6. BUREAUCRATIC MANAGEMENT

The function of bureaucratic management is to control the disposition of the financial, technological, human, and physical resources of the organization so that it can continue to grow. Bureaucratic management is thus an adaptive response to successful growth and emerges when the successful, professionally managed corporation has become so large and complex that corporate ability to plan and control is endangered by the decentralization that was necessary in order to get decision-making and control closer to the marketplace.

The Management Style

Labels for systems of organization are convenient but may be misleading. This is certainly true in the case of bureaucratic management, which has increasingly negative connotations for the private sector (and perhaps even the public sector) because of its reference to government patterns of control of both organizations and individuals—some would call it interference.

But labels aside, the bureaucratic management style, with its proliferation of systems and structures and its accumulation of staff people at corporate and group levels, is essential to the control of sizable organizations.

Corporate staffs require enormous amounts of information in order to do their analyzing and planning, information that can only be supplied by lower level employees in the several units who in a bureaucracy are now required to fill out the forms and send in the data. Simultaneously the corporate staff imposes procedures and specifications in their attempt to upgrade the various functional and line organizations. The rationalization for such standardization is of course to promote and control the quality of professional efforts. For some reason, people seem surprised and resentful when the standards thus set, along with the mechanisms for auditing them, lead inexorably to standardization with the resulting inhibition of creativity and decisiveness. During this time, managers with financial background tend to rise to the top, and data processing begins to dominate the organization's systems. The corporation controls its resources by being sure that any decision with respect to the acquisition, use, or dispersion of corporate resources must be reviewed by those especially responsible for the best use of these resources.

The Human Relations Contract

In response to the extremes that often accompany the performance–reward system, the bureaucratic human relations contract retreats to the less demanding relation of conformity–stability. The employer says in effect, "If you will please conform (i.e., not make waves), we will define policies and expectancies so precisely that you will have a stable life without risk." The employee answers by saying, "I will conform if the organization remains consistent and stable."

This rather weak and impersonal contract nevertheless seems to make everyone comfortable. Since the emphasis is on detailing clearly how things should be done, neither the organization nor the individual assumes risk. The company assumes that its planning systems will determine the best strategies and decisions, and it purchases the conformity of employees to those systems with secure, clear-cut, obtainable expectations and requirements.

The Crisis

No better symbol of the bureaucratic crisis exists than its inevitable red tape. Systems and procedures, standards and forms, all proliferate until the firm's very vitality is threatened.

Decision and action no longer keep up with growth opportunities. Everyone perceives that the rigidity of systems for reporting, controlling, and supplying information stifles initiative and creativity; but in the bureaucratic set-up there appears to be little that anyone can do about it. The dilemma is real: how to preserve an integrated, central corporate planning and control responsibility, certainly a necessary function, and at the same time assign decision making, strategy development, and similar activities, also necessary functions, to lower levels where greater responsiveness is possible.

Capsule: Bureaucratic Management

This phase sees the reemergence of functional control in the form of staff entities. In addition to basic functions (marketing, manufacturing, technology), the service functions (finance, personnel, legal, planning) attain major management importance. These staff entities are gradually superimposed on the line structures. The staff–functional reporting structure was often shown as dotted-line configurations superimposed on solid-line structures on organization charts, until the complexity of such drawings made the final result confusing and impractical. Modern bureaucracies do not even attempt to chart the intricate line-staff interfaces. Staffs get their power through their control of negotiations for corporate resources. They operate through systems and systems programs to enable the corporation to strategically deploy its resources worldwide over long-range time frames.

Transition to Matrix Management

So, in response to a need for greater flexibility and for responsibility at lower levels, bureaucracies have experimented with various forms of project management, product-marketing management, brand management, and other forms of committee, task force management, hoping thereby to solve the dilemma. All these digressions from bureaucracy are efforts to cut the team loose from organizational shackles. Through the years such efforts as these have led to a multidimensional approach to management which removes some of the emphasis on gaining control only through systems, procedures, and staff units. It is called matrix management.

As we consider it, we must keep in mind that it is a difficult, demanding and, as yet, imperfectly designed organization form. Whether, in truth, it will prove to be a predictable next stage in organizational evolution or simply an elaborate and tricky organizational alternative is still to be proven.

7. MATRIX MANAGEMENT

The Function

Matrix management's primary function is to provide decentralization and centralization simultaneously. Greiner[7] calls matrix management a collaborative process which in some way makes solid-line and dotted-line reporting obsolete. Matrix management[8] allows a centralized functional control over the major areas of the corporation while, at the same time, it decentralizes product or business responsibility. In matrix management, each function—marketing, manufacturing, technology, and so forth—is consolidated so that each forms a professional organization. Hence, a major resource of the corporation can now be managed by functional executives without having to go through divisional general management. The corporate functional executives implement their plans and controls within their functions almost as though they had direct line-control. At the same time, product-line management and/or business management consolidates its functional lines. These entities determine the strategies for their product lines or businesses in collaboration with functional product-managers, who report to them as well as to their functional executives. These functional product-managers are centralized in their functional reporting and decentralized in their specific product-line reporting assignments.

The Management Style

Matrix management is a revolution in management style, not just a departure from classical organization theory. Actu-

---

[7]Greiner, op. cit.
[8]Willim C. Groggin, "How the Multidimensional Structure Works at Dow Corning," *Harvard Business Review*, January-February, 1974. Davis and Lawrence, *Matrix*, Addison Wesley Publishing Co., Boston, Mass. 1977. Groggins, and Davis and Lawrence provide excellent reviews of the theory and practice of matrix management.

ally, in many respects it is diametrically opposed to the classical theory whereby each manager reports in a direct line to one boss and whereby shared responsibilities are clearly shown by a dotted-line relation on the organization chart. Matrix managers on the other hand report to two bosses: they have both a full functional-team membership and a full business-team membership. Matrix management style is hence heavily participative and team oriented; decisions of any consequence are invariably made within a group structure and require many internal negotiations; authority derives from either functional or business expertise. The usual problems with the psychological aspects of absolute authority and interpersonal dominance appear to be refreshingly irrelevant within this management system. Since responsibility is shared, the opportunity for ambiguity is high; those with an intolerance for ambiguity find matrix management stressful, confusing, and unresponsive.

The Human Relations Contract

The contract within the matrix management system is even more informal and nonspecific than in the bureaucratic system. It seems to be a trade-off between adaptation and job freedom. The employer says, "If you learn to work effectively through this complex and ambiguous system, we will allow you maximum flexibility and minimum direct supervision." The employee answers by saying, "I will tolerate this ambiguity and learn this complex system if I am allowed maximum freedom so I can control my own efforts." This contract therefore involves only those in matrix positions; the remainder of the employees remain on the bureaucratic contract.

The Crisis

One writer about matrix management speculates that the crisis of this system may be "psychological saturation" because of its emotional demands. Our RHR experience, however, suggests that the crisis may have more to do with the eventual inability of the corporation to define and communicate its mission as multiple interfaces proliferate and internal preoccupations predominate. Matrix management is probably more a response to the complexity of corporations than it is to growth. It enables organizations with highly technical or complex businesses to accomplish strategic planning more effectively. In the long run, its impact may be to allow a shrinkage in the human resources of an organization while it participates in more and more complex business ventures. The advancement of data-processing technology will no doubt allow a continued reduction in both staff and middle management. The matrix system is thus ideally suited continually to balance the resources of the functions and businesses of the organization while carefully controlling the head count.

But at the same time, its very complexity taxes the ability of most employees to discern a central theme or purpose with which they can identify. This in itself may be a more significant organization problem than the stress on employees of ambiguity or the effects of multiple supervisors; and it may even result in the reintroduction of the traditional pyramidal structures within the matrix.

Capsule: Matrix Management

Matrix management simply recognizes both structuring dimensions, line and staff, as legitimate and, rather than imposing one on the other, conceptualizes the structure as a two-dimensional matrix. This is done primarily with the basic functions (marketing, manufacturing, technology). The service functions generally are superimposed on the functional dimension. The new matrix unit is the basic structuring element and consists of product-line managers from each function who report to a product (business, program) manager as well as to their functional superior. The product manager exerts leadership over all strategic product and profit planning for that product segment. The functional manager exerts leadership over the development and delivery of his unit's functional performance in each product segment. This organization form allows a high technology, complex business to plan and control more effectively without endless addition of more and more staffs and systems.

8. GENERAL OBSERVATIONS

Ontogeny Recapitulates Phylogeny: A Perspective on Organizational Evolution

In the biological development of the human being there is a fascinating phenomenon called "ontogeny recapitulates phylogeny." These scientific terms refer to the interesting fact that the human embryo, during its development in the womb, passes through physical stages of development that appear to parallel in microcosmic form the evolutionary development of the human species. For example, at one point the embryo develops gills and later loses them as it grows. At another point the embryo has a tail which it (fortunately) also loses. People are occasionally born with vestiges of organs appropriate to more primitive forms of animals, such as additional nipples.

How does ontogeny recapitulate phylogeny in the social organism? The answer is quite obvious as we look at the history of organizations in the United States and the relative development of industry in various other nations of the world. The evolution of the modern industrial organization has its roots in the years surrounding the industrial revolution in the mid-nineteenth century. Merchant, craft, and guild organizations had obviously gone before, but the combination of the industrial revolution and a democratic free market provided the developmental determinants that released the full evolutionary force of the modern organization. Some of the early business entrepreneurs were enormously successful. They flourished in an era when the exploitation of new technologies and untapped resources could proceed without restraint. The entrepreneur with a competitive advantage reaped enormous wealth and power. He became known as the robber baron. This entrepreneurial form of organization with its characteristic management style endured as the predominant form, even though some businesses grew to be very large. The business environment during that period was relatively simple and straightforward. The entrepreneur did not have unions and complex labor negotiations on his agenda. He did not have local, state, and federal regulatory agencies to confound his strategies. Consumer and environmentalist pressure groups were unknown. The entrepreneur founded family dynasties and moved into thoroughly paternalistic, personal, or family management forms protected from competition by their monopoly status. This was obviously an entrepreneurial period in United States history.

The modern entrepreneur differs only in degree from his antecedents. Most modern entrepreneurs show the characteristics of the robber baron, although moderated today by more restrained business values and by much less potential power. However, today's beleaguered businessman gets a certain satisfaction from reading humorous job descriptions culled from retail establishments of the Victorian era. In addition to performing clerical duties, the Victorian employee had to arrive early, start the fire in the coal stove, dust the counters, take out the ashes in the evening, and attend Sunday School.

The paternalistic, loyalty–security, personally managed business was the natural successor to the entrepreneur. It endured as a predominant form until the government imposed antitrust legislation to break up large monopolies and then imposed huge, punitive inheritance taxes. This latter tactic acted then, and acts today, to force family-controlled businesses to go public, sell out, or merge, thus combining with business forces to precipitate the next evolutionary stage.

Professional management as a broad evolutionary wave in the historical development of organization emerged by the 1930s. No more pertinent example could be cited than the development of General Motors during the 20s and 30s.[9] While other automotive corporations were wallowing in the crises of overextended centralized personal management, Alfred P. Sloan and the General Motors management went about fashioning the profit centers and professional management system and style which allowed it to become the world's largest corporation. At the time this was happening, Henry Ford was almost destroying his corporation with antiquated entrepreneurial and paternalistic management. Studebaker Corporation became the pure and extreme example of the family or personal business; it loved to project an image of one big happy family; local newspapers repeatedly pictured three generations of Studebaker families. For years Stude-

[9]Alfred P. Sloan, Jr., *My Years With General Motors*, Garden City, New York: Doubleday and Co., Inc. 1964.

baker boasted of having never laid off anyone, even though such was the growing practice in other automotive companies. Studebaker employees participated with the company management in a rich variety of company-sponsored civic and social activities. Studebaker never relinquished its style of personal management but never lived to enter successfully the professional management era.

As professional management evolved from the 20s through the 40s, management technology and management science were being fashioned by the universities. The graduate schools of business focused on the development of the general professional manager. The professionally managed business now had a strong ally in developing the technology and the human resources to fuel an insatiable appetite for growth through the creation or the acquisition of profit centers, a growth spurt that dominated the 50s and 60s.

During this period the demand for professional managers elicited a number of developments in the personnel and management process side of business. Management development became a significant corporate function. College recruitment programs, management trainee programs, programs to provide developmental transfer within the company, internal and external training programs—all became elements of a major management responsibility to develop general managers. Performance review systems were developed to monitor progress and to determine compensation. The management-by-objective system was developed to tie together management processes, manager development, and corporate business goals and objectives. For a brief period of time the nontechnical, liberal arts student was even looked upon with favor because it was felt his breadth of training might give him a head start along the road to professional management. As the bureaucratic nature of the encroaching systems and planning cycles became prominent, human resource systems, organization development techniques and procedures, and computerized management inventory approaches gradually eroded the individual focus of manager development and in many businesses relieved the manager from personal involvement in the development of his subordinates. This tendency, rather than red tape, may have been the real Achilles' heel of bureaucratic management.

The rapid growth unleashed by the development of professional management in the 20s and 30s inevitably required the institution of systems and controls that would enable management to harness the resulting giant enterprises. More and more elaborate and formal systems were devised for functions such as purchasing, production control, inventory control, materials flow, cost analysis, pricing, capital appropriation, etc. These systems gradually encased most large corporations in a bureaucratic cocoon that demanded the emergence of a new business form.

Most eras appear to overlap; their boundaries are indistinct. However, the final era does not appear to be insidious in its arrival. Matrix management arrived with the space age. If we were labeling eras by market forces or socio-economic variables, we could just as easily have labeled this the zero-growth era. While businesses were serenely pursuing a growth period during the 60s, the American culture was undergoing its well-known and well-publicized cultural revolution. While the power of institutionalized business was being eroded along with the institutionalized powers of community, family, government, and religion, business continued to plan its strategies with one thing in mind—growth. Almost unnoticed during this time, out of project management in the space industries, the elements of matrix management were developing. In 1970-71 there was a recession. In 1972-73 there was an economic boom that seemed to tax the manufacturing capacity of every manufacturer in the world. 1974-75 saw another sudden recession. Out of this roller coaster sequence, and as a part of the cultural realignment of priorities, there came a sudden 180 degree reversal of the corporate attitude toward growth. In the 60s a typical plant manager, general manager, or president bragged not just about the amount of increasing sales and profit if things were going well but also about how much larger the company was in people: "Our plant now employs 1100 people" was a statement made with pride. "This company employs twice as many people as it did ten years ago" was not a statement of concern but of realized growth aspirations.

But in the mid-1970s a human inventory control spontaneously emerged, marking a revolution in the corporate attitude toward human resources. A rigid head-count or human accounting system became the way of life. Now the president might more likely brag, "Our volume is up 8 percent and our profits are up 12 percent, and we are doing this with fewer people than we had last year." Everywhere, executives were suddenly under pressure to hold the head-count down. This had an immediate effect on personnel and management development systems and activities. Suddenly, campus recruitment was only for engineers, chemists, or accountants. By the mid-70s most of the management trainee programs had disappeared. Practically no one would hire a liberal arts graduate off the college campus. Whereas before, most corporations had one department of relatively routine functions which was a dumping ground for plateaued, obsolete, or poorly performing professional and managerial employees, now managers of such departments were required to become as fully professional and efficient and contributory to the bottom line as any other department.

Likewise, a decade ago most organizations alloted additional resources to at least one department whose functions were ideal for introductory training of young technical or professional people. Now, this departmental role has disappeared since all organizational slack is removed from the system. In the process of creating a lean, muscular organization, many training and development positions have disappeared. In the professional management era it was common practice to divide departments into additional units in order to create more supervisory positions as promotions for "comers"; commonly, assistant manager positions were added for the same reasons, and extra levels of management were often shoehorned between existing levels. But in the 1970s, businesses reversed this process, eliminated some management levels, abandoned the assistant and assistant-to positions, and consolidated staffs, divisions, and functions into more efficient units.

This final management era appears to have brought under intensive control a huge area of expense, i.e., the cost of organization growth. One can speculate that this happened for a simple economic reason—the tremendous inflationary increase in the cost of people. However, it would also seem to be directly related to the cultural upheaval of the 60s. The sexual revolution with its erosion of the family with distinct and familiar sex roles; the environmental protection movement; and the general antitechnology, antiautomobile, antiprogress, antibusiness movements—all seemed to be the result of some sort of cultural evolution that would finally contain overpopulation. From an evolutionary point of view, we may speculate that the matrix management era may provide a flexible organizational structure and management process within which the human elements that make up the organization can be conserved and utilized with greater efficiency and flexibility.

Multinational Business

As we consider organizational evolution within this broader framework, we must also consider implications for multinational corporations. If the United States has had its own evolutionary course with regard to industrial organization, then we must assume that other nations, particularly those of the West and the Third World, will also have their own evolutionary timetable. For example, European business has only been developing its full professional management era during the 1960s and 70s. (When we talk about an era in a given country we are, of course, referring to an average business condition.) Management science and management technology have advanced enormously in the last two decades in Europe, even though many European businesses remain heavily paternalistic, functionally dominated, and tightly controlled. Japanese business is famous for its family nature; the loyalty–security contract is nowhere in the world more adhered to than there. The evolutionary theory predicts, however, that over time in a free world market Japanese business will lose its competitive advantage and will have to move to another organizational stage if it is to keep its present position. Similarly, the Third World countries must capitalize upon the great advantages of the entrepreneurial organization to secure shares of the world market through lower cost employees and a more immediate and resourceful response to the marketplace.

The Evolutionary Profile

The five evolutionary stages have been presented as discrete and significantly different organizational profiles characteristic of all business in a given evolutionary phase. The truth of the matter, however, is that organizations, like people, are continuously unfolding wholes, changing in emphasis and experiencing crises but showing from an early age a definite personality and temperament. Probably all organizations contain the predispositions and postphase elements of all the evolutionary stages. All organizations can, no doubt, be described by using a profile for each organizational stage and defining the stage that predominates.

Entrepreneurial vitality may be the initial determining characteristic for the survival of an organization regardless of its stage of growth. It may become relatively dormant during the personal management era when the corporation appears to have a large share of a given market locked up; but new product development and technological innovation must reassert themselves if the company is to have more than a very short life cycle. In automotive and other consumer products businesses, planned obsolescence appears to be a strategy used at later stages of evolution to keep the entrepreneurial drive alive and the markets young and responsive.

The personal management factor incorporates the organization's basic mission. It is the time that an identity is firmly established and the loyalty of employees and customers firmly secured. Most famous brand names come out of this period and often carry the family name of the founders. Although organizations lose their simple dedication to a product or service, they must attend occasionally to the care and maintenance of such loyalties and to the definition of their fundamental mission. This is particularly true in the later stages of organization development where traditions, pushing from the past, and bureaucratic controls, encompassing the present, obscure for the organization what it is really trying to accomplish.

The results-oriented style of professional management most certainly has been a part of business to some degree during all stages, and must certainly not be lost completely in any stage if the business is to remain healthy and growing. All organizations must eventually be measured against the yardstick of bottom-line results.

The system and control that comes with the bureaucratic era also must have been in the embryo stage throughout the organization's existence. No organization can exist without some understandings and the disciplines of procedures. The fundamental nature of all organizations demands that the individual subordinate his own individuality to the procedural requirements of group action.

The matrix factor provides a certain conservation and fluidity of the management process through collaborative effort. In the early stages of organization, people are apt to wear several hats and thus to share responsibility as a natural consequence of their more primitive structure. Teamwork and highly participatory management often dwell side by side with paternalism and one-man rule. When matrix management succeeds one-man rule, it has the support in many organizations of years of participatory management influences. Those organizations that have been throughout their history to some extent involved with a shared management will embrace the matrix style much more easily than organizations which have had rigid lines with firm, authoritarian control.

The obvious conclusion is that at any given time one can find all of the management factors operative in any organization. Those factors that predominate will define the evolutionary stage of the enterprise. Occasionally, one will see a phenomenon, comparable to psychological fixation, in which the organization will have moved on to a later stage of organization evolution but will still show a strong underlying predisposition towards an earlier factor. For example, a two-billion-dollar, high-technology corporation that emerged suddenly on the office machines market and grew rapidly for several decades based on a patent advantage, is moving appropriately into the later stages of organization evolution. However, this corporation is so inbred, its company mission so deeply imprinted, its functional areas so thoroughly tangled in traditional and highly beneficent corporate policies, that the professional phase, the bureaucracy, and the new matrix management they are introducing, will not for a long time replace its basic personal management nature.

The sequential nature of the evolutionary process is further complicated by the fact that organizations often do bring in elements of other developmental stages long before the existing developmental stage really requires it. An enlightened family manager will bring in professional management influences long before his era is really over. If this simply means more decentralized management, better job descriptions, and better bottom-line controls, his efforts will be productive. If this means that he brings in a professional manager at a high level without altering his organization's fundamental management style and structure, then his efforts will result in failure. The professional manager will be rejected in much the same way that an organ transplant in a human body is rejected. A professional manager brought in by the entrepreneur can only succeed if the entrepreneur steps aside and if the company has proceeded far enough in its evolution to benefit from pro-

fessional management. There are few situations more pathetic
than the professional manager trying to organize and delegate
in a situation where the entrepreneurial nature of the business
dictates that everyone leap into the fray and get his hands
dirty. It is perhaps just as unfortunate to see a bureaucratic
business hire or acquire a successful entrepreneur only to see
him slowly smothered by bureaucratic caution. By the same
token, however, it is the fortunate entrepreneur who perceives
soon enough that he must acquire some kind of management
item if the organization is to continue to grow. The most insightful entrepreneurs are those who, recognizing that they
cannot change their own style, either retire early and stay out
of the way of the business or seek acquisition by a professionally managed firm. The insightful executives in a personally managed firm can gradually bring in professional managers and with persistence and intelligence reorient their
organization to a more decentralized and professional stance.
It is unfortunate that more often the family management
hangs on until they are gobbled up by a larger firm after a
long period of crisis.

A second unfortunate scenario takes place when the
ownership, after several years of slipping profits and decreasing share of market, uses a recession and its resultant disastrous bottom line as the excuse to bring in new leadership.
The new president too often uses the recession crisis to rationalize the wholesale discharge of the personal management
team and its replacement by professional managers. Companies that are forced to make management changes in crisis
cannot afford the time nor the expense to make changes compatible with the needs and requirements of its individual elements. People get hurt when organizations change only because of a crisis. Orderly change, however, can be planned
for and can be realized when management understands the
organization's personality and stage of evolution.

9. CONCLUSION—EVALUATING AN ORGANIZATION'S STAGE IN THE LIFE CYCLE

Each stage of the life cycle of an organization has its
unique functional management style, human relations contract, and management crises. It is critical to the viability of

the organization that it move from one stage to another in spite of trauma. And it can do so if management is sensitive and knowledgeable about the organization's dynamics, its needs, and its present stage of growth.

Throughout this chapter we have emphasized the need to understand the dynamics of any organization before taking steps to improve it. Should an individual or a group in an organization want to study that organization formally, the following Table of Organization Life Cycles may be useful. The point should be stressed that the table should be used as a guide only; there is no presumption that the list of characteristics of each stage in the life cycle of an organization is necessarily complete nor are all the items always applicable to every organization.

INSTRUCTIONS

The purpose of this Table of Organizational Life Cycles is to identify the conditions or characteristics or situations that need to be changed if the organization that is rated is to grow. In the table the characteristics or qualities of (1) the structure and function, (2) the management style, (3) the human relation contact, and (4) the crisis are listed for each of the five phases. Please check each item as to whether in general you agree (A), disagree(B), or are uncertain (C) about whether the characteristics or qualities apply to the organization you are rating. After this analysis—and one should not be puristic about the evaluations—go back and star the item(s) that seem to be especially significant. Upon the conclusion of the evaluation, the "scores" can be summarized on the attached Summary Table to make it easier to determine priorities, i.e., what needs remedying or changing first, what second, etc.

TABLE OF ORGANIZATIONAL LIFE CYCLES	A Agree	B Disagree.	C Uncertain	D Significant.
PHASE I — ENTREPRENEURIAL MANAGEMENT CHARACTERISTICS				
1. Structure and Function a. One-man management b. Absence of planning, systems, organization structure c. One product or service predominates d. Small, flexible, competitive e. Still establishing a business; seeking a competitive advantage				
2. Management Style a. Impulsive, opportunistic b. Paternalistic but informal c. "Seat-of-the-pants" management d. Few or no formal job definitions or lines of authority				
3. Human Relations Contract a. Only one real boss; he makes all decisions of consequence b. Most employees relatively low paid for the industry c. Everyone goes to the CEO with any problems, whether business or personal d. Very few highly trained or widely experienced professionals in the business				
4. Crisis a. "The CEO is too busy; we can't get to him for important decisions." b. A growing feeling that the organization is getting too big for a one-man rule c. It's getting more and more difficult to operate without defining some lines of authority. d. Our growth will stop unless we can attract and hold some good upper management people. e. The CEO is running the business more and more by slogans and dicta. f. We must develop a management team if the company is to survive.				
	A	B	C	D
Summary: a) Total items: b) In the D column, star any item that seems to you to be especially important.				

Entrepreneurial Management

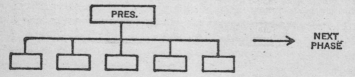

PRES.

NEXT PHASE

	A Agree	B Disagree	C Uncertain	D Significant
PHASE II — PERSONAL MANAGEMENT CHARACTERISTICS				
1. Structure and Function				
a. Top management is a small team with close personal ties to the CEO.				
b. Operations are controlled by functional V.P.'s who are mostly concerned with their own departments.				
c. "Nobody else has our know-how in our product (service) line."				
d. "Our profit margins are large because of our preeminence in the field."				
e. The management's main job is to protect our competitive advantage.				
2. Management Style				
a. "We have developed our own way of managing this business; no outsider could manage us."				
b. "Most decisions are made on the basis of our long experience and heavy traditions."				
c. "Our managers are homegrown rather than professional."				
3. Human Relations Contract				
a. "We are basically still a family-type business."				
b. "Our people are very loyal."				
c. Few people are ever discharged.				
d. The employees personally identify with our product (service) and its quality.				
e. The company takes a personal interest in the employees.				
f. There is a strong sense of belonging among employees.				
4. Crisis				
a. "We are now so diversified we don't know what business we're in."				
b. "Our divisions are going their own way and are completely out of control."				
c. Division general managers hoard their good people.				
d. Corporate staff cannot visit division people even in their own areas without the division manager's permission.				
e. Each division has its own systems and policies.				
f. Corporate priorities are difficult if not impossible to establish.				
g. Top management doesn't really control the corporation's resources.				
h. Corporate management is usually unable to promote growth of the business in the markets that we should be aiming for.				
	A	B	C	D
Summary: 1. Totals 2. Number of starred items				

(Continued)

PHASE II — PERSONAL MANAGEMENT CHARACTERISTICS (Continued)

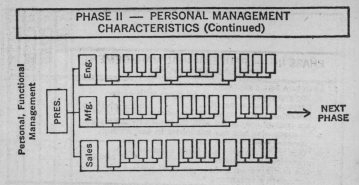

	A Agree	B Disagree	C Uncertain	D Significant
PHASE III — PROFESSIONAL MANAGEMENT CHARACTERISTICS				
1. Structure and Function a. Is organized around profit centers. b. Is quite decentralized; great authority is given to division general managers. c. Line authority is all important; little if any real emphasis is on staff.				
2. Management Style a. Management is primarily concerned with short-term profits. b. Management demands results. c. To develop general managers is a basic need throughout the organization. d. Tough-minded cost-cutting is required of all managers.				
3. Human Relations Contract a. Employees expect to be compensated for the quality of their performance. b. Management gradually weeds out nonperformers. c. Employees are not as secure in their jobs as they used to be. d. Ambitious employees often leave the organization if they are not promoted as soon as they think they should be.				
4. Crisis a. "We are losing our competitive advantage." b. "The competition often beats us on price." c. "Our top management is too old-fashioned and traditional." d. "We now have several product lines (services), but we still operate as if we had only one." e. "We have a lot of obsolescent people." f. Employees are not rewarded for performance, just longevity. g. "The market is changing and the competition is catching up." h. Top management lives in the past.				
	A	B	C	D
Summary: 1. Totals 2. Number of starred characteristics				

(Continued)

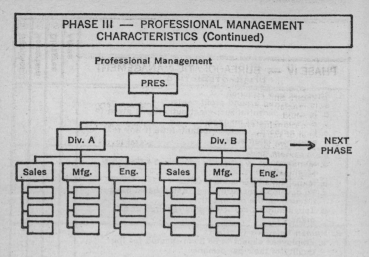

PHASE III — PROFESSIONAL MANAGEMENT CHARACTERISTICS (Continued)

Professional Management

PRES.

Div. A   Div. B   → NEXT PHASE

Sales | Mfg. | Eng. | Sales | Mfg. | Eng.

	A Agree	B Disagree	C Uncertain	D Significant
PHASE IV — BUREAUCRATIC MANAGEMENT CHARACTERISTICS				
1. Structure and Function a. Financial reporting and control systems are very detailed. b. The planning and budgeting process takes a great deal of the manager's time. c. There are strong staff functions at several levels (corporate, division). d. Charts really no longer describe all of the organization's dimensions and relations.				
2. Management Style a. There is a gigantic, computerized management information system. b. Management tries to cover or anticipate every eventuality by establishing a prescribed procedure or policy. c. Most decisions, before being implemented, must be checked with several staff functions and/or levels of management. d. Detailed reports regularly are required from all visits and also must accompany all requests.				
3. Human Relations Contract a. Most personnel questions, problems, or decisions are settled by the policy manual's provisions rather than by a manager. b. Employees with very, very few exceptions, are required to conform to standards and procedures. c. No one person makes an important decision or takes any personal risk on company matters. d. Relations between supervisors and subordinates are based primarily on the performance of the employee.				
4. Crisis a. Systems, procedures, standards, and forms proliferate. b. Rigidity of systems for reporting, controlling, and supplying information stifles initiative. c. Functional control is often in the form of staff entities; service functions attain major importance. d. Staffs have power through their control of negotiations for corporate resources. e. Decision and action no longer keep up with growth opportunities.				
	A	B	C	D
Summary: 1. Total 　　　　　2. Number of starred characteristics				

(Continued)

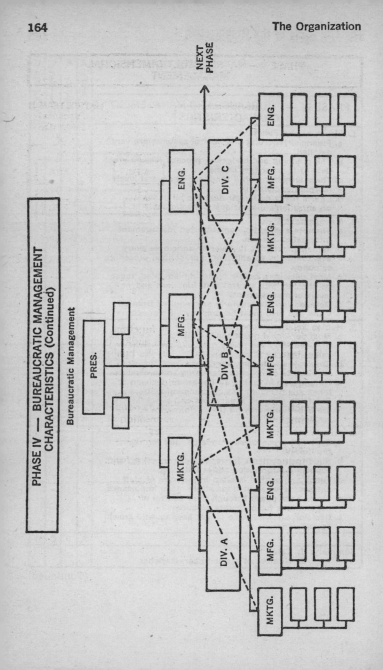

PHASE IV — BUREAUCRATIC MANAGEMENT
CHARACTERISTICS (Continued)

Bureaucratic Management

NEXT
PHASE

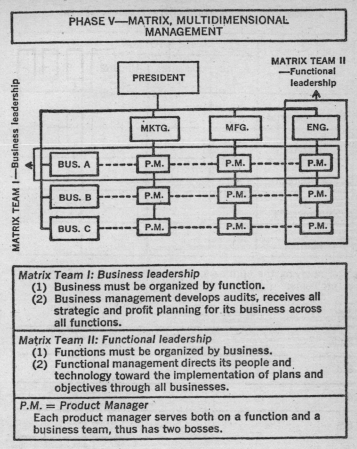

PHASE V—MATRIX, MULTIDIMENSIONAL
MANAGEMENT

Matrix Team I: Business leadership
(1) Business must be organized by function.
(2) Business management develops audits, receives all
strategic and profit planning for its business across
all functions.

Matrix Team II: Functional leadership
(1) Functions must be organized by business.
(2) Functional management directs its people and
technology toward the implementation of plans and
objectives through all businesses.

P.M. = Product Manager
Each product manager serves both on a function and a
business team, thus has two bosses.

SUMMARY OF EVALUATION OF LIFE CYCLE

PHASE	TOTALS			
	Agree A	Disagree B	Uncertain C	Starred D
I Entrepreneurial				
II Personal				
III Professional				
IV Bureaucratic				
V Matrix				

After studying the summary, these appear to be the priorities of problems:

1st
_____

2nd
_____

3rd
_____

4th
_____

5th
_____

6th
_____

7th
_____

CHARACTERISTICS OF THE EVOLUTIONARY STAGES OF THE ORGANIZATION

	ENTREPRE-NEURIAL MANAGEMENT	PERSONAL MANAGEMENT	PROFESSIONAL MANAGEMENT	BUREAUCRATIC MANAGEMENT	MATRIX MANAGEMENT
MANAGEMENT STYLE	One-Man Paternalistic	Maintenance Team Paternalistic	Profit Center Autonomous	Systems Impersonal	MultiDimensional Collaborative
HUMAN RELATIONS CONTRACT	Leader-Follower	Loyalty-Security	Performance-Reward	Conformity-Stability	Adaptability Job Satisfaction
CRISES	Leadership Crisis	Autonomy Crisis	Control Crisis	Red Tape Crisis	Purpose Crisis
ORGANIZATIONAL CONTROL	Centralized One-Man	Centralized Functional Team	Decentralized Profit Center	Centralized Staff	Simultaneously Centralized & Decentralized

CHAPTER IX.
Vital Signs of Effectiveness

I. INTRODUCTION

Objectively assessing the effectiveness of an organization is an extremely important but also a very difficult task. Perhaps a primary reason for this difficulty is the fact that any organization is already being evaluated constantly, although very informally, by employees, competitors, its community, and government agencies, to list only a few, who, with or without comprehensive knowledge, have opinions about its quality. Even those responsible for its viability, the directors and officers who are intimately involved, often feel that "We know all that we need to know about our company; so what's the need for a formal evaluation?"

Furthermore, the task of evaluation may seem to be unnecessary because the traditional signs of successful performance are easy to read. Bottom-line proof of profitability (for a commercial enterprise), high morale as proved by low turnover, growth in volume and/or size, and ostensible progress toward stated objectives are frequently cited as evidences that "We must know what we're doing." With such indications of success, some managements conclude there seems to be no need for a formal evaluative effort.

Another obstacle arises from the difficulty that members of

the organization have in being objective as they study themselves. How can one be detached, be scrupulously fact oriented, if one is looking in the mirror? Even physicians restrict themselves from operating on members of their own families. How then can management be expected to do an unbiased, scientific study of the organization?

But perhaps the most significant block to a formal organizational assessment is the sheer difficulty in studying a living organism with all of its intangible aspects and limited number of hard facts. Any organization, like any human being, is a complex of tendencies and processes that make an in-depth knowledge difficult to obtain. And when the organization is in motion, as it certainly must be if it is alive, the findings of a formal evaluation would seem to be too temporary, too evanescent, to be of any permanent worth.

Such considerations as these, of course, have merit and, although they may not be voiced, are nevertheless pertinent to the reluctance of many conscientious managements to assess their organizations for effectiveness. But in spite of such obstacles, the need for doing a formal, objective, and systematic assessment remains. As discussed elsewhere[1] the years ahead promise bigger challenges and opportunities for the competent but unending horror for the inept.

This chapter, therefore, without dogmatically citing any unbreakable rules or proposing any absolutes, explores some concepts that may provide insights into what's going on in an organization and details criteria of effectiveness that can serve as guidelines in assessing an organization. These concepts also can help managers assess the needs, strengths, and weaknesses of the organization.

2. CONCEPTS OF ORGANIZATION

The first step in assessing any organization's effectiveness is to determine what is to be assessed, which is not as obvious a matter as one usually assumes. For what is meant by "organization" determines not only what is to be examined but how

[1]See Chapter I, "The Individual in the Organization," Chapter IV, "The Roles of the Manager," Chapter XI, "The Changing World of the Director," and Chapter X, "The Concerns of Top Management."

best to proceed. There are two major concepts of organization—the structural model and the biological model. These will be defined and evaluated; then we will discuss the criteria by which to judge their respective usefulness.

The Structural Model

Organization is almost universally thought of as structure that can best be shown in a pyramidal arrangement of lines and boxes which illustrates how functions and the people relate in a hierarchy.

Thoughts, plans, and actions are thus based on this diagramable structure. When the question is asked, "How are you organized?" the response is almost invariably in the form of one or several charts. Some organizations are even proud of their intricate, arcane book of charts, beautifully updated even weekly to keep them current with the inevitable changes in personnel or in functions or in reporting relations. There are also many organizations where charts are relatively straightforward, enabling a discerning examiner to understand quickly how the organization is at least intended to operate. As an expression of a concept of organization, the chart is useful, particularly in certain phases of an organization's evolution. It can then express in traditional form the purpose of the organization, its typical functions, and how it is set up to fulfill its role in the economic and social environment. The chart has particular value—one might call it shock value—when the charts of five years ago, of today, and of five years hence are laid side by side with the ages of incumbents in the boxes. Then the inevitable changes brought about by normal attrition as well as the critical need for planning replacements are both dramatically highlighted.

But, unfortunately, there are some hazards in the use of charts. For one thing, the sheer drawing of a chart is an onerous chore which in and of itself may cause some resistance to badly needed change. In addition, since the chart is an official document, known to all as a statement by top management, a change in it must mean a change in the thinking of top management. And that calls for explanations, perhaps rationalizations, and may produce some mindless tongue-wagging (What do you suppose *they* mean by this?) or may exacerbate normal resistance to change.

A more serious hazard is the use of charts by executives

who are so addicted to them that they genuinely think of the organization as boxes on a piece of paper, neatly labeled by function and jobholder. Too often such thinking becomes stereotyped. Organizational problems are presumably (but erroneously) solved by moving the boxes on the chart. "Personnel is always over budget; it's out of control. Let's make the controller responsible for personnel. He's a good watchdog on expenses." So such a move is made with blissful unawareness of basic functional and logical relations.

Another hazard in the use of charts arises from the mental compartmentalization that results from an overdependence on structure. When an ambiguous problem arises, it is too easy to think the problem will go away because it is really in someone else's department—in another box, so to speak. The duties and responsibilities of each department are clearly identified on the chart, so "We don't need to worry about that. After all, handling grievances belongs to personnel, not to us in manufacturing." In addition there may often be little understanding of the problems, failures, successes, or opportunities of other parts of the organization. The quality of the organization's integration may crumble under the impact of the tendency to compartmentalize that a chart often seems to promote. This situation is particularly disadvantageous when the organization is in rapid evolution or when for other reasons its circumstances are exceptionally fluid. Matters of importance can go unheeded because they've fallen between the boxes of the chart without anyone noticing. And such problems, as most administrators of tightly structured organizations know from bitter experience, can return to haunt.

At the opposite extreme in the use and/or misuse of charts is their absolute prohibition. For instance, one CEO of a major corporation forbade their use, rationalizing that the minute you drew up a chart you tended to lock people into boxes, you restricted top executives' freedom to involve the best available experience and ability, regardless of position, and you stressed the hierarchy instead of a feeling of responsibility for the best job the company could do. The CEO and his colleagues of course paid a price for not having any kind of chart, although they felt the price was worth it. For one thing, new faces on executive row would spend quite a bit of time on their new jobs before they felt they knew how they fit into the working relations of the company's executives. In addition, there was always likely to be some confusion as to who was finally responsible for what, the most persuasive one or the one with the best judgment. With no authority from a hierarchical position to compel others to accept one's opinion, a plan or project or decision that was finally adopted certainly had to win its way on merit.

The Biological Model

If the traditional, structural model of organization has limited usefulness, what is a better alternative? Is there a concept of organization that is equally tangible and clear-cut, one that compels acceptance because it is readily understood?

One extremely useful approach is to see an organization as a living entity, an organism (see Chapter VIII). The parallels with living organisms are numerous: both the organism and the organization go through life cycles; both are "alive" in the sense that they are moving, dynamic, everchanging entities; both have many characteristics and qualities in common with other members of the species, yet still both are unique in and of themselves; both are integrated organisms whose functions are intricately interrelated; and both evolve and adapt, grow and develop, and show countless other signs of what biologists call life.

To view an organization as a living entity, therefore, can be very helpful in understanding it. Such a view avoids the pitfalls of the structural model and provides insight into the processes of the organization that may be involved in planning, controlling, interpersonal relations, morale, and the many other aspects of organizational life that the structured model cannot picture at all.

Simply stated, living systems do three things: (1) They regulate their internal environment (internal services in the organization). (2) They relate to their external environment (operations). (3) They reproduce (development).

1. Internal Services

The first process of an organism, regulation of its internal environment (termed homeostasis by biologists), occurs through the use of automatic, self-adjusting mechanisms, such as the digestive processes, that enable the organism to function easily and consistently. In organizational life, homeostatic processes are those internal services, such as needed

management information and payables and receivables, that
provide ease of operation and dependability.

2. Operations

The second process, transaction with the external environment, is commonly called regulatory behavior. Organisms
take in a variety of substances, depending on whether they
are grazing animals or predators or living in the sea or moving on wings. Whatever is consumed helps the animal to adjust, adapt, and maintain its internal environment. These
types of processes, when applied to an organization, can be
thought of as regulatory for they define what the organization
does to what it takes in. The organization converts its inputs,
such as raw materials, into a final product, which in turn is
eventually transmitted to the marketplace. These functions,
systems, and activities are typically called operations.

3. Development

The third function of organisms, reproduction, is often the
missing element in the organization's life. The reproductive
function, of course, includes the mechanisms and systems that
guarantee organizational continuity. Without such continuity
for living species, all is lost. And so it is with the organization. Corporate life has no terminal objective in the normal
sense. It does not arrive and then settle down to exist in an
unchanging state forever like a rock on the hillside.

Organisms reproduce tissues by the replacement of defec-
tive material or parts as in healing a wound or reproducing
its kind. Organizations likewise may maintain their viability
and continuity by a variety of forward-looking systems and
mechanisms. (Unfortunately it is considerably less common
to find an organization that aggressively looks forward and
values the concept of perpetuation.) Strategies, planning for
the provision of capital, the development of management potential, the creation of systems that insure the necessary inputs and functions to allow the organization a future—these
are some of the reproductive functions of an organization.

Perhaps these processes could avoid the biological connotations of reproduction by being termed instead "development,"
for in truth the organization without thought about development or without procedures that presumably guarantee continuity is indeed dead already, in effect if not in actuality.

Use of the Biological Model

The three-part biological model of organization stresses dynamic functions, processes, and interrelations. What does operations need from the controller? What does development need from marketing services? What manager training by personnel is needed by the research division? The "bio" model easily shows how one person, group or function affects the whole.

Even more importantly, the use of the biological model makes the identification of needs and problems easier. As an organization "ingests" its raw materials, "digests" them (i.e., makes a product from them in operations, and then supplies the product to the market)—in short, engages in its basic life activity, it uses many subprocesses: the raw materials come from different sources, production involves many different steps, and selling varies from easy to difficult for the same product in different markets or at different times or against different competitors. Each of these subprocesses can be examined carefully to determine with accuracy if there are needs or problems that require a change in personnel, procedure, or policy.

From the point of view of the structural model, on the other hand, all functions tend to be generally or broadly conceived; and regrettably the labels on the functions—engineering, manufacturing, personnel, etc.—are often used loosely as substitutes for precise thought. "Yeah," says one manager, "engineering never comes out with anything on time." "Never," answers another, "with anything." With such thinking (engineering, it must be remembered, is one box on the chart) how can the problems and needs in engineering be identified?

The value of the biological model is intrinsic to its very nature. If the life of an organization is dynamic, an ever-changing kaleidoscope of people, functions, purposes, and environments, then the static framework of the structured model is as limited as would be one's understanding of a person from a single snapshot. But the biological model, being in itself a concept that encompasses vital forces, is more likely to provide in-depth understanding.

3. ASSESSMENT

With the concept clearly in mind of an organization as an organism, one can assess the effectiveness of its subprocesses. The subprocesses are in effect the characteristic elements of the organization and occur as surely as do a living entity's digestion or heart action. There are eight of these characteristic factors to be found in any organization: purpose, philosophy, leadership, integration, viability, structure, communication systems, and environmental relations.

Presumably the most effective organization would exhibit a high quality of performance of each process. By the same token, deficient performance of a process would certainly point up a problem. In essence, therefore, the eight characteristics are eight criteria of effectiveness. An examination of each readily shows its relevance.

Purpose

It is axiomatic that each human behavior serves the individual in some way. Sleeping, yawning, jogging, talking, laughing, crying, breathing, eating, digesting: all meet some need of the organism. Similarly, organizations behave purposefully to meet needs, whether these are articulated or unspoken, clear-cut or obscure, practical or impractical. Even though some organizations regularly muddle through without defining their purposes, their efforts are less effective than those of organizations whose purposes are clearly defined. Defining purposes requires a clear and current definition of the product or service and an understanding of how that product or service meets needs, whether simple or complex, temporary or permanent, tangible or intangible.

Perhaps everyone says at first and in effect, "Sure, I know our purpose. We're an organization that produces chairs," but then on second thought, adds, "Come to think of it, I don't really know why we make only collapsible patio chairs." Even long-established concerns will have many managers who consciously (or otherwise) never have thought much about why their organizations exist. Such an attitude, common though it is, may seem adequate; but in truth the assurance that comes from knowing why one is doing what one is paid for is lost. The result is at best a loss of potential; at worst, a listless effort.

A clearly stated and well understood basic purpose serves to keep the organization focused and moving in a common direction. It keeps the people aware of why the organization exists and alerts them to additional opportunities. But in order to have an impact, the basic purpose needs to be reexamined and reaffirmed from time to time. The corporation or institution that fails to do so often loses its sense of direction or fails to recognize opportunities.

An interesting case in point is the car rental company that deemed its purpose was to provide temporary transportation for people away from home. After a certain number of months or miles the cars were considered scrap and were wholesaled at the best price. Now a new purpose developed when they saw that there was a need for well maintained, relatively new, used cars. They saw that, in effect, they were producers of used cars, sold them at retail and considerably enhanced their return on investment by meeting an additional need. All that it took was a review of their single basic purpose, now outmoded, by the addition of a broader purpose.

A classic error made by otherwise competent organizations is to think of the production of net profit as their basic purpose. This is like saying that breathing is the purpose of life.

A major conglomerate had net profit as its purpose and used this as its main criterion in evaluating acquisitions. Over time, the conglomerate consisted of an array (or disarray, if you please) of profitable companies in several kinds of businesses and services—at least profitable at the time of their acquisition. But as the conglomerate decreed the formulae for profitability, thereby interfering with the style of the subsidiaries that originally had made them profitable, the profits often eroded. Something had happened to the purposes of the acquirees; what formerly guided them and made them profitable was gone. Now their purpose was only to make profits, an overriding purpose that upset their usual planning, organizing, coping, product development, and all of the other aspects of their former effective organizational life. Expediency and opportunism became the guides. And too often long-term, bottom-line failure resulted.

As with human organisms, to remain effective an organization requires consistency between purpose and action, for consistency provides stability. People then are not confused about why they are doing what they are doing. Employees and executives alike are not at cross purposes. Behavior is predictable. But inconsistency brings a high price. The organization with an original basic purpose to provide a high quality product that then allows cost-cutting to dominate its action runs a serious risk of losing both its market and its effectiveness.

Hand in glove with a purpose is a plan, with both short-range and long-range objectives, for accomplishing the purpose. The organization must have a plan, whether formal or informal; otherwise each executive and manager develops his own. Without a plan, actions are reactions with all of the potential difficulties that may come from impulsive, *ad hoc* behavior. A long-range plan is one way of turning the kaleidoscope of activities into a desirable pattern. When a mass of iron filings are dropped on a plate of glass, they are indeed a jumble; but when a magnet is passed under the glass, the iron filings quickly establish themselves into a recognizable pattern. A long-range plan is like that magnet, organizing a jumble of individual activities, objectives, and desires into an integrated effort.

How long is long-range? It means different lengths of time, depending on the nature of the business. For example, the electric utilities industry typically plans ahead a minimum of ten years, since the construction of new plants alone has at least that much lead time. For a company in a short-cycle business, such as retailing, where seasons or styling are factors, the long-range plan could be much shorter.

Long-range objectives are different from targets and goals. Targets are immediate, very short-range; goals are intermediate, such as one to five years; whereas objectives are long-range, a general vision. What is important in doing long-range planning or setting long-range objectives is to measure against what has been done and ask, "Do we need to change?" This is the concept of the moving objective. It is not engraved in stone; it is constantly reevaluated and perhaps revised.

In large organizations where communications are necessarily complex, a plan is most often written down. But whether the plan is written or not, the process of developing the plan is more important than the plan itself. The thinking that people do as they determine options is more important than what is finally put down on paper.

The people who take part in the planning process get the greatest value out of it. Sometimes this way of organization planning is called bottoms-up-and-top-down planning. If people are not involved in making the plan, the likelihood of ineffective response is fairly great because the plan as written down is likely to be merely a statement of words, rather than a realization of what those words mean. This is why the planning jobs are often rotated by good companies. A person is put on the planning group for a year and then replaced; but now there are two people in the same department who have been through planning. Bottoms-up-top-down planning, when it is done effectively, is usually carried on with both superiors and subordinates talking about how they together are going to achieve the overall plan.

However, even such an estimable activity as planning can be overdone, and extensive participation, unless controlled, can slide crabwise into running the organization via committee and making planning decisions by consensus. The way to avoid subsequent organizational paralysis is to confine participation to the input stage and have the decisions made by appropriate persons in authority.

Philosophy

It is probably true that a statement of philosophy for an organization is one of the most overrated, uninfluential, and yet common things on the American business scene. The problem is that such a statement may come from some individual, perhaps a chief executive or the company's founder, with a strong personal philosophy that he pastes like a decal on the organization, regardless of its purpose. Sometimes (and too often) a chief executive is persuaded that a statement of philosophy is simply a good thing to have; so he puts some noble words together and passes it on to the organization as a *fait accompli.*

In spite of such misuses of a statement of philosophy, an organization without one, written or not, risks falling apart. Philosophy is the thread that ties together the basic values of an organization (if it can be said that an organization, per se, has values). Philosophy is not a creed or a statement of values; rather, it is something that says that these values we

have are important to us and are tied together in such a way
that they are internally consistent. Thus an organization's philosophy is the connector between business purpose, management style, and long-range objectives; it ties them together
and integrates them.

For instance, a professional service organization may have
a philosophy of commitment to the free enterprise system and
of sharing risks, opportunities, and rewards with the entire
staff. This philosophy integrates the purpose (providing the
highest quality of professional service to business and industry), the management style (personal professional involvement of the top officers and the inclusion of all staff in the
professional decision process), and long-range objectives
(maximum growth in professional excellence and numbers of
staff in order to have a greater impact on business effectiveness).

Furthermore, a philosophy is a statement of principles that
guides the organization in accomplishing its purposes. Philosophy refers to the reasons for the organization's beliefs;
values refer to the beliefs themselves. For example, an organization can express a belief in equal rights for women by
granting equal pay for equal work (a value) because all
people are created equal before the law and in society (philosophy).

A major corporation's philosophy stated, among other
things, that the organization (a) would strive to be a good and
independent citizen by contributing to the welfare of our society and (b) valued the free enterprise system. So one sum-
mer the corporation set up a very large fund to help
underprivileged, unskilled teenagers to find employment in
ten major cities, the fund to be administered by the Labor
Department of the government and monitored by the company. Usually such programs are funded through tax dollars,
with private industry's cooperation in training. But this corporation's philosophy required it to give some leadership to
beneficent programs for society rather than to leave the improvement of society only up to government.

The philosophy of a business organization, while considered essential, presents the greatest difficulty to top managers, partly because they are more action oriented than
contemplative and partly because a philosophy must be global
enough to cover areas beyond each executive's immediate

concern but yet specific enough to be applicable to each executive.

This need to be both global and applicable creates a number of potential problems. Should a philosophy be written down? It depends. In entrepreneurial organizations, headed by a strong leader whose personal philosophy comes through to all in the consistency of his actions and reactions, the philosophy of the organization (i.e., of the leader) could be unstated but very effective. On the other hand, in a large multinational organization where the CEO may have great authority as a leader but relatively little personal contact, a written statement of philosophy may be absolutely necessary in order to communicate to the far corners of that large corporation what the leadership stands for.

But there are risks in writing down a philosophy, not the least of which is that behavior cannot belie the words, for belief in a philosophy rests on what is done, not on what is said. If a leader voices a lot of sweet talk but is ruthless in his actions, there is bound to be distrust and cynicism. Conversely, if the written philosophy is adamant in its demands of people but the leader's actions are inconsistently soft, the written statement is worthless and may, in fact, do more harm than good.

A major task of a chief executive is to insure that the organization and its systems allow people to function on their jobs in terms of the established purposes and philosophy of the leader. Too many times the systems work to the contrary. For example, a compensation system which gives a bonus only for tangible increases in sales volume rewards behavior that is inconsistent with the philosophy of rewarding the employees for growth on the job.

Leadership

An organization has to have a leader, either titular or actual. This criterion asks for a determination of the quality of that leadership. How does the leader control the behavior of others? Through fear? By personal charisma? By introducing stimulating ideas? In personal relations? By a strong sense of responsibility? By authority of office? Whatever the style of leadership, it must be appropriate to the needs of the organization, its stage of life, and its economic-social milieu.

Even though an organization may continue fairly well for

a while after a leader has left because of retirement, resignation, or death, it must soon replace him. Determining such a succession is an extremely critical matter. A new leader may have a different philosophy or a different style, but the organization remains the same. Thus the two may not fit, not because of any inadequacy on the part of the new leader or of the organization, but simply because of a fundamental incompatibility. It is thus tremendously important that the new leader be appropriate to the philosophy and the style of management and in addition, perhaps more importantly, meet the needs of the organization.

Examples abound of organizations where the leader or the organization had to change in order to continue to be effective.

In the case of one company that had been very effective under founder's leadership, there was no way of continuing that pattern of organization under new leadership; it just didn't fit. The old leader could walk out into the plant—a metal bending plant with much clatter and banging—and would know immediately that the No. 4 press was down. When the new president came in with a different background of experience and sensitivity, there was no possible way he could identify that the No. 4 press was down. So he had to resort to a system of reports (generally disliked, initially at least).

For another example, a large organization was charged with illegalities in its foreign dealings on the part of several members of the top management. The reputation of the company was at stake. A new leader was brought in with an international reputation for integrity, candor, and honesty. He represented the bulk of the organization in his character and was able in a short peried of time to sweep away the intimations of corruption and reestablish the organization on the world business front as trustworthy. In this instance, the organization did not change; the leadership did.

Another consideration is the management style of the leader, its effect on those he leads, and its appropriateness to the personality of the employees. Management style goes hand in glove with philosophy, for style is the expression of how to get things done through the organization. More than management techniques and theories, style is the internal and external expression of feelings about people.

Management style can be described in many ways—low

key, authoritative, democratic, participative. It does not by itself denote either purpose or philosophy. A very authoritative
management style may value social responsibility; a democratic style may be unconcerned about the organization's
obligation to society.

One difficulty for some people is that they have adopted a
management style that doesn't fit either their personality or
their philosophy. Their style thereby is a technique rather
than a natural, consistent way of operating.

One organization which has a strong commitment to service to the customer and concern for the employees has a
management style that puts people under extreme pressure.
This pressure undercuts the basic commitment because protecting one's self becomes more important than customer
service and concern for employees.

The question arises, must a personal management style, in
order to be effective, be acceptable to the entire organization?
Clearly, when the conflict is strong, the individual is released
or voluntarily leaves. To have a manager with a personally
authoritative style living in a very democratic organization
with its more slow-moving, decision-by-consensus way of operating would be internally awkward if not destructive. But in
between total rejection and total acceptance is tolerance. No
environment is likely to be perfectly satisfactory to all. But if
the overall management style is just a little out of phase with
one's own, it can both be understood and tolerated. At least
general acceptance of purpose, philosophy, and style is essential.

Integration

By definition, integration is the meshing of the activities of
people who share a common goal. When purposes are clear
and accepted and when objectives are seen as worthwhile,
then integration is relatively easy to reach. The question of
this criterion, therefore, is not so much do people work together well, but why. If not, why not? Since the causes of integration (or disintegration) are also more important to
determine than the exact degree of it, any assessment of an
organization's effectiveness should not be sidetracked by a futile effort to quantify such an intangible as a reason why
people work in an integrated fashion. Furthermore, one
should not be fooled by unproductive integration. It is

conceivable, of course, that people could enjoy working together so that, superficially there is a high degree of integration; but a closer examination might reveal that their
contentment is ineffective. They might be happy, but still unproductive. And since the name of the game is results, not integration of activities for its own sake, it becomes clear that
integration, or at least some degree of it, is a by-product of
effectiveness, not an end in itself. When there is integration
but poor productivity, the likelihood exists of a real talent
deficiency, plus a lack of clear goals.

Integration has a strong element of feeling in it, an element
that in a sense defies logic. As a consequence, the assessment
of integration is difficult because the evidence for or against
its presence must be subjectively determined. Feelings, emo-
tions, the quality of interpersonal relations, the bonds that
tie people together, the commonly held values—these are
some of the things to study in determining the quality of integration.

Viability

This criterion asks, How alive is the organization? Is there
a prevalent, positive feeling that "we know where we're going" and that "we enjoy being part of this effort?"

Like integration, viability is a symptom of such underlying
causes as a clear-cut, accepted purpose, common values, and
consistent philosophy. Also, like integration, viability is likely
to be greatest when the organization is experiencing success,
when it competently accomplishes what it sets out to accomplish, and when it feels capable of coping effectively with
inevitable difficulties and changes. In an organization, viability is the same as joy of life in an individual—a healthy,
robust, glad-to-be-alive feeling.

Evidences of viability are legion and may vary from the
amount of camaraderie and laughter in the lunchroom to the
relative percent of turnover, from the attitude of the recep-
tionist to the manifest pride of workmanship about the product or the services of the organization.

Also, like integration, viability is a feeling tone, something
that, like invigorating mountain air, is unseen but vitalizing.
To generate viability is beyond the capability of any applied
techniques, for after all to try to produce viability is to try,
and certainly in vain, to change a cause by attacking its

symptom. And the common causes of viability or of its lack-luster opposite are not only numerous, but also specific to the organizational situation. What turns one group on, colloquially speaking, may leave another group cold.

Viability is the capacity of the organization to cope with change while maintaining functional integrity. Management feels fully responsible and, furthermore, assumes correctly that the quality of management makes a difference. Without such viability, the organization is likely to be on a long, slow slope downward. But when viability is the primary end of management, the functions that fall into the category of development in the biological model—planning, evaluation, strategizing, etc.—come to the forefront.

A mistake made all too often that threatens effectiveness by threatening the quality of viability is to fit the organization to available personnel. This is particularly true when a new chief executive comes in or someone is promoted to that post and basically says, "Here is what we have, and therefore this is what we are going to organize around." Jobs are sometimes created, and even whole divisions are adjusted, to fit a particular individual. Sometimes this is done on the basis of the individual's special strengths; sometimes on the basis of the individual's weaknesses. But even though it may be necessary temporarily to construct or systematize jobs or patterns of organization on this basis, it should never be done unless it has already been determined what is the best kind of organization for that business, that market, and that philosophy. The communication of "what we aim to become" lets the people know that top management recognizes that the present situation is only a step toward the structure that is most appropriate.

Organizational Structure

This criterion does not ask, "How are you organized?" but it does inquire whether or not a group of people *is* organized. There are of course many patterns or systems of organization (see Chapter VIII). The critical question of this criterion, however, is whether or not a given organizational structure is appropriate to the group at this moment and, in addition, is understood by its members. Does the structure fit the function and purpose of the organization? Is it wired up like a cow when it is supposed to be a predator? For example, is it set up for static conditions when market penetration or new product development are the keys to success? The structure of the organization must be devised not only for its members but also, more importantly, for its purpose, its pattern of functioning, and its environmental requirements.

Communications

In essence, this criterion asks how ideas, information, or feelings are transmitted from the mind of one to the mind of another. Formal communications—memos, letters, speeches, problem-centered discussions, etc.—are relatively easy to identify; it is not so easy, however, to identify, let alone evaluate, the characteristic pattern of the grapevine, the casual encounter at the water cooler, the after-hours bull session, or the many other informal ways of communicating. This criterion essentially asks about the nature of communications in the organization. The answers will tell a lot about how members of the group find out about objectives, progress toward goals, changes in procedures or policies, the reasons for the changes, and a host of other communicable matters.

To communicate fully, frequently, and fairly will certainly be necessary to organizational strength in the near future in order to facilitate involvement in decision making, planning, and controlling, to cite only a few functions. In addition, there are two other factors that make communication especially critical: the burgeoning of computerization that makes much more information readily available (see Chapter VII) and, second, the finding that managers spend more time in getting and giving information, usually orally, than is usually supposed (see Chapter V).

Environmental Relations

There are four environments in which an organization functions. Three are external: its community—local, national, and international; its industry/profession—associations as well as competition; and its physical environment—the water, air, and land it affects. The fourth is made up of groups that strive to protect and/or salvage the environment. The critical question of this criterion is whether the organization actually lives in isolation (or seeks to) or acts as a good citizen; whether it contributes by its concerns and actions to the general quality of life, or whether it is complacently parasitic. One environment is internal: the relationships of its members. It could be a healthy or unhealthy environment. A good illustration of a healthy response to the unwelcome sunshine law which opens up the employee's personnel file to personal inspection occurred in a forward-looking California company. Their competition responded by heavy-handed resistance to the law and fought the law by fostering an amendment to the State Labor Code. But the progressive company instead purged all old materials from its personnel files, moved documents with plans of management for personnel to other files, and then publicized the fact that any employee could schedule a date for the personal review and examination of his or her file. Although few requested such an opportunity, the employees felt good in knowing they could.

4. EARLY WARNING SYSTEMS

Finally, the effective organization has its own tried-and-true ways of anticipating both impending disaster and probable opportunity. Such ways are vitally important. To be surprised by a devastating disaster—a breakthrough in a manufacturing process by the competition, for example—can so panic an organization that it makes unwise moves, for its plans may be suddenly irrelevant, its procedures instantly outmoded, and its market position severely threatened. By the same token, to miss an opportunity can open up new avenues for the competition and can lead to lowered morale as people live with the rueful feeling, "It might have been."

Few people in one industry clearly saw the impact of foreign competition with its low-cost labor markets. When finally this factor was noted, the industry then compounded its troubles by not anticipating the rapid movement of labor markets from one country to another—from Japan to Korea to Taiwan to Brazil. And then the raw materials came in short supply to the surprise of American manufacturers who had overlooked the fact that they depended on foreign countries almost totally for their raw materials. Another industry effectively anticipated sharp changes in competitive circumstance and carefully planned for them by developing a standardization of the components for its products, thus making

American production far superior and less costly than even one of the world's best and least expensive labor markets.

Use of Scenarios

Some organizations anticipate both disaster and opportunity by setting up what are called scenarios, i.e., if this kind of situation occurs, this is how we will respond. Organizations that use scenarios are no better prognosticators than anyone else, but their development of scenarios compels them to look ahead constantly to evaluate what might be coming. They have not got their heads tucked down, nor are they saying, Buggy whips are really going great.

Use of History

An organization can also develop its sensitivities to potential difficulties and opportunities by carefully studying its history, rather than just accepting it. When an organization merely accepts its history, it tends to want to replicate its successes, and the greatest breeder of rigidity is success.

A very large organization tried to deal with a problem of reduced profit by reemphasizing practices that brought it to its present large size. The result was a dramatic and continuing loss of sales volume and profitability. It failed to recognize sharp changes in the nature of its clientele and its competition. This illustrates the need to appreciate changes that are taking place and to realize that if there are no changes, there is no need for management. In the biological model of organization structure, management is comparable to the central nervous system. Clearly, sedentary, unchanging amoebalike organisms with simple response parameters need no such extensive nervous system.

Spotting Inconsistencies

Inconsistencies are warning signs that spell trouble ahead. There may be inconsistencies between the basic business purpose and the way the market is developing; for example, an organization's purpose is to provide high quality, moderately priced writing instruments but the market is going toward inexpensive, throwaway pens. There may be inconsistencies between the nature of the organization and the changes in customer demands; perhaps the organization has different in-

formation in three separate locations about the dealer's order
and now finds that the dealer needs all the information simultaneously. Or there may be inconsistencies between the systems and the kind of people in the organization; when a
sophisticated computer system is installed for use by untrained people there may well be difficulty ahead.

Monitoring

Effective organizations devise better ways to anticipate the
future. Of course the usual methods for determining "how
we're doing" are maintained as checks and balances—cash
control accounting, percent of market share, and the like. But
beyond these systems, which work after rather than before
the fact, sensitive monitoring methods can be used to cali-
brate the quality of the crucial life forces within the organization and its industry. Such methods constitute a genuine
service function that evaluates proper forward goals and provides needed information for timely remedial action. Assuming that human resource planning should thoroughly
document potential future management, several progressive
companies, for example, hold annual personnel reviews, division by division and department by department. In these, the
manager discusses with supervisors (and the personnel vice-
president) the appraisals of his people together with plans for
their on-the-job development and job future. Such a system is
manifestly more than after-the-fact monitoring of how the organization is doing.

Another monitoring method is a continual examination of
the compensation system. Does it reward employees for
desired behavior? Since people do effectively what they are
rewarded for, it is important to know whether a salesman's
bonus, for instance, is based on his quantity of sales regardless of quality of sales.

To monitor the communication systems is still another effective method for checking on the causes of problems that
may arise from misunderstandings. When everyone works under one roof, it may be an acceptable communication system
to say, "I'll tell him when I see him," but when people are
separated geographically, it is obvious that another system for
effective communication is needed. And this principle becomes more critical with the plethora of communications that

are not only possible but probably will be actual in the Computer Age.

5. CONCLUSION—IMPLICATIONS OF CHANGE IN THE ORGANIZATION

The organization, apart from the individuals in it, is a dynamic entity that exists as a result of as many forces and possesses as many characteristics and behaves in as many inscrutable ways as any human being. The implications, therefore, of what organizational life will be like in the future are hard to forecast with exactness; but just as the behavior of any person who is well understood is generally predictable so is the life of the organization and how management may or must react.

A summary of some principal implications shows how organizational effectiveness will be particularly crucial but also difficult to achieve in the 80s and 90s.

1. Frequency and rapidity of change will be the hallmarks of organizational life.

2. Rapid technological advances will continue to promote revolutions in communications, data processing, and the burgeoning microtechnology of electronics. So much information will be generated so easily that, to keep from being completely inundated, managers will need to control the flow so that it produces only what to them is essential information.

3. Pressures from external forces will multiply beyond those of the 70s. Environmentalists will continue to state their cases before regulatory, legislative, and corporate bodies.

4. Special-interest groups of new, unimagined kinds will come to the forefront along with many groups that were born in the 70s.

5. We can probably also assume that governmental regulation and interference in business will reach crisis proportions in the 80s.

6. Antipathy to the private enterprise system by the media, the public, and legislators may congeal into a virtual mass movement. Effective methods for educating such groups about the fundamental nature of American business will be needed. In other words, business and industry will need to tell their story in a considerably more cogent fashion, stressing

the political, economic, and psychological value of business to the individual in our society, not merely our system's productivity of more and better products.

7. A factor that will affect organizational pattern and style, perhaps one even more difficult to develop, is a change in managerial attitudes. Executives who depend upon the authority of their positions and who perpetuate organizational or departmental separateness will find the going very tough.

Organizations will need to work aggressively to combat such debilitating attitudes. Instead, they will need to focus on joint processes for which responsibility is shared, rather than on autocratic or hierarchical authority. Executives will be forced to accept interaction in problem-solving, accountability, and other responsibilities as a method for achieving organizational success. They will need to learn now to welcome rather than merely tolerate this interaction.

8. During the near future it will be more important than ever before to keep a watchful eye on how the organization must evolve to maintain its viability and its growing edge. Creating a function which looks toward the future of the organization can be a significant step in trying to anticipate changes in the marketplace, in the external environment, and in society. Just as animal species must adapt to their environments in order to survive, so must organizations.

9. Only by thinking of organizations as dynamic, living entities rather than as structurally rigid systems can there be much hope for survival, both now or in the future. Survival clearly depends on responsiveness to the environment and a deft harnessing of internal capabilities in order to adapt to an ever-changing world. Therefore, knowing the resources and dynamics of the organization is essential for viability today and a guarantee of survival tomorrow.

PART FOUR
The Leadership

CHAPTER X.
The Concerns of Top Management

1. INTRODUCTION

In previous chapters we have delved into the various aspects of organizational life and of course made observations about the nature and the quality of organizational leadership, the work that leaders do, the responsibilities of their jobs, the problems they face, and the errors they sometimes commit.

However, there is one significant aspect of leadership left that we have covered only by implication and imputation—the concerns of top management. What goes on within the inner world of CEO's? What are their worries and fears as well as their determinations and positive thoughts? Certainly matters such as these would have a strong bearing on how the leaders lead.

To find out about this inner world, we interviewed a sampling of the CEO's of our one thousand client organizations. This chapter is the report of those interviews.

Our procedure was simple. When a member of top management of an RHR client—the chairman, the president, or the chief executive officer—agreed to be interviewed, we provided in advance these four questions for discussion:

1. What are the major problems or concerns that *you see ahead?*
2. What specific pressures or influences do you perceive as influencing top management in the *performance* of their jobs in the years ahead?
3. What other factors (not mentioned in Questions 1 or 2) do you feel will affect the way you *can* operate in the future?
4. Finally, thinking of the preceding three questions, *how* do you think that *your role* or the way in which you operate will have to *change* in the near future?

The interviews took from two to four hours; the questions, obviously open-ended and unrestricted, were usually used as kick-off points for a candid, conscientious discussion. Since each CEO as the head of a client organization has a professional relation with the RHR psychological consultant who serves that client and who interviewed him for the purpose of this survey, the interviews were unique and revealing. Each of forty RHR consultants talked with several clients, all business organizations ranging in size from a volume of 10 million dollars to a volume of several billion dollars, from purely local to multinational companies, and from young or family-owned businesses to behemoths; each class is about equally represented in the survey. Half of the clients interviewed are among *Fortune*'s 500 businessess, banks, and insurance companies.

2. QUESTION ONE

The first question, "What are the major problems or concerns that you see ahead?" attempted to get at those persistent, nagging, worrisome concerns of CEO's. The four listed in Figure 1 (page 193) were cited by enough respondents to call them commonly held.

Changes in American Society

The most common concern is the pervasive change in American social-cultural conditions. CEO's of organizations of all sizes are concerned, particularly those in the billion-dollar-or-over corporations. Here are excerpts from their remarks:

. . . [There is a] higher value placed on leisure time than work time; [there are] rising expectations as to what should be earned from one's work.

. . . A major issue is quality of work life. We need to work toward letting workers think and function as humans versus an emphasis upon extrinsic job factors such as pay and working conditions.

. . . [Several] questioned society's values, the pattern of consumer advocacy, the challenging of the free enterprise systems.

FIGURE 1

Rank Order of Major Problems
(Question One)

PROBLEM	RANK ORDER
Social-cultural conditions in the U.S. (changes in values; "quality of life" interest)	1
Inflation-energy	2
Government regulations; business climate in general, both here and abroad	3
Organizational and personnel problems	4

These CEO's now see themselves responsible—if they want to insure a viable organization—for providing a "quality of life on the job." Even more than that, and it's especially startling, is that top executives seem to feel responsible as leaders, as policymakers, and as good citizens for providing a great deal of employees' quality of life, whether on the job or not.

"We will have to change a helluva lot," says one CEO. "A premium is now placed on our flexibility and adaptability," observes another. "Many industrial organizations will be hard-pressed in the early 80s to cope with these problems," says a third.

Inflation and Energy

Second among major concerns is inflation and energy, two mighty forces in the economy. The respondents not only cite inflation and energy as major problems, but almost always also cite government bungling and incompetence as a major reason that these difficulties continue to plague us.

The concern for inflation and energy causes more frustration and even anger than does any other problem. Costs of raw materials, for example, are climbing, and when passed on to consumers (as is necessary), invoke criticism and calumny. The availability of energy seems to depend on the OPEC countries' whims. And currently the United States has no comprehensive plan for energy development.

Here are some of the CEO's comments, some of which are almost plaintive.

. . . How can I run a business, plan in advance, and predict how to build a product at a profit?

. . . How can I keep the machines running and keep the doors open while we have this energy crunch?

. . . Energy resources . . . affect so many other things. Although we will have more income per family, there will be less discretionary money to spend.

. . . (There's) no way to see a slowdown [in inflation.] Evidence is all to the contrary. Because government spending [local, state, federal] is so high, the controls on economic cycles that once existed no longer exist.

. . . (There's) long-term inflation—and the public is not ready to accept higher levels of corporate profitability.

. . . (We're) dealing with consumers about the pricing of energy [says the CEO of a utility]. They go to legislators who take a punitive approach toward the energy companies. And this puts tremendous pressure on management.

. . . We face times of shortages . . . energy, particularly fossil fuels, is only one of the shortages; others might be just as serious or more so, such as shortages of the materials that we use in production—copper and manganese and various and sundry exotic metals that give special properties to metals and plastics. All of these types of things may be in shortage and we need to think of new ways of doing things. The whole world cannot use in the same abundance as the Western world did in the developing years of the Industrial Revolution. One of the significant differences from Colonial days is that now worldwide communications have made it possible for everyone, even the most backward nations, to know what we have in the developed world; and as a consequence they all want the same thing; and the idea of sacrifice and acceptance of shortages is going to be very difficult to sell because of the attitude that says, "You got yours and now we want ours."

All in all, the energy and inflation crisis casts a pall over the present and dims the future outlook.

Government Regulations

Close to inflation and energy in rank order of concerns (and likewise provoking anger and frustration) is the proliferation of government regulations. So many of these hamper business by demanding many man-hours of irrelevant paperwork and long delays in responding to inquiry or report.

... We have to demand our liberty back from bureaucrats. For example, the excess cost to X Corporation to comply with government regulations was 20 million dollars. Now that's what worries me.

Some CEO's called the government generally non-business in its orientation but often came perilously close to labeling it anti-business. In general, the government is seen by most as something far less than a partner in the conduct of business.

However, government regulations, unlike energy and inflation, constitute a concern about which CEO's believe they can do something.

... [Ours] is a business which is regulated by both federal and state laws. The CEO must pay continuous attention not only to existing regulations but to how to get them revised, how to lobby, what new ones to add, and which to drop.

... Rapprochement between business and government is an absolute necessity for the 80s. ... We need to get better students into our government, for example, so that there can be better quality on both sides of the fence. In much of Europe and Japan, an opposite kind of situation exists: The better students traditionally go into government, whereas business is only for those less skilled and less "noble."

The People Factor

Other areas of major concern as CEO's prepare for the decade ahead are the quality of personnel and the general effectiveness of the present organization style and structure.

. . . (We have) a strong need for experienced, capable managers.

. . . Companies have to make better use of the people-resources—challenges are no longer just technological.

. . . We are going to have to do more at the corporate level in hiring broad-gauge, competent people and place them into various units to get experience; otherwise our system is never going to generate people who can come to the top with the breadth and vision we need.

. . . In light of what the 80s are likely to be, we will have to restructure our organization to get more flexibility and more participation by so-called lower management in planning and major policy decisions.

Thus among the problems that CEO's can do something about, much concern is focused on the people factor, specifically the need to upgrade the caliber of the workforce, especially of managers and technicians.

. . . (Problems include) getting the people and the ability to come up with innovations.

. . . (We'd) better develop our human resources through technical training and through advanced training in the ideals of free enterprise, individual recognition, and liberty.

. . . Managers are brighter and better schooled than ever . . . [and] need to be.

. . . We need more M.B.A. educated people in order to strengthen the abilities of our managers better to analyze and appreciate the things that affect profitability.

. . . [We need to] attract and retain a skilled and competent work force, especially managers.

. . . [I'm] having a harder and harder time hiring people who want to work. In a stone quarry, for example, the truck drivers want an air-conditioned cab with stereo and FM-radio.

. . . Competent personnel are going to be harder to find.

This need for greater capability does not necessarily mean that CEO's think that organizations today are crippled by ineptitude, but it does mean that CEO's generally expect the demands on people in the future to be more rigorous, requiring greater knowledge and skill. Clearly, the awareness is growing that increasingly effective people mean an increasingly effective organization.

Furthermore, the trend of the times to change the positions within the workforce of minorities compels attention to who does what in the organization and of course how well it is done.

. . . People (are) taking on responsibilities at a younger age.

. . . (More) women's roles include a career outside the home.

. . . (There's a) problem of transmitting experience acquired by managers to their successors . . . Managerial experience is often lost in the transition from one generation to the other.

Several CEO's commented that government regulations and societal trends are complicating organizational patterns. In addition, more skilled workers require technical specialization beyond the current capability of schools and other resources to supply. More and more organizations are developing their own training centers as well as rehabilitation programs to facilitate skills training.

. . . The scarcity of skilled technicians is a big concern today.

. . . Younger employees demand more training and look forward to moving ahead faster—they're better educated and expecting more.

. . . People problems are going to be compounded.

. . . The nature of top management will change. There will be a partnership form of governance. We must profes-

sionalize management. Each top manager must have an
equivalent—not a subordinate role.

3. QUESTION TWO

The second question, "What specific pressures or influences do
you perceive as influencing top management in the performance of their jobs in the years ahead?" also stimulated provocative discussion.

Government Regulations

More than anything else, top managers expect government
controls to affect their performance as executives. The strong,
oft-repeated concern is that government hampers business
with regulations that too often are picayunish, with demands
for irrelevant paper work, with a proliferation of unnecessary
studies, and, too often, with blatant incompetence. No one
objected, of course, to what was felt to be sensible federal
regulation that really protects the American public. The following excerpts from the reports of the interviews give the
substance and flavor of the reaction to regulations.

Some CEO's are appalled at the sheer cost of regulations
to a company.

. . . Increasing taxation at the corporate, federal, state,
and local levels (like) real estate taxes and Social Security
taxes all erode the profit prospects.

. . . [Regulations] are found in every direction you turn
and have a cost burden and stifling effect on all business.

. . . To obtain all the permits needed to build a coal
generating-plant from federal, state, and local agencies cost
this company about six to eight months' time plus nearly
one million dollars in cash for the studies and for employees' time . . . Ten years ago it cost only enough to determine if the soil would support the foundation for the
plant—$10,000 or less.

Others were more concerned about the cost in time and effort.

. . . Much more of my time [said the CEO of a 500-million-dollar company] is spent with issues that touch on regulatory agencies. We have a packet of cases pending that is about two inches thick—cases dealing with environmental issues, fraudulent claims by disgruntled employees. We're justifiably proud of our compliance with EEOC and of our many affirmative action programs; but when a minority person comes to one of our plants, supposedly looking for employment, walks right past the employment office and into the factory through swinging doors with the sign on them Employees Only and is then told by a foreman to go to the personnel office and while doing so gently takes her elbow and reverses her direction so she is now facing the swinging doors; and then when she walked right on by the employment office and instead apparently went straight to the EEO office and filed a complaint, charging us with refusing to hire a minority person and besides with mistreating her—I think "manhandling" was the term used—why, then I get damned disgusted; but later, when a young investigator from this EEO comes over, clipboard in hand and cigarette dangling from his mouth, and begins to quiz our people in a supercilious manner and smiles cynically in disbelief when they tell him what happened; and so then we go to court and spend a lot of money and time to assure a not guilty verdict—why, then, thinking back on that whole experience, I get damned mad at a government agency that in this case at least was incompetent and, maybe worse than that, dishonestly making trouble for us by deliberately planting that woman.

There was certainly agreement that government regulations are proliferating at an unconscionable rate.

. . . I can't even keep up with pending government regulations that affect our business. For example, there was just a change in the tax code dealing with employees earning a certain amount. It involves a rebate on taxes and a new way of calculating weekly earnings. I learned about it by accident about three weeks before it went into effect. Fortunately, the government delayed its implementation for six months; otherwise a large number of companies would have been in significant violation without even hearing about it.

. . . A most important influence on how I expect to do my job comes from the increasing amount of government control and regulation. It is inundating us now and it's not improving. It will continue to affect us and will grow.

. . . Government has leapfrogged, grown, become loaded with bureaucracies and we are ensnarled.

. . . We are stymied by a creeping paralysis evolving from continuing and increased government regulation.

Sometimes the respondents cited specific agencies whose regulations were proving troublesome:

. . . EEOC for one area; they seem to have an anti-business attitude that is irritating. When they came in they assumed we were guilty, and it was up to us to prove we were not. ERISA was particularly time-consuming—no better plan, just different. Government in these areas almost seems to be attempting to control our communications.

. . . My major problems are OSHA and EPA. I sold off one of my business areas. The trial judge agreed that we were protecting our people better than if we did what OSHA told us to do. I took the case to the Appellate Court and lost.

Many thoughtful respondents were concerned because the proliferation of government regulations seemed to augur poorly for a continuation of the basic economic philosophy of the United States.

. . . Government is making it more difficult to have a free choice in setting up boards of directors. Government is forming special-interest representation on boards. There is great pressure for representation of social issues rather than stockholder interests.

. . . Inherent in the governmental response to various special-interest groups is an underlying lack of confidence in our American free enterprise system. It imparts a lack of confidence in the social concern and integrity of American business executives and interferes with their freedom to operate their businesses in the best interests of their shareholders.

. . . There is heavy competition between the federal agencies and the state agencies for the right to regulate our industry.

. . . Too many decisions are being made poorly because too much attention is being paid to the political aspects of things. The influence of politics on judgment is just too heavy.

. . . The government has a necessary role in a free economic system to protect the public. But the government of the United States looks on all business with suspicion.

Business Climate

One in two CEO's feels that changes in the business climate will demand personal flexibility as well as newer ways of organizing, communicating, and controlling. Interestingly, the larger the organization the more significant to top management become the changes in the climate for business. While a fourth of the 10-mllion to 100-million-dollar companies expect the changes in the business climate to exert a strong influence on how business is done, nine out of ten of the billion-dollar-and-over corporations anticipate heavy pressure.

The intrusion of government into the world of business is the biggest factor affecting the quality of the business climate.

. . . [There is] a growing tendency to give token compliance rather than patriotic compliance [to government demands]. We are forced to look for loopholes, to balance noncompliance against compliance.

. . . Management will have to learn to deal with some very difficult legalistic challenges as audiences learn to use the legal system for harassment, personal gain, etc.

. . . Government . . . government . . . government.

. . . [Management must study] the demographic curve. There are changes coming in the under 40 age group. Unstable government and economics do not make people comfortable in making long-term investment decisions. We need to have a more predictable environment.

The CEO's of very large multinational companies see the climate in which they carry on business around the world as changing also.

. . . In spite of trade arrangements, treaties, the European economic community, the opening up of China and other Iron Curtain countries to trade, nationalism will become more prevalent and will cause more and more difficulties in world trade. There will be control of imports and a great deal of protectionism. The larger American multinationals with 100 percent equity in their foreign operations should seriously reexamine their position. We should manufacture in more places and procure parts in more other countries; we should not attempt to have 100 percent equity or we are going to be in serious trouble. The multinational will survive if it is flexible enough, but [if it's] stiff-necked it won't make it. Multinationals will survive because the countries need the expertise and capabilities of the multinationals. In spite of their nationalism, they have to invite these organizations in to help them meet their own needs. In fact, the impact on local economy is very, very great. One multinational I know of has more cash at its disposal than all but nine of the countries in the world.

. . . The speed of communication has changed things. We will have to emerge as a community of nations. You know, nothing will happen unless there is a crisis, for that really moves people to act on something important. We will have to develop flexibility in how to live with our neighbors. Our economic problems will force us to solve our social problems.

Caliber of Managers

Many CEO's expect the future demands for organizational effectiveness to raise the caliber of managers.

. . . Participative management will demand that our executive group explain what they are doing and why, both more readily and more completely.

. . . We are not getting enough able people to run the business.

. . . The demand for flexible hours [will] continue to accelerate.

. . . This is a period of changing loyalties of employees—people no longer identify with the institution or the company—but usually with a particular man or leader.

Consumerism

Somewhat surprisingly, only a third cited consumerism or threats of product liability as a circumstance that might affect their way of managing. This doesn't necessarily indicate a lack of concern. The negative feeling toward irresponsible consumer advocacy—one person called it "tantamount to witch-hunting"—is actually very intense. But it is likely that most CEO's know how to cope with occasional product deficiency, as the recent and voluntary recall of automobiles demonstrates. Only those who find the consumer advocacy movement "sneaky and subversive", in the words of one respondent, bothered to cite it as an expected pressure.

The Forgotten Shareholder

Many executives are concerned over the plight of the stockholder. Even though the stockholders own the business (it is their investment that, technically at least, makes the business possible) CEO's feel that unless something is done soon, the shareholders will indeed be shortchanged. The banks, the unions, the employees, the consumers, the customers, the government agencies, and even the managements are each threatening to take over control. The shareholder may growl and complain or urge the professional stockholder to needle the management, but he is generally forgotten, the lowly owner of the place.

. . . There has to be a whole new relationship. Gadflies have been an unfortunate waste of time, but shareholders have to be considered.

. . . [We must be] much more responsive to shareholders from whom we now are getting conflicting expectations.

. . . The biggest single challenge will be trying to relate the shareholders' best interest to being coincident with public interest. For example, if ——— Company (an oil company) declares a significant increase in profits, the public says this is bad—and forgets that much of these profits go into pension funds that allow retirees to sun in Florida.

. . . The poor stockholder is going to be largely ignored. Other than the recent capital gains tax reform, nothing has been done for shareholders.

On the other hand, some top executives hold quite a different view.

. . . The joint stock companies were a wonderful invention that worked extremely well for 300 years and were used to develop the Colonies. From them evolved the modern corporation. But the modern corporation cannot afford to be purely for the benefit of stockholders, as in former days. If we don't recognize we have several priorities— stockholders, employees, government, and society in general—we are headed for serious trouble.

. . . Attitudes of stockholders will not be a problem other than for their legitimate desire for proper return on their investment.

Whether or not stockholders are in for a bad time in the 80s is not as significant as is the fact that only a third of the CEO's in the survey mention any concern for the shareholder, although the third who do are intensely concerned. This may be a shift in top management thinking. There was a time only a decade or two ago when most CEO's felt that they had two sets of bosses—the board and the stockholders. And they seemed then to be constantly aware of both groups. Now only a third of the CEO's even think to mention the shareholders as an influence or a pressure on them in the future.

A Compelled Social Activist

Except for the responses that cited lack of productivity as a probable future problem, all of the other influences that CEO's anticipate are out of their normal sphere of control such as the activities of the environmentalists, the waning of the free enterprise system, government agencies, and the problems of energy and inflation. Many CEO's are therefore planning to broaden the scope of their interests and activities and to influence the business climate of American society. They feel almost compelled to become, as one said, "a social activist." Several have resolved to step up their personal efforts to influence the government and other "society makers."

4. QUESTION THREE

By the time the interviews reached the third question of the survey, "What other factors (not mentioned in response to questions one and two) do you feel will affect the way in which you can operate in the 80s?" the CEO's had already stated what problems were uppermost in their minds and which would be the most difficult to solve. Nevertheless, their responses to question three are not insignificant. Quite the contrary, as an examination of Figure 2 on page 206 quickly shows. Interestingly, in answering question three the CEO's began to talk about what they must do, can do, and plan to do to cope with the situations they expect to face in the 80s.

Responses to question three fall into two groups; those factors that CEO's feel they cannot directly control and, like the cost of energy for example, can only adjust to; and, second, those factors that they feel they can influence. Top management people are unlike Don Quixote. They don't fight windmills. They assess what can possibly be changed and work to make the change; they decide what cannot be changed and adjust as best they can to the inevitable.

5. QUESTION FOUR

The responses to question four, "Finally, thinking of the preceding three questions, how do you think your role or the way in which you operate will have to change in the immediate future?" are especially illuminating. All of the selected top managers discussed what actions they planned to take to cope with their problems.

FIGURE 2

Responses to Question Three

What other factors (not mentioned in answering questions one and two) do you feel will affect the way in which you can operate?

FACTORS TOP MANAGEMENT FEEL THEY CANNOT DIRECTLY CONTROL

	Rank Order
1. Cost and availability of energy	1
2. Cost of money	2
3. Cost of materials	3.5
4. Inflation	3.5

Others cited: labor costs, emphasis on "quality of life," environment and safety requirements, increase in socialism, government regulations, union philosophy, consumerism, competitiveness

---

FACTORS TOP MANAGEMENT THINK THEY CAN CONTROL OR INFLUENCE

	Rank Order
1. Need for more capable people	1
2. Building a more diverse work force (women, ethnics)	2
3. Need for more technically skilled people	3.3
4. Conservatism on the increase	3.3
5. Increased relations with the government	3.3

Others cited: internationalism, "quality of life" emphasis, communication, changes in organization, participative management, tightened controls, greater flexibility by top management

Improved Personal Effectiveness

One in three said he would make better use of his personal time and effort. The duties and obligations of their offices, they felt, need continuing review if not reappraisal in light of today's and tomorrow's management world. Their comments clearly indicate that this determination to improve personally is not self-flagellation or a subtle admission of fault. Rather, their comments underline their conviction that required changes in an organization's attitude, skill, or insight begin at the top. The familiar adage, "An organization is but the lengthened shadow of one man," expresses metaphorically the personal burden of responsibility that CEO's feel. And this is most likely why they start to change their organizations by changing themselves. Here are selections from their responses to question four:

> . . . A CEO now must become a change agent or a facilitator . . . to be on the leading edge . . . to create a new style of management . . . for example, where the vice-president of human resources would know that his decisions were final because he would make better decisions than if he knew they would be reviewed by someone else.

> . . . We must involve others in CEO-like activities, decision making, etc. The job of CEO has become too complex for one man.

> . . . I will restructure the organization . . . so I will be involved in issue management, not short-term monitoring of operations.

> . . . [CEO's] will need to be more sophisticated . . . to rely more on experts.

> . . . [CEO's] will need to become more flexible . . . to change as the times require.

Emphasize Manager Development

One in four plans greater stress on manager development as a hedge against trouble ahead. To them this means stepping up recruiting efforts, refining and adding training programs, involving managers more at all levels in general management, and improving the personnel policies and systems by continuing reappraisal. Here's what some CEO's say they need to do:

... have more incentives to keep top people.

... be more willing to negotiate with subordinates, peers, and customers.

... build a stronger top management team.

... secure more participation in management by all managers.

... be more aware of people.

... get our employees on our side by letting them know we care.

... lead better and to force the development of people.

... be more attentive to developing professional managers.

... set up and monitor an MBO or other system of evaluating performance.

... increase emphasis on finding, training, and involving better managers.

The bland assumption that the typical American lives by the work ethic and is motivated to do a job, work hard, and have a career is challenged, if not extinct, in today's world. So CEO's in their concern for developing people in the organization are recognizing the validity of the probable changes in many employees' values, interests, and drive.

Furthermore, this commitment of CEO's reflects the advance in knowledge about human behavior, its causes, and dynamics. When RHR psychologists first began consulting with managements in the mid-40s, CEOs' knowledge about human behavior was much more intuitive than studied. Now it's a rare CEO, let alone a top management staff, who is not knowledgeable about the principles of human behavior. In recent years a host of behavioral science seminars have proliferated on the executive scene—courses about psychological phenomena such as motivation, learning, forgetting, etc., as well as "how to" programs about recruiting techniques, interviewing methods, and organizational systems. The effect is a top management that is much more sophisticated, sensitive, and knowledgeable. So when CEO's say that in order to cope with the problems of the present they are going to emphasize the people factor in their organizations, they are capitalizing on a trend of the last thirty years and speak on the basis of considerable knowledge and awareness.

Become a Social Activist

As CEO's observe how society not only impinges on organizations but also increasingly controls them, they are committing themselves to local, state, and national activities. This is more than "if you can't beat them, join them." This expresses a belief that organizations, especially businesses, are citizens who are responsible for contributing to the goals and general life of society. Such a belief goes beyond the oft-quoted assertion that what was good for our country was good for General Motors, and *vice versa*, for it says in effect, "our organization is part of the United States; as we go, so goes the country; as the country goes, so go we."

Business organizations are being pushed to take on social responsibilities. Ever since the days of the robber barons who unashamedly exploited labor and in so doing laid the groundwork for much of today's rebellious consumerism and parasocialism, business leaders have often kept aloof from society. Their jobs have usually been all-consuming, engulfing their time, abilities and interests.

Now they are saying that as business leaders who live in a society they must become more actively involved. Contributing one's time, talents, and experience to shaping society is an ever greater part of the CEO's responsibility.

. . . (We'll need to) interpret what we are doing to all five publics—customers, suppliers, community, shareholders, and employees.

. . . (We) will need greater awareness of and sensitivity to actual and possible publics by identifying frames of reference of other people, anticipating [them], keeping current with [them].

. . . (I've got to) keep my eye on external factors.

. . . [We] must serve all publics.

. . . (There's going to be) more time spent on external influences.

Of course many top managers have already become involved as protectors of our system. Years ago, for example, a large chemical company staged small group seminars on the meaning of free enterprise; all employees were invited to attend. Furthermore, all employees had the option of buying company stock up to a percentage of their annual wage at a current market value but redeemable by the company at that value at any time. One in three employees participated in this realistic effort to involve them in the free enterprise system. CEO's are appearing on TV talk shows and are being interviewed by the press with respect to their feelings about the American free enterprise system in newspapers, magazines, house organs, and other publicity vehicles. Some executives have even taken a six-month leave of absence in order to live on university campuses as "resident businessmen" in the business-administration department.

Be More Flexible

The actions listed so far will require flexibility, say CEO's. This apparently means greater willingness to roll with the punches, to adapt to new demands and new circumstances, to be more effectively resilient.

. . . We will have to be flexible enough and adaptive enough to keep up with the rapid pace of change.

. . . To react properly to change is to be sensitive to the evolving process.

It is clear that flexibility does not involve an abdication of responsibility, an abandonment of goals and objectives, or a watering down of principles. It simply means that CEO's, acutely aware of the changes in society and hence changes in what in reality will work in their organizations, are determined to keep moving forward rather than to risk losing out by living in the past.

6. CONCLUSION

The responses of top management to the survey's four questions contain of course much reiteration and repetition; but the following four areas cover the points that give the business leaders most concern:

1. *The impact of the cultural revolution.* There is clear recognition that enormous changes in American values and attitudes are creating a markedly different business climate. Finding ways of organizing, providing a quality of life to employees, surviving in spite of a subtle erosion of the free enterprise system—these are some of the challenges of the decades ahead.

2. *The twin monsters—inflation and energy.* The interviewees felt essentially hopeless about the uncontrollability of both of these powerful forces in the economy. Most felt that only better government could rectify the situation.

3. *The super bureaucracy of the government.* CEO's consistently decry the intrusion of government regulations into the business world but are almost unanimous in their determination to do something personally to reduce unwarranted government control. They plan to support lobbying efforts, to influence legislators, to serve on association committees—in short, to do what they can to change government's attitude of nonbusiness to one of cooperative partnership.

4. *Personal change in style and commitment.* A large majority are committing themselves to "come out from behind the desk" in order to work constructively as concerned citizens to help shape American society. Many feel that their responsibility as business leaders is to serve all of mankind, not just the shareholders.

In general, there is no evidence that business leaders are knuckling under to pressures that confront them today nor are they retreating from the more difficult areas. Rather, it appears that they are gathering their efforts and thoughts and enlisting the aid of others in coming to grips with most difficult problems. It could well be that the social activist's role which is being discussed today is the most significant finding of this survey.

The concerns of top management are about gargantuan issues, but their view of the issues as challenges and their determination and commitment to resolve them augurs very well for the effectiveness of the American business organization in the future.

CHAPTER XI.
The Changing World of the Director

1. INTRODUCTION

Of the many changes in the world of management, one of the most dramatic is in the role of the board of directors. The changes began subtly in the late 60s. Before then, the economy was good; there were few scandals, few suits, few reasons for a director to be held liable. Directors were selected for their stature, for being well-known, or for their potential to contribute directly to the company's success. For example, directors of banks were expected to shift major portions of their businesses to the bank they served. Closed fraternities of interlocking directorates were common.

In the late 60s and the 70s events compelled changes: bankruptcies; Watergate, with its aftermath of public suspicion of government officials as both a President and a Vice-President of the United States resigned; charges of bribery of foreign governments; the consumerism movement; the recall of many autos; college students suing universities for canceling catalogued courses; correspondence students suing because they couldn't get jobs as promised; and widespread class-action suits.

Even in the 1960s board members periodically met to discuss operations and review the information provided by man-

agement but left the real business of running the organization
to the company's executives. Even in the rare case of a director being charged with liability for his actions or inaction,
the so-called best-business-judgment rule was a strong de-
fense. Time and the actions of many shareholders and outside
groups have changed this; directors have been held financially
accountable for what they have done as well as for what they
have failed to do. No longer is a directorship of an American
corporation a sinecure. Since 1967 the number of suits filed
against directors has increased 900 percent. These suits
charged mismanagement, including error, omission, and mal-
feasance.

So current circumstances compel the modern board to take
a new look at its functions, make-up, procedures, and operating conditions. This has resulted in a modification of the
ways in which boards now discharge their standard, age-old
responsibilities, and the change is continuing. It's truly a matter of new wine in old bottles; the labels are the same but the
contents are different.

2. OLD FUNCTIONS AND NEW PRACTICES
Accountability and Liability

Boards of directors are more and more frequently referred
to as working boards. This simply means that they must take
an increasingly active role in insuring effective fulfillment of
all functions critical to the viability of an organization. One
standard function, monitoring the performance of the organization, must be handled differently because of current conditions. Directors are finding themselves liable for the legal
responsibilities of directorship and are extremely vulnerable
as individuals. The managements of organizations that produce the questionable products or services are not legally accountable, but the directors could be—and often are held
accountable.

In some instances, boards of directors are strongly
pressured to divest their companies of investments in South
Africa, on the grounds that such financial support is patently
racist. *Time* magazine in its June 11, 1979, issue reports that
divestment totals are creeping up as the result of such
pressures. For example, Harvard students boycotted classes

for a day and picketed the trustees. And Yale's Advisory Committee on Investor Responsibility recently recommended that the college sell 900,000 dollars worth of stock in a bank which lends money to the South African government. The committee put their case with remarkable candor, reports *Time*: "We recognize that divestiture is of little practical consequence and hence is almost entirely symbolic. Still, symbols and gestures are important in the realm of moral and humane concerns."

So directors are taking prudent protective steps. If they are responsible for what is going on in the organization, they had better know what is going on. They need detailed knowledge of their own as the basis for their decisions; the recommendations, information, and insights by internal management, however trustworthy, are insufficient. Even if the board decisions prove to be wrong, they must be made at least with some effort to get the facts. After all, a director cannot be held liable for a bad decision, but for an insupportable "rubber stamp" decision he certainly can be. One knowledgeable firm of consultants made the following suggestions that might help a director avoid personal liability for certain actions:[1]

Do Your Homework

Know the business and all its operations. Keep current with business developments in general and your company in particular. Read the company's current financial statements and reports. Request information (including meeting agendas) well in advance of scheduled board meetings to allow adequate preparation time. Know the corporation's constitution and by-laws and what types of action they allow. Examine minutes of board meetings you've missed to stay up to date on the corporation's affairs.

Document Your Actions

Document all proceedings, including votes on important items, as well as the reasons for the decisions. Review minutes of board meetings to ascertain whether actions have been accurately recorded—especially your comments thereon.

Obtain Outside Assistance

Obtain professional advice concerning complex develop-

---

[1]Deloitte, Haskins & Sells, in its corporate publication of June 29, 1979, *The Week in Review*.

ments (e.g., formation of a pension or profit-sharing plan).
Consult with an attorney if you are unsure whether certain
actions may be beyond the corporation's powers.

Avoid Conflicts of interest

Avoid them whenever possible, but if a conflict does arise,
report it to the board and have such disclosure documented
in the minutes and abstain from any votes regarding the
matter.

Some boards have instituted their own procedures and policies for measuring how the organization is doing and insuring
ethical practice. For example, not many years ago it was rare
for a board member to go directly to a staff member; now it
is a fairly common practice. Whatever boards of directors
must do to validate their legal control of the organization,
they are now doing more frequently. Of course, they are now
protecting themselves from unwarranted attacks by extensive
liability insurance. Let's not forget, however, that liability insurance does not cover such things as libel and slander, director actions for personal gain, or a disregard of legal and
reporting requirements, to cite just a few exceptions.

Succession

Another of the board's responsibilities, and one that is generally taken most seriously, is to determine succession of
leadership by its election of officers. More and more boards
want to observe for themselves the performance of candidates
for board-elected offices and are insisting that an effective
performance review system be used throughout the organization so that people are upgraded for quality performance
rather than for such superficial reasons as tenure or friend-
ship. Boards thus are increasingly monitoring the performance review system and using its data in reaching their
personnel decisions.

In one corporation, the chairman and president, along with
any other board members who happen to be in the area,
spend a day with the manager of each subsidiary division as
he reports on his business and on his people. This is an annual review. Notes are taken, and even a color slide of the
manager's present organization chart with names, ages, positions, retirement dates, and ratings on it is duplicated and
will be hauled out a year later for comparison. In another organization the board holds a session twice a year with the

vice-president of human resources as he discusses the plans and programs of manager development within the organization. In one large corporation there is a human resources committee of the board that is composed of directors with a track record of having developed strong organizations with strong people. This committee meets regularly to monitor the progress of a list of identified potential executives, approves their career paths, and serves as a sounding board as well as counsel to the chief executive with respect to senior management changes. This committee has access to all members of management as well as to outside consultants who are working with the company in the area of manager development.

Obviously, all of this adds up to a strong trend among boards to monitor continually all efforts to develop managerial potential. When the times comes for selecting a new chairman, a new president, or the appointment of new officers, the board is caught neither by surprise nor by a dearth of information.

Foundations

Another common board function, the control and disposition of foundation funds, was for many years a casual but altruistic duty. Now, under the glare of movements such as consumerism and individual rights, because of the social responsibilities expected of commercial enterprises, and because of all of the pressures to control the disposal of the organization's profits, the decisions to disperse foundation funds are crucial and often publicly scrutinized. To be knowledgeable of what the foundation should contribute and why takes time and study. For example, one sizable foundation wished to contribute extensively to the liberal arts education provided by independent colleges in its state. First, however, the board determined what it considered to be a liberal arts education. It then employed experts to survey the independent colleges of the state as to their effectiveness in providing such a liberal arts education. The results of that survey then became a significant factor in determining the size of the foundation's contribution.

Special Expertise

Selected board members may act as informal counsel to the chairman, who serves alone at the top; he can check his thinking in the embryo stage about succession or about whether to acquire or about sensitive long-range plans. Outsiders (i.e., nonorganization members) with special expertise are often given special assignments by the chairman or by the board as a whole. One board assigned a director who was an effective real estate broker to look at the company's properties.

Public Relations

Boards today are also often asked to perform a public relations function. In speaking to reporters they represent the organization, particularly if there is a contentious issue and if they are respected in the business community. Their public relations function is not so much a direct assignment as it is a natural outgrowth of board membership. Their presence asserts their support of the company's philosophy and objectives. It says that directors subscribe to the goals of the company, what it represents, and that they have become a part of it. Many boards insist upon a written publishable code of ethics.

Educating Directors

One of the problems that generally has not been resolved very well involves the educating of board members. The more successful organizations, however, whose board members are expected to be contributors, are developing both well-structured orientation programs for new directors and procedures that enable new board members to fulfill their responsibilities quickly and effectively. The demand now by the board is for open, thorough, and detailed communication. And such a demand has created a need for modified procedures and somewhat altered relations with the staff of the organization. Directors must make a determined, planned effort to develop their competence to respond to today's increasingly complex world.

3. CHANGES IN MAKE-UP

Insiders vs. Outsiders

The question of inside versus outside directors is being debated today and has important implications for the future. Now that the "old boy" syndrome of interlocking directorates amounting almost to a closed fraternity is disappearing and now that the individual rights movement is cascading, there is a potential storm brewing over this issue. Is the board an extension of the operating top management, except for a few people of special skills or values? Or is the board, if it is to control and objectively evaluate the organization, likely to be tainted by insiders whose self-interest prevents their passing objective judgments on themselves? The present head of the SEC urges all organizations to eliminate all but one insider. One consumer advocate is said to have gone to the extreme of asserting that there should be no insiders on an organization's board.

Either position not only impugns the character of an insider on the board, probably the president of the organization, but runs other risks as well. In the first place, directors are responsible for succession. If the only insider on the board decides to retire early or takes another job or dies, there is no other insider who has had any board experience in decision making at the policy level or in relating to other directors. Few large-company presidents have agreed with the chairman of the SEC and said that they don't want any insiders on the board except themselves. This also seems to be an untenable procedure in the eyes of a working board who are trying to make knowledgeable decisions about succession and other major problems. For the president to be their sole channel of information is risky. It would be a rare individual indeed who could convey accurately to the board the thinking of all of senior management. Secondly, board members are limited in their opportunity to judge performance of possible successors; they cannot have had first-hand exposure as to how a nonboard-member executive handles himself or how he thinks.

The probable best solution is a balance between insiders

and outsiders, with the majority being from the outside. A more typical ratio would be three to four insiders (the chairman and the president and perhaps a couple senior executive VP's who get elected to the board at the time that they are considered potential chairman and/or president) and the remainder of eight to ten outsiders. Having the company's key officers on the board enables the directors to ask tough, critical questions of those who are responsible for day-to-day operations and who should know the answers and are expected to know them.

Then there is the matter of representation on the board, a direct reflection of social pressures today to recognize the rights of special interest groups in the workforce—blacks, women, blue-collar workers, etc. To appoint a person to the board primarily for public relations effect is a mistake in judgment. The objective in developing a board is to create a balance of expertise which will fulfill the responsibility of the board and enable the organization to meet its objectives. So all board members should be selected not because they represent a constituency *per se*, but because they can bring balance to a board as it considers a broad range of issues.

4. CHANGES IN PROCEDURES

Selecting Directors

Because of these conditions and circumstances the selection of board members is critical. One obvious step in this selection process is to use a search firm to find an outside director. But such a procedure may raise a question about the organization's network of acquaintanceship in the community or in its area of activity. If these are so limited that the organization feels forced to use a search firm to find candidates for an outside directorship, there may well be a severe need to become less parochial.

Before a new board member is selected, there are critical questions to be answered. What are the present and anticipated needs of the organization that require contributions from the directors? What are the long-range plans of the company with respect to new business and/or acquisitions? For example, one large corporation, whose directors are nearly all insiders, is thinking of acquiring a company in a completely unrelated business. How effective will that board be in assessing the acquisition, developing strategic policies, and assisting in the integration of the two companies? What is the balance of training and experience of the board with respect to its critical functions? What is the board's balance as to age and tenure? Answers to these and other questions will define at least the parameters of the qualifications of the new board member.

The new role of the board has gradually changed the selection process because of the reluctance by some to run the risks of a directorship. On the other hand, there is a change toward the positive since more and more board members now are wholesomely motivated to accept membership because they feel they can contribute through their special expertise and interests to the life of the organization, whether commercial or nonprofit. Thus the constituency of boards is gradually changing to fulfill the new responsibilities that society has forced upon them. They are aware of the legal, environmental, and social factors affecting the organization. They are willing to play an active role in monitoring performance and in determining succession of key executive positions, functions that today demand strength of character, personal courage, and the ability to act with confidence and assurance based upon professionalism and a deep knowledge of the work of the organization.

Board Size

The question of board size is another area of change. The requirement to have three standing committees—audit, compensation, and nomination—determines the minimum size of nine to twelve people. The maximum size of a board is determined by the requirement that it be a working board.

In the days when appointments were made largely in recognition of service to the company or personal loyalty to a chairman and when there was no mandatory retirement age, boards often grew to an unmanageable size. Although those days are gone, their existence has a lingering effect today in that reducing board size is a painful, laborious process. Those who value staying on the board to assure retirement income now are asked to change the bylaws so as to require mandatory retirement, a difficult choice for those oldtimers who must vote to give up their enjoyable socialization with friends of many years' standing at a monthly or quarterly get-to-gether for a day and an evening. It is thus neither an easy nor automatic matter to create a working board that defines tenure, requires mandatory retirement, and generates all of the conditions for effective functioning.

Independence of Committees

Board committees are becoming more independent, thereby benefitting the organization's effectiveness.

The audit committee, of course, is legally required to employ outside firms and is therefore automatically independent in at least the performance of that task. But the trend grows stronger for audit committees to be functionally independent as well. Now audit committees are wisely establishing, for example, clear-cut criteria by which to evaluate the performances of both the outside auditing firm as well as the internal auditor. If the committee is displeased with an outside firm's failure to come up to standard, it changes firms. Such increasingly stringent demands require, of course, a thorough understanding of significant accounting problems and their proposed solutions as well as the knowledge by which to judge whether the accounting procedures and results meet the committee's own criteria. Such knowledge is essential to the committee's effectiveness in dealing with management and auditors, both internal and external.

There is a fine line between proper governance and assumption of management's responsibility. William Kanaga, chairman of Arthur Young & Co., discussed this fine line between governance and interference in a recent speech. "The committee should have the freedom to probe any activity, ask any questions, and obtain any information [from any source] consistent with its objective and the scope of its activities. Such freedom, of course, carries with it an obligation to allow company management freedom to exercise its own prerogatives—to make decisions, to allocate resources, and to take appropriate risks without second-guessing. In short, a good audit commiteee resists ritual on the one hand and meddling on the other."

The compensation committee, also increasingly independent, is now no longer likely to rubber-stamp the president's or chairman's recommendations for compensation changes.

The committee, with or without outside consultation, evaluates the work of executives themselves before approving changes in compensation. For example, perhaps a fairly typical one, a certain board compensation committee got recommendations from the president and the chairman for salary changes for other officers and from the chairman for the president. The committee then conducted its own investigation of comparable salary ranges, studied the evaluations of the officers, and considered the validity of the company's pattern of compensation. True, their final recommendations to the board were similar to those of the president and the chairman; but the significant thing is that they needn't have been. Such independence as this would rarely have existed in the 60s for fear of upsetting the chairman or creating tensions caused by nonconformity.

Committees and the Chairman

Consistent with the trend toward independence of board committees is their relation with the chairman who appointed them. The chairman is an ex-officio member of all board committees; he meets with them if he wishes and participates in their discussions, voicing his opinions and judgments about the people or the functions that the committees are responsible for. The committee members who may well be more knowledgeable on some matters are thus helpful to the chairman because of their nonadversary, constructive, and advisory relation. The chairman, still in control and still finally responsible for board action, gets support, ideas, and other positive contributions from the independent committees who thereby go a long way toward ensuring sound decisions and strengthened viability for the organization.

The nominating committee, which formerly carried out its legal function by rubber-stamping the chairman's recommendations for new directors, may now question such recommendations and insist that candidates meet the specific future needs of the board of directors and the company.

It must be concluded that the independence of the board committees assures the chairman of objective decisions, the best expertise available, and protection of the organization's best interests. Effective independent functioning depends, of course, on an advisory, not at all an adversary, relation with the chairman. (Woe be to the chairman who must fight his directors, who doesn't trust them, and who must constantly protect his flanks and engage in endless bickering and politicking!)

Should board members go directly to staff in seeking more information about a report made yesterday, incidentally to probe an individual's capability for his job? Certainly this is not commonly done. It is risky because it implies that the officers are supplying unreliable information to the board. Nevertheless, for purposes other than investigation, any board member who is on an independent committee may need to gather necessary information and should have the right to go to any staff person for the purpose of clarification without subterfuge or secrecy. .

The trend is for the board to require functional heads to report personally at the regularly scheduled board meetings. The board then gets to know the respective executives—how they think, how they perform against budget, their record of anticipating problems and situations, and their ingenuity in proposing solutions. After all, these executives should be the most knowledgeable people in the organization about their particular areas. Thus, over time, both the executives and the board members become well acquainted. When issues of succession or compensation arise, decisions can be made on the basis of firsthand knowledge.

5. CHANGES IN CONDITIONS

Compensation

The compensation of board members is also changing. In working boards the trend continues upward. Directors who are truly experts in their fields must be compensated adequately for the increasing demands on their time and rewarded for the contributions expected of them. In August, 1975, Towers, Perrin, Forster, and Crosby, an international management consulting firm, reported a study in which the outside directors' fees averaged $12,594. Three years later they reported that 90 of 100 largest industrial companies paid fees ranging from $4,000 to $22,500. Eighty-six percent of these companies also paid fees of $250 to $1,500 to their outside directors for each regular board meeting attended; committee meeting fees ranged from $200 to $1,500 per meeting.

Many institutions, such as colleges, the YMCA, and hospitals have no compensation for board membership. What motivates the board member is a desire to contribute and to grow. Even though compensation is increasing, people who serve on boards are generally there because they are wanted and because of their capacity to make a contribution, not because they need extra income.

Government Regulations

Another major trend which will most surely continue is government regulations that bear on the work of boards. We seem now to be in a period of regulatory overkill. As one board member said, "I don't know how we're going to get out of this except by responding the way that I think a board ought to respond—to do things as they should be done rather than the way the government seems to want them done. Make good, objective judgments based on full communication and adequate knowledge." Mr. Lazarus, chairman of the board and CEO of Federated Department Stores, Inc., stated it best: "The business establishment is suffering the same disenchantment that the public at large appears to feel about so many of our institutions. When this kind of distrust is pervasive, we are always in danger of the enactment of ill-considered legislation or regulations that can be more harmful in the long run to the public interest than the transgression such laws are designed to eliminate. And, frankly, business cannot, year in and year out, tolerate a never-ending proliferation of regulations. This is at least one compelling reason why we have to devise effective procedures for our self-governance and convince those who would impose new regulations on us that we fully intend to live up to our commitments. If we cannot at least do this, we cannot expect to remain free of the burdens of additional formal regulation. If we cannot be persuasive in making a case for our own self-governance, we will suffer a steady erosion of our capacity to be flexible, entrepreneurial, and competitive. The quality of our economic system will be diminished, and, in turn our quality of life will suffer."[2]

In recent years government regulations seem to have had a

[2]Ralph Lazarus, Chairman of the Board and Chief Executive Officer of Federated Department Stores, Inc., *The President*, Volume 14, No. 12, (December 1978).

negative impact on boards. They are now individually liable for the product of the organization. They have to be wary of a conflict of interest between the organization on whose board they sit and their own companies. They are battered by a plethora of regulatory agencies (the FDA, the SEC, etc.) as well as by many public pressure groups. For example, the *Weekly Legal Times* of Washington conducted a survey in 1978 of the 100 largest corporations and 150 others to keep track of two trends: the rise in fees paid to law firms that have a partner serving in the dual role of director and corporate counsel and the increase in the number of in-house lawyers employed by corporations. Even though the practice of having a lawyer serve on a corporate board of directors while the lawyer's firm represents the corporation is neither illegal nor improper, Harold M. Williams, chairman of the Securities Exchange Commission, has unofficially been urging corporations to discontinue the practice *before the federal government bars it with legislation.*[3] (Author's italics.)

In Spite of Stifling Regulations

Yet in spite of all these presumably inhibiting regulations that take up so much of a board's time, there are strong boards who are exercising highly positive leadership by seeing to it that their organizations contribute to the welfare of society. One such specific contribution is through the personal activities of the chairman. In many organizations at present the chief executive has less than half of his time available for the business, and the trend is in the direction of even less time. In ten years the average chairman will have only one fourth the time to attend specifically to the business; the rest of the time will be devoted to external relations—contributing to community boards, serving on government *ad hoc* committees, spearheading movements to clean up inner city ghettos, and the like. Almost every board meeting nowadays has social issues to consider and fervid discussions as to the posture of the organization. It takes knowledgeable leadership of such discussions to determine perceptive stances.

[3]Reported by Gary R. Clark in *The Cleveland Plain Dealer*, July 12, 1979.

Tenure

Mandatory retirement and tenure are tied together, and the trend in both instances is toward shorter terms. The criterion for retirement is becoming less a matter of age than of active involvement in the business community (if the organization is a business corporation). More and more, the trend is toward retirement as a director when one retires from normal business and/or organizational activities; one organization, for example, requires retirement from the board within a year after retirement from a board member's principal employment. If an individual who retires at age 62 is still on a board at age 70, the feeling is that he is too much out of touch to be effective. But, more importantly, tenure is increasingly determined by such logical considerations as the probable length of time a board member can make good contributions to meeting the needs of the organization. If an individual, for example, is no longer on other boards and has retired from a principal occupation, it is questionable whether a contribution can continue to be made. On the other hand, a "professional" board member who serves almost full time on numerous boards can continue to bring a wide range of experience and knowledge. So the chairman of the future must ask tough questions: Is the make-up of the board related to the needs of the organization? Should changes in its make-up be recommended, even if some long-term directors will not be proposed for reelection? The whole point in establishing tenure is to foster, whenever possible, the working board idea.

6. CHANGES BECAUSE OF INTERNATIONALISM

Differences between the United States and other countries in which an organization has developed subsidiaries can be deep and severe, making central control by the board especially difficult. Conflicts in management cultures and styles; disparity in benefit programs, compensation systems, and the like; and, of course, the well-known ethical differences in business practices, are all potentially hazardous to any integrated, organized, and international effort that the board is responsible for.

If the trend continues toward internationalism (but with a nationalistic emphasis) and away from parochialism and provincialism, the board member of the future must be equipped to live comfortably in a one-world of work. He may well be an unofficial ambassador who avoids conflict (even wars) by spearheading mutually satisfying methods of working together. Operations as such function across national boundaries within a framework of policies, objectives, and general procedures that stem from an international understanding and point of view. Certainly the kind of board member who fulfills such responsibilities and seeks such opportunities is of a special cut. And, like Abou Ben Adhem, his tribe may be increasing.

Another implication of growing internationalism is experimentation in the systems for organizing board activities, for communicating, and for the use of specialists as consultants. One major American international company with extensive European operations, for example, has one European board member. He, in turn, is chairman of an advisory board made up of four leading European executives from four different countries. They are advisory to their chairman in the sense that they know the economic conditions in their respective countries, the mores of doing business, the laws, and commercial opportunities. They occasionally meet with the full American board and, of course, are constantly informed by their chairman of progress and problems. In other instances, advisory boards are specialists, such as scientists, who meet with the major board, among themselves, and/or with the executives to contribute proposals, monitor progress toward objectives, and in other ways function as consultants who are in the family but not of it.

7. CHANGES IN THE ROLE OF THE CHAIRMAN

While the functions of the chairman are in substance unchanged, the current conditions and the trends that will undoubtedly hold well into the 80s are creating intensified demands. The chairman traditionally of course has had a hand in running board meetings, controlling the board, and determining what the directors considered in their meetings. But in all of these traditional functions there is today and will be to-morrow a shift in emphasis, if not in concept.

Board Meetings

For instance, such routine duties of the chairman as setting up an agenda, chairing the meeting, and thereby determining the general style of the meetings are now more likely to change subtly. The board is now a working board—or if not, certainly will be in the near future. The agenda will call for committee reports, proposals, decisions to be made, and probably a heavy load of matters to consider in the time allotted. All of this could mean more formality, less time-wasting informality, better premeeting preparations, and more informed discussions, less meeting time consumed by fact-finding or by bringing some directors up to date and so on. The chairman sets the tone and the climate of the meetings; and these in turn symbolize the style of leadership of the organization.

An effective chairman is keenly aware of how some matters on the agenda will be sensitive issues and could indeed provoke wearing discussion and even rifts among the directors. Accordingly, a chairman in anticipation of such a contentious issue may discuss the matter privately with those directors who are likely to be upset, thereby doing what can be done to avoid infighting and disruption.

Control of the Board

The chairman has two major methods for maintaining control: one, by chairing the executive committee; and two, by deciding the make-up of board committees. In both methods the chairman sets the standard of behavior and of expected contribution. This gives the chairman control because directors can then be held accountable for measuring up to standards; if they do not, the chairman is warranted by the circumstance of clear expectation and requirement as to performance to exercise authority in some form. In short, even though the relation among directors is that of peers and not superior-subordinate, the chairman is functional leader and thus can control the board.

Identifying Needs

Finally, there is no more significant aspect of a chairman's responsibility than analyzing and predicting the organization's needs. It is the chairman who most of all senses what the organization's real problems are today and, perhaps more importantly, what they are likely to be tomorrow. A chairman of a large bank never fails to predict for his board what the financial world will be like in the immediate future; a chairman of a large multinational corporation is consistently prophetic, anticipating for the directors the shifts in emphasis or product or direction that the organization will have to make down the road. Such predictions go beyond fact and logic; they depend upon wisdom, intuition, insight, and experience, as well as knowledge. This is why, of course, the job of chairman is critical to the effectiveness of the whole organization.

8. CONCLUSION—CRITERIA FOR TODAY'S AND TOMORROW'S BOARDS

Experience to date supports the idea that an effective board of directors will meet these criteria:

1. *Balance.* Two balances are necessary: one, a balance between insiders and outsiders; and two, a balance among the kinds of expertise required by the organization's needs.

The latter refers to the need for a board to have within its membership at any moment the specialized expertise required to understand the basic functions of the organization. Partly this is as obvious a matter as having an expert in electronics on the board of a company that manufactures computers; partly it is as nebulous a matter as the future make-up of the organization. For example, if a relatively small organization of partners decided to incorporate so that ownership could be shared by the employees, but no partner was a financial expert, this would be an area of expertise much needed by the partners-turned-directors. Furthermore, as needs change so do the requirements for expertise, a fact which has marked implications for tenure. It is possible for a director's expertise to be no longer needed, and the board, in order to get back into balance, must replace him with one whose expertise is now required. The need for balance in expertise, therefore, underlines the concept that board membership, no longer the lifetime sinecure it often was in the past, is now more likely to depend on capacity to contribute to the meeting of current or future needs. Increasingly, the director is cast in the role of a resource, especially to the critical functions of the organization. And of course as functions change through time, so must the nature of the resources for them. The chairman of the board is continually responsible for monitoring those changes in directorships that are required by long-range plans.

2. *Consultants*. Members of the board will be able to use outside consultants effectively, such as auditing firms, compensation specialists, and organization and management-development consultants. To use consultants effectively means, among other things, that a director knows how to evaluate a consultant's credibility; how to work with a consultant by providing him with objectives, necessary background information, and clear-cut definitions of problems; and finally how to recognize the gaps in his own knowledge compared with the consultant's expertise.

In addition, to work effectively with consultants means to have access to outside consultants, even privately, to enhance one's capability to contribute by a broadened knowledge of operations, of manpower resources, of compensation plans and systems, and of acquisition and merger strategy. A director must also ensure that (1) a consultant's opinions and recommendations are consistent with and supportive of the organization's long-range objectives; and, that (2) the financial resources allocated to outside consultants will indeed serve the long-range strength of the organization.

3. *Pattern of Contribution*. Each director will be motivated increasingly to contribute to the organization's viability through unique experience, knowledge, or skill.

a. Directors on a truly working board will in the future devote a far greater amount of time to board activities.

b. Directors will serve on fewer boards.

c. Directors will be paid considerably more for the basic membership as well as for board meetings and committee meetings.

d. Directors will demand that their particular expertise be fully used.

4. *Tenure*. As indicated above, tenure is now in many instances and will be for certain in the future completely de-

pendent on the capability of a director to contribute to meeting the assessed needs of the organization. Such tenure requirements, it may be well to reiterate, are finally the chairman's responsibility to judge at election time. And such decisions may indeed be difficult, since the close association between chairman and board director now must be objectively evaluated, even if it hurts.

5. *Characteristics*. What qualities are required of an effective director? These can be divided into nonpersonal and personal factors, as follows:

Nonpersonal Characteristics

1. The potential director's status in the organization's world is a significant factor. In this context, status refers to standing. Experience and contribution in some relevant area—community, business, social—will have already earned the candidate respect, that precious, nonpurchasable quality that to be merited can only be earned.

2. One of the key facets of such respect is the reputation for integrity, also an unpurchasable, intangible quality. The significance of integrity to a board is that the slightest suspicion that one director in the group lacks it will somehow, like a drop of ink in a barrel of water, taint the whole group.

3. Of course relevant experience is also essential to a competent directorship. The key word is *relevant*, i.e., experience related to the critical functions or to the future areas of the organization (such as international business) or to the philosophy it is concerned about promulgating (e.g., a liberal arts college interested in furthering a nontechnical educational program).

Personal Characteristics

More than casual study and acquaintance are required to determine the presence of these qualities, outlined below:

1. Mental ability
   a. the ability to think conceptually
      (This is most critical, since all policies with which the board almost exclusively deals are in essence statements of concept, usually in abstract terms.)
   b. intellectually curious, alert and inquisitive
   c. the ability to reach sound decisions under heavy pressure without panic or impulse but with due deliberation

 2. An integrated personality with a clear-cut personal philosophy and thought-through goals
 3. Social adjustment
  a. reasonable insight into why others feel and act as they do
  b. more of a leader than a follower
  c. ability to work with others who are also strong personalities, to have power with and through others as opposed to needing power over others.
 4. Self-understanding
  a. realistically accepts himself for what he is without pretense or false pride
  b. can laugh at himself without loss of self-respect
  c. is secure enough in his self-image to live with a diversity of personalities without defensiveness or fear or undue compensation
 5. Ability to organize and direct others
  a. carries assigned authority over others with ease
  b. understands how to communicate well
  c. easily identifies with management—gets things done through others

No aspect of organizational life is more affected by the changing world of management than is the role of the board of directors. The traditional board functions are being practiced in new ways. Accountability for decisions and liability for actions are very real. Succession of leadership is more than ever being astutely planned. Special expertise is often required. Board members represent their organizations via all media and in public appearances. All of these usual functions are now almost always differently, and sometimes more intensively, performed and require special attention to the educating of board members.

PART FIVE
Implications

CHAPTER XII.
The Changing World of Management

1. INTRODUCTION

The root cause of change in the world of management is a change in the values of our American society. Change in values is a wrenching, sometimes even threatening tremor that upsets customs, forces habits to change, and seems to undercut many of the acceptable principles of managing.

Why is such an ideological shift so shockingly and vitally important? Simply because of the nature of values, those perceptions and beliefs that a society holds to be right. These are the determinants of actions, laws, and systems; they fix purposes and political systems and thus define how a society is striving to live.

Changes in values should not be confused, although it is easy to do so, with different ways of behaving brought about by technology. The telegraph, radio, automobile, television, plastics, the Salk vaccine, sound and color movies, the voyage to the moon—a long list of technical developments have changed our world dramatically from that of even one generation ago. When the Shah of Iran died in Egypt on a Sunday morning, the entire world could instantly speculate on its significance through the magic of satellite communication. But such changes in technology are what management has traditionally adjusted to with relative ease.

It's the change in values that makes managing difficult and challenging. For value changes, while intangible, are potent in their impact on human behavior. Values deeply affect people's expectations, demands, hopes, dreams, needs, and wants. They are motivational. To understand them, therefore, is step one in understanding the effects of changes in the world of management. For example, if one were to assume that as in yesteryear the work ethic was a value of most employees, then traditional systems of compensation, promotion, job assignment, appraisal, labor relations, and pensions would be valid. But what a difference if one correctly were to assume today that the so-called quality of life was an ethical demand of many employees. Then, as detailed in Chapter I, the employee's expectations, wants, needs, and hopes will be different.

2. A NEW REQUIREMENT OF BUSINESS

Historically, our society provides an open opportunity for any entrepreneur to produce in his own way a product or service that the public is willing to pay for. Thus, the major purpose of a business has been to generate a profit for the entrepreneur or shareholder for providing a product or service that was wanted or needed, whether hoola-hoops or steel, bread or home computers—all without any expectation that the entrepreneur owes society anything in return.

Some of the wealthier, more altruistic captains of industry—the Mellons, Carnegies, Hannas, and Rockefellers—contributed, of course, to the welfare of American society. They granted scholarships, built libraries and museums, and supported research on social problems ranging from health hazards to slum conditions. But their largesse was voluntary and, although appreciated, was not expected, let alone demanded.

Now, the social responsibility of a business organization to be a good citizen, formerly expressed only by the social conscience or the religious beliefs of the executives, is more often considered the social obligation of the organization, even a debt to be paid for the opportunity to produce a product or service that the public will pay for. What formerly was a matter of personal conviction on the part of the CEO or the board is now increasingly being cranked into a company's long-range planning.

The question of how society's needs are determined is difficult to answer explicitly, even though precise knowledge of how a different need emerges would be extremely useful for management's necessary response to it. No individual can be cited as a determiner of a social need. Abraham Lincoln did not cause the Emancipation Proclamation nor can Gloria Steinem be credited with women's liberation even though both, because they articulated and activated the feelings and ideas of influential thinkers, are often cited as the creators of their causes. So it appears now to be incumbent on management to be alert to social movements and to exercise astute judgment about the probability of trends being transformed into relatively permanent values. Historically, managements have generally been good in judging the economic opportunities of changes in society. But on the sociological and psychological fronts, managements seem to be less skilled in judging the impact of changes in values, tending to assume that people will react today as they formerly did. (As an aside, it might well be predicted that progressive managements may well add to their top staffs some formal capability for gauging the value shifts among their employees and customers.)

The next question is when and how will a business organization know it is discharging its social obligation? Will scrupulous compliance with every government regulation be satisfactory? Will intent and desire earn credit even though the resulting efforts may be somewhat inept? Will some single local or federal agency be a watchdog—or will several—so that official approval will be evidence enough? Will the whole matter be voluntary? If so, will a nonconforming business run the risk of society's disapproval with a possible threat of employee rebellion, with or without union sanction? Also, if so, must a business which feels it is meeting its social obligation sell its program of social obligation as a matter of self-protection?

Thus, each question leads to more questions and to so much uncertainty that one may correctly conclude that whatever satisfies the conscience of the organization is sufficient evidence. (And let's not even attempt to prescribe what conscience should dictate!) Suffice it to say, tomorrow's world will require a business organization somehow to satisfy its shareholders, executives, other employees, customers, and even the general public that it is meeting its social obligation.

Social Obligation, Good Or Bad?

It may seem that this concept of the social obligation of a business is a regrettable development; and that an awareness of its responsibility to foster rather than to harm the welfare of people and to improve rather than to damage the environment poses a threat to a business's existence. Nothing could be farther from the truth. Business has always met social needs by supplying goods and services, by providing jobs, and by creating wealth that raises the standard of living. Business has always been dependent on the perceptions of its customers. In point of fact, business's survival depends upon its social awareness. In this age when not even nations can long survive on their own, the demand that obliges business both legally and conceptually to contribute to society's welfare is really only necessary self-interest. Conflict comes only when the "needs" of society run counter to the survival needs of a business.

Economic survival compels interdependence or, to define it differently, a mutual need for others. Such raw materials as manganese and chromium, for example, both essential to American manufactured products, are available almost exclusively in South Africa, Zimbabwe, and the U.S.S.R. Since these countries in turn need our technology and production expertise, there is created a practical condition of mutual need.

Over and above such an obvious, even simplistic, condition of interdependence are the complex needs of all societies for each other, especially by those in the so-called Third World. Not only are there material needs for food, shelter, and jobs but also what amount to psychological, even spiritual, needs such as a recognition of human rights, of self-determination, and of a peaceful existence with law and order. (At least, such are thought by our society to be needs that are created by values which we consider inviolable.)

Given the interdependence of societies in the world, even a small organization in a miniscule fashion affects the world community. As one American executive put it: "We simply cannot afford protectionism and isolationism. We're going to have to become partners . . . of these underdeveloped coun-

tries or we'll be cut off from something we can't do without."
In short, our self-interest is served by meeting the needs of
others.

Our society can in part meet needs in other societies for
education, skills training, and technical expertise. And the
Western world's private enterprise systems will have to be the
major element in providing the underdeveloped countries
with such resources since, at least on the face of it, our systems produce more and better. In fact, even the leadership in
a worldwide effort to improve societies will have to come
from the business segment, not the government or the public
service segment such as the church or even the well-inten-
tioned eleemosynary organizations like the Red Cross. If the
business segment were really to lead in meeting the needs
of other societies as they meet ours, then truly a social obligation on a grand scale will have been discharged.

Realizing such a noble goal as this is also a matter of very
pertinent self-interest. For example, the "one world" concept
postulates a one-market world. But if other societies are to
consume our products and produce products that America
needs, they must first be able to earn more, even more than
they can from the sale of their raw materials. To earn more,
they need a viable economy; and to have such requires education and skills training. The logic of Henry Ford is applicable on a worldwide basis. He wanted his employees to be
consumers—of Fords, of course. So he broke the wage bar-
rier by paying more than three times the going rate of that
time. Then employees could afford a car. Ford thus struck at
the heart of how to build a viable economy, simple as it may
be: enable the consumers to buy what they want and need.

3. THE NEW CEO

This emphasis on the social responsibility of a business organization means that executives, particularly the CEO and
the chairman, will spend more time, even up to fifty percent
of their working time, on outside matters. This is not speculation. Many of the CEO's in the RHR survey reported in
Chapter X are already committing themselves to come out
from behind the desk in order to become activists—that is, to
spend time to influence legislation through personal contacts

and lobbying, to speak up for the free enterprise system via media interviews and public presentations, and to cultivate potential partners in other countries. A clear implication of this shift in the CEO's responsibility is that he will become more of a social philosopher, even a kind of cultural anthropologist who is comfortable and knowledgeable in dealing with those in other cultures about matters of mutual concern other than sheer financial and business issues.

For a long time, businesses have been fundamentally a matter of either manufacturing, engineering, or finance. Most CEO's come from these disciplines; very few from psychology, personnel, the social sciences—the people disciplines. Now the expectation is common that people problems, the development of managers, and the whole range of concerns with why people work and how best to organize their activities will be dealt with more forcefully. Whereas in the past, people problems could be deftly delegated to resourceful vice-presidents of personnel, the future holds no such relatively easy out. Rarely, in the past or even in the present, has human resource planning and utilization been truly integrated in the total planning of the organization. Manpower planning, management succession, redundancy planning (the current euphemism for layoffs), have seldom been a part of the strategic planning efforts; in the future they almost certainly will be.

Oddly enough, to be effective in this world of people problems is difficult for many CEO's. They usually have been reared in an environment where the man of action is the hero. The nicest compliment a CEO traditionally can get is that "our CEO really runs this business" or that he can perform any job. So to move into a world of diplomacy and negotiation and of public speaking and legislation-influencing may be challenging to some, but to most it means doing less and less of what one has always done best, namely, to size up a problem, devise a solution or plan, authorize action, and monitor the result.

Another implication, if managers are fulfilling this responsibility for influencing people, is that there must be a somewhat different preparation for any top-level job. One way, already implemented by some divisionalized companies, is to create for each division a board whose function is to serve the CEO of the division in the same way that the major board serves the corporation, thereby giving a division head experience with a board of directors. Another way is to have meaningful decentralization with genuine delegation of decision-making responsibility. It is important to stress meaningful since in most companies that say they have it, they in fact do not. There usually are strings attached, such as reviews by the top CEO of critical vice-presidential or divisional CEO decisions. Perhaps a real commitment to decentralization would be shown by having the functional equivalent of a chief executive officer or even more than one executive officer in order to divide the functions and responsibilities of the traditional CEO. For instance, one such executive officer could concentrate on international matters, another on the critical problems of long-range planning and the development of strategies; one could specialize in handling internal financial matters; another, production.

While the CEO is engaged on outside matters, the executives at home must keep the business operating. Hence, another implication of this trend in the CEO's pattern of job activities and one that amounts to training and preparation for a top-level job is a change in job assignments to realign decision-making responsibility. For example, under the CEO a layer of executives could be assigned, each having for his particular functions, the same decision-making power and accountability as the CEO. Thus the personnel V.P. may make a final decision on any issue, however sensitive and critical, without being second-guessed, since presumably the personnel V.P. is more knowledgeable of his functional area than the CEO and perhaps has more wisdom about it. The CEO may retain veto power, of course, when the issue involves broader considerations than the vice-president is accountable for.

Or, if it were not feasible to reorganize in such a way, perhaps an organization could retain the old titles but have different roles and thereby create new learning situations. The chairman, for example, rather than the CEO, could be responsible for strategic planning, working with the board on controls, auditing, dealing with the outside and perhaps having veto power because he has the broad picture in mind. But the chairman would then have nothing to do with day-to-day execution of anything except to make sure that the operating people are functioning within the plan and within policy and are working toward the same strategic, long-range goals. Such a role could be labeled chairman or perhaps more accurately chief strategic officer.

4. THE NEW POPULATION

Clearly, a major implication of the changes that will affect management in the near future, especially long-range and strategic planning, lies in the demographics of population trends, birth rates, and longevity. The usual expectation of a steady wave of people going through the organization so that the losses from attrition are steadily replaced by new and younger employees is no longer predictable. Because of declining birth rates, greater longevity, and new rules that prescribe different retirement patterns, the balance of age in the employee workforce is upset. There may be more retirees on pensions that must be funded by the contributions of fewer younger employees. The grim reality of insufficient pension funds is not here yet, but the demographics say it will not be too long before the probem is on us unless some significant changes are made in how business is done and in how pensions are funded.

5. PARTNERSHIP

A comprehensive response to the changes in values in American society requires management and government to link arms in a meaningful partnership. True partnerships are both binding and voluntary, expressing the desire of the partners to accomplish together what neither can nor wants to do alone. The CEO's in the RHR survey almost unanimously said they wanted to work with the government in creating enabling legislation rather than passively waiting as at present for regulations to be foisted on them by disinterested, even antagonistic, legislatures.

And it is probable that many government officials would respond positively to businessmen if managements were unified in their desire to cooperate as partners. Such a partnership, for example, might generate some legislation that included incentives on earnings' capability. Then executives, instead of greeting the legislation as usual with groans and exclamations of disgust, might say, "Hurrah. Look, I can increase dividends, invest in research and product development, and share more with employees as well as delight the shareholders if we can meet these government plans." Again as an example, if management were initially involved with legislators in developing the social legislation that the new values require, executives, who are experienced in implementing plans, could enhance the social impact of the new regulations. Only good could come from cooperation, a genuine partnership between government and business, between legislators and executives. Each group is responsible to the public, the legislators for the voice of the people on how to live together, and the executives for the wherewithal to live. What could be more natural than a partnership? Furthermore, without impugning their leadership qualities, it is true that legislators fall far behind executives as men of action rather than reaction. The heads of organizations are those who make things happen; the legislators react to what a majority want to have happen and then design the regulations which legalize it. How powerful an impact a real partnership could have, especially in the area of America's relation to the needs of the developing countries of the Third World (and of our needs for them). Executives could and already have made significant contributions. As leaders and as partners, they could contribute even more if in coexistence with government, the plans, policies, and programs for developing a better world were devised.

6. A PUZZLE AND A SOLUTION

One executive succinctly stated a puzzling problem for management: "The changes in social values, it seems to me, give us [in management] a road to tread that is narrow but laid out between two ditches. The most vicious strikes and debilitating union difficulties often occur in organizations that have really done a super job of taking care of their people. They are almost paternalistic with their long-standing history of good relations, they pay their employees well; but when the union comes around, there is often a helluva fight. Did they go too far in helping and in fostering participation versus hanging back and getting labeled as a mossback? Why is it that well-meaning organizations who get involved in social betterment programs seem actually to create serious problems for themselves? For instance, some companies already have flex hours; and people work seasonally. But productivity often goes down, people cannot be relied on to show up for work (even during the working season), and management cannot tell the employees anything or pay them more. Employees always seem to feel that only their personal needs come first. Okay. How then do you serve these values, these cultural changes? It would take Solomon's wisdom, it seems to me, to stay on track. We want to do right by people, but we still have to produce a product at a profit for the shareholders."

This poses a conundrum without an obvious answer. It is a truism that, human nature being what it is, one tends to bite the hand that feeds him—when there is any intimation by the feeder's actions or attitude that the recipient is unable to care for himself. Essentially, the trouble with paternalism toward adults is that it denies the adult any degree of self-determination. Psychologically, people resent being slaves, either physically or ideologically; thus when they're cared for by beneficent programs, they are being told, in effect, "You can't take care of yourself so we'll take care of you."

Fortunately, the new value many employees place on having a hand in deciding the nature of their jobs and their future may well be the best answer to the conundrum. For who can revolt against what he had a hand in devising? This concept is sharply reminiscent of Dr. Perry L. Rohrer's frequent dictum: "The strongest managements are those who strive for power *with* others rather than power *over* others." The very basis for American democracy is the premise that people must determine their own destiny. In other words, one cannot for long get away with telling others how to live or what to believe without provoking protest and rebellion.

7. CONCLUSION—A SUMMARY OF INJUNCTIONS

Changes in the policies and practices in the world of management are inevitable and imminent. Our effort in this book has been to highlight them, to cite enough evidence of their probability to be convincing, and yet not to prescribe any answers. Nevertheless, we would be remiss if in summarizing this final chapter we did not attempt to state in brief what managements must surely think about if their organizations are to survive, let alone thrive, in the immediate future.

1. *Management must educate, train, teach, explain, and exhort.* There is nothing about the free enterprise system that cannot be taught, explained, illustrated, and otherwise examined. Managements implicitly accept the precepts of free enterprise but they too often incorrectly assume that others in our society share that philosophy. The need now is to become vocal protagonists of what organization life is all about. It can be sold; it must be sold.

2. *Management must select employees with greater care and knowledge.* To be careful in selection is so axiomatic as to be trite. Yet in today's and tomorrow's world the need for astuteness in selection is extraordinarily critical, since no organization can remain viable for long without a resourceful manpower development plan. At many places in previous chapters has the crucial nature of selection been pointed out: when employees are appraised, when there is some participative management, when compatability between jobholder and job assignment is sought, when there is a dearth of potential managers, when delegation of decision-making occurs, etc. In almost all of these instances, the selection of people because of their values (or their amenability to learn to accept desirable values) is as important as the usual qualifications of capability and experience. All of this is not to say that values should be prescribed for an employee; but it does assert that values, beliefs, and attitudes must be examined because they account for drive, motive, and interpersonal relations, the key determinants of effectiveness on the job.

Once selected by an organization, the employee may become a permanent fixture. Already in Belgium, for example, an employee cannot be released after ninety days of employment without the employer's giving the departed employee a significant separation allowance. There are intimations in the United States of trends in the same direction that protect the employee from whimsical as well as justifiable release. As a consequence, it is reasonably predictable that there is likely to be less firing and therefore less hiring. Put this possibility together with the quality of life syndrome which puts the brakes on mobility, the change in retirement pattern, and the

EEOC regulations, and the results are likely to be a more stable work force, whether wanted or not. Thus, to add an employee is a critical matter which, like marriage, may well be "until death do us part" but without the relatively easy divorce.

3. *Management must be flexible.* The so-called flexibility of management is too often only superficial. "Of course," they say, "we adjust, adapt, make do, roll with the punches—always have. We're flexible because we have to be." But such behavior shows resiliency, not flexibility; it is a bending before a strong wind of change to avoid breaking but without any difference in understanding or knowledge or conviction.

The kind of flexibility required of today's and probably tomorrow's management is a gut-level, basic change in insight, concept, and perception. It is the antithesis of blind dogmatism with its unyielding, absolutist, righteous positions on the one hand and of weak, unctuous agreeableness on the other. Flexibility takes such inner strength and certainty as to one's directions and goals that necessary compromises or modifications in policy and practice are neither threats nor defeats. True flexibility expresses one's ability to change his mind because he's learned something and has seen a better way of implementing a principle.

The power of managements in the United States to influence changes is inestimable. There are thousands of organizations which are managed by many thousands of capable, action-oriented, vital people. Most belong to one or more of several hundred associations—the AMA, industry groups, chambers of commerce, etc., most of which focus in their agendas and programs on the techniques of management or the promotion of a product. Little attention is given to the philosophical underpinnings of the free enterprise system or to the principles involved in the management of social change.

The challenge to those who manage is to speak with one voice as they work together to make our society what it can be. There is no more powerful group in America.